Security Automation with Python

Practical Python solutions for automating and scaling security operations

Corey Charles Sr.

Security Automation with Python

Group Product Manager: Dhruv Jagdish Kataria

Publishing Product Manager: Khushboo Samkaria

Book Project Manager: Uma Devi Lakshmikanth

Senior Editor: Sujata Tripathi

Technical Editor: Rajat Sharma

Copy Editor: Safis Editing

Proofreader: Sujata Tripathi

Indexer: Pratik Shirodkar

Production Designer: Joshua Misquitta and Prashant Ghare

Senior Developer Relations Marketing Executive: Marylou De Mello

First published: February 2025

Production reference: 1130125

Published by Packt Publishing Ltd.

Grosvenor House

11 St Paul's Square

Birmingham

B3 1RB, UK

ISBN 978-1-80512-510-5

www.packtpub.com

To my wife and kids, for your unwavering support and inspiration. This journey wouldn't have been possible without you.

Foreword

In today's fast-paced digital landscape, the need for efficient, scalable, security solutions has never been more critical. As cyber threats continue to evolve in both complexity and frequency, the ability to respond quickly and accurately is paramount for security teams across the globe. Enter Corey Charles Sr., a seasoned cybersecurity professional with years of hands-on experience, particularly in the realm of security automation.

I've had the pleasure of watching Corey navigate the intricate challenges of cybersecurity throughout his career. What sets him apart is not only his technical expertise but also his relentless pursuit of innovation. He understands that modern security operations cannot rely solely on manual processes. Corey's work in automating critical security tasks, such as vulnerability scanning and incident response, has demonstrated how leveraging tools such as Python can drive operational efficiency while maintaining robust security postures.

Security Automation with Python is a reflection of Corey's deep understanding of both the strategic and technical aspects of security. This book distills his knowledge into practical, actionable insights that security professionals can use to stay ahead of evolving threats. Corey's approach to automation goes beyond the basics, offering real-world examples and applications that can transform security operations from reactive to proactive.

What I admire most about Corey is his ability to communicate complex ideas in a way that's accessible to everyone, regardless of their coding experience. Whether you're a seasoned security expert or new to automation, Corey's clear guidance and passion for the subject make this book an invaluable resource.

I'm confident that this book will not only enhance your understanding of security automation but also inspire you to embrace new technologies to elevate your security operations. Corey Charles Sr. has created a roadmap for the future of cybersecurity, and I encourage you to explore and apply the principles in this book to protect against the ever-growing threats in today's digital world.

Frank McMahon

Retired CISO

Contributors

About the author

Corey Charles Sr. is an experienced security professional with 18 years of experience in risk management, information security, and IT technology. His expertise spans various roles and certifications, including **Information security roles** working on implementing and overseeing security measures, including vulnerability management, threat detection, and response; **IT leadership** where he has a proven track record in leading IT security teams, guiding project execution, and supporting security initiatives across organizations. He holds certifications in Qualys vulnerability management, **Project Management Professional (PMP)**, Google Cloud, Microsoft Azure, and **Certified Information Security Manager (CISM)**, showcasing his commitment to advanced security practices and technology expertise.

Corey brings a balanced skill set in both strategic oversight and hands-on technical proficiency, making him adept at managing security programs and aligning them with organizational goals.

This book is the result of invaluable contributions from many people. I would like to thank my mentor, colleagues, and fellow professionals who have generously shared their knowledge and insights with me. Special thanks to my family for their endless encouragement throughout this journey. I am also deeply grateful to my readers, whose curiosity and passion for learning drive the exploration of automation in security.

About the reviewers

Guven Boyraz is a cybersecurity engineer and manager with a wide technical breadth and deep understanding of many systems. He boasts over a decade of experience in the computer science and IT industry. Throughout his career, he has provided cybersecurity consultancy services to a wide range of clients, including both enterprise-level customers and start-ups, primarily in London, UK. With a B.Sc. in electrical and electronics engineering and several certifications in computer science, Boyraz has acquired a strong educational foundation. In addition to his consulting work, he has also made significant contributions as a trainer and speaker at numerous international conferences. He is a professional member of the British Computer Society.

Dr. Manish Kumar holds a Ph.D. in computer science from Bangalore University. With 16 years of teaching experience, he is an associate professor at the School of Computer Science and Engineering at RV University, Bangalore. Specializing in information security and digital forensics, he is also a subject matter expert in cybersecurity for IBM, Coursera, and edX. He has presented numerous research papers in reputed conferences and published them in journals. Actively involved in research and consultancy, he delivers workshops, technical talks, and training for engineering institutions, researchers, law enforcement, and the judiciary. He is a life member of CSI, ISTE, and ISCA, and a senior member of ACM and IAENG.

Gourav Nagar is the director of information security at BILL Holdings, Inc., where he leads the information security engineering and security operations team. With over a decade of experience in cybersecurity, Gourav has built robust security programs across various domains, including security engineering, incident response, threat detection, cloud security, and digital forensics. His career includes key roles at industry leaders such as Uber, Apple, and EY. Gourav holds a master of science degree in management information systems from Texas A&M University and multiple industry certifications, including CISSP, CISM, CHFI, and **GIAC Certified Forensic Analyst (GCFA)**.

Table of Contents

3

Scripting Basics – Python Essentials for Security Tasks   71

Part 2: Automation of the Security Practice

4

5

6

Web Application Security Automation Using Python   171

Part 3: Case Study and Trends in Security Automation Using Python

7

Case Studies – Real-World Applications of Python Security Automation   199

Preface

The rapid evolution of technology has brought an unprecedented rise in security threats, compelling organizations and professionals to adopt more efficient, automated solutions. *Security Automation with Python*, was born from the increasing demand to streamline security operations, where manual processes are no longer sufficient to keep pace with the evolving threat landscape.

Throughout my career in cybersecurity, I've seen firsthand how repetitive tasks can overwhelm teams, diverting focus from more strategic, high-priority issues. This prompted me to explore Python as a solution for automating essential security operations—from vulnerability management to incident response. Python's versatility, simplicity, and widespread use make it an ideal tool for building scalable, customizable solutions in security automation.

The inspiration for this book came from a recognition that while many security professionals are experts in their field, they often lack coding and automation skills. This book seeks to bridge that gap by providing practical, hands-on guidance for implementing Python in real-world security scenarios. Whether you're a security analyst, engineer, or someone looking to enhance your cybersecurity skills, this book will empower you to automate time-consuming tasks, freeing up valuable resources for proactive threat detection and mitigation.

I am deeply grateful to my wife and children for their unwavering support, and to my mentors, colleagues, and fellow professionals who have contributed their insights and experiences along the way. Their influence has been instrumental in shaping the content of this book, and their commitment to advancing cybersecurity continues to inspire me.

This book is structured around key areas of security automation, from vulnerability scanning to incident response, each designed to equip you with the tools and knowledge to enhance your security operations. As you work through each chapter, I encourage you to approach the material with curiosity and a desire to apply these solutions to your own security challenges.

My hope is that *Security Automation with Python* will empower you to take control of your security processes and help you build more resilient, efficient systems. I trust that this book will inspire you to push the boundaries of what's possible with automation in the ever evolving world of cybersecurity.

Who this book is for

The target audience for this book includes security professionals, DevOps engineers, and IT administrators with a foundational understanding of Python programming and cybersecurity principles. You should ideally have experience with basic scripting, familiarity with network security concepts, and an interest in automating security tasks. Those with knowledge of vulnerability management, incident response, and general IT systems will benefit most, as the book delves into using Python and tools such as Ansible for practical automation in these areas. While prior exposure to automation frameworks is helpful, the book provides step-by-step guidance to bridge any knowledge gaps.

What this book covers

Chapter 1, Introduction to Security Automation with Python, introduces the fundamentals of security automation and highlights Python's role in streamlining security processes. It explores common automation use cases in cybersecurity, setting the stage for how Python can address repetitive tasks, increase efficiency, and enhance security outcomes.

Chapter 2, Configuring Python - Setting Up Your Development Environment, shows you how to configure a Python environment specifically for security automation. This chapter covers essential tools, libraries, and best practices for creating a reliable setup, including virtual environments and dependency management, ensuring a stable and organized development foundation.

Chapter 3, Scripting Basics - Python Essentials for Security Tasks, revisits core Python programming concepts relevant to security automation. Topics such as data handling, file I/O, and control structures are presented with a focus on applying them to security-related tasks, equipping you with the essentials for scripting in a security context.

Chapter 4, Automating Vulnerability Scanning with Python, explores automated vulnerability scanning, and guides you through using Python scripts to conduct scans, interpret results, and generate reports. It demonstrates integrations with popular vulnerability scanning tools, enhancing your ability to automate detection and reporting.

Chapter 5, Network Security Automation with Python, dives into network security tasks, showing how Python can automate network monitoring, firewall rule management, and intrusion detection. You will learn how to leverage libraries such as Scapy and Python' socket module for effective network security operations.

Chapter 6, Web Application Security Automation Using Python, focuses on web application security and covers Python-driven methods for testing vulnerabilities such as SQL injection and **cross-site scripting (XSS)**. It explores popular tools and libraries, guiding you on building scripts that enhance web app security assessment.

Chapter 7, Case Studies - Real-World Applications of Python Security Automation, presents a case study on SecureBank that illustrates practical applications of security automation in the financial sector. This chapter demonstrates how Python was used to improve vulnerability scanning, incident response, and compliance, providing a real-world example of security automation's impact.

Chapter 8, Future Trends - Machine Learning and AI in Security Automation with Python, explores emerging trends in AI and machine learning within security automation. You will gain insight into how Python supports AI-driven security solutions and learn about tools and frameworks that are shaping the future of automated threat detection and response.

Chapter 9, Empowering Security Teams Through Python Automation, recaps key takeaways and emphasizes the practical benefits of security automation. It encourages you to apply the techniques and tools discussed, empowering security teams to work more efficiently and effectively in a constantly evolving threat landscape.

To get the most out of this book

To ensure compatibility with the code in this book, you should have Python 3.10 or newer, as this version supports the latest libraries and security features. The recommended development environment includes **Ansible 2.17**, along with tools such as `pip` and virtual environments (e.g., `venv` or `conda`) for package management. For OS compatibility, a modern Linux distribution (e.g., Ubuntu 20.04 or newer), macOS 11.0 or newer, or Windows 10 (64-bit) is necessary. Additionally, having at least 8 GB of RAM and a dual-core processor will ensure smooth operation for larger automation tasks and simulations.

Software/hardware covered in the book	Operating system requirements
Python 3.12	• Windows: Windows 8.1 and later, including Windows 10 and Windows 11. Both 32-bit and 64-bit versions are supported, though 64-bit is recommended. • macOS: macOS 10.9 and newer. • Linux: Python 3.12 should work on most modern Linux distributions, with many package managers offering installation options for it.
Tenable Nessus, version 10.8.3	• Linux: Compatible with distributions such as Amazon Linux 2, CentOS Stream 9, Debian 11/12, Fedora 38/39, and several versions of Red Hat (up to version 9) and SUSE Enterprise. It also supports Ubuntu versions 14.04 to 22.04. • Windows: Supported on Windows 10, 11, and Windows Server versions 2012 through 2022. Note that Windows systems must have the latest Universal C Runtime library and PowerShell 5.0 or newer installed for optimal performance. • macOS: Works on macOS versions 12, 13, and 14, supporting both Intel and Apple Silicon architectures.
Ansible is version 10.0, with Ansible Core currently at 2.17	Ansible requires Python 3.9 or newer

If you are using the digital version of this book, we advise you to type the code yourself. Doing so will help you avoid any potential errors related to the copying and pasting of code.

Download the example code files

You can download the example code files for this book from GitHub at `https://github.com/PacktPublishing/Security-Automation-with-Python`. If there's an update to the code, it will be updated in the GitHub repository.

Conventions used

There are a number of text conventions used throughout this book.

`Code in text`: Indicates code words in text, database table names, folder names, filenames, file extensions, pathnames, dummy URLs, user input, and Twitter handles. Here is an example: "The same approach can be extended to other firewall vendors by modifying `rule_command`."

A block of code is set as follows:

```
import paramiko

def create_firewall_rule(host, username, password, rule_command):
    ssh = paramiko.SSHClient()
    ssh.set_missing_host_key_policy(paramiko.AutoAddPolicy())
    ssh.connect(host, username=username, password=password)

    stdin, stdout, stderr = ssh.exec_command(rule_command)
    print(stdout.read().decode())
    ssh.close()

# Example rule command for Cisco ASA firewall
rule_command = "access-list outside_in extended permit tcp any host 192.168.1.100 eq 80"
create_firewall_rule("firewall_ip_address", "admin", "password", rule_command)
```

Any command-line input or output is written as follows:

```
npm install -g newman
```

> **Tips or important notes**
> Appear like this.

Get in touch

Feedback from our readers is always welcome.

General feedback: If you have questions about any aspect of this book, email us at customercare@packtpub.com and mention the book title in the subject of your message.

Errata: Although we have taken every care to ensure the accuracy of our content, mistakes do happen. If you have found a mistake in this book, we would be grateful if you would report this to us. Please visit www.packtpub.com/support/errata and fill in the form.

Piracy: If you come across any illegal copies of our works in any form on the internet, we would be grateful if you would provide us with the location address or website name. Please contact us at copyright@packt.com with a link to the material.

If you are interested in becoming an author: If there is a topic that you have expertise in and you are interested in either writing or contributing to a book, please visit authors.packtpub.com.

Share your thoughts

Once you've read *Security Automation with Python*, we'd love to hear your thoughts! Scan the QR code below to go straight to the Amazon review page for this book and share your feedback.

https://packt.link/r/1805125109

Your review is important to us and the tech community and will help us make sure we're delivering excellent quality content.

Download a free PDF copy of this book

Thanks for purchasing this book!

Do you like to read on the go but are unable to carry your print books everywhere?

Is your eBook purchase not compatible with the device of your choice?

Don't worry, now with every Packt book you get a DRM-free PDF version of that book at no cost.

Read anywhere, any place, on any device. Search, copy, and paste code from your favorite technical books directly into your application.

The perks don't stop there, you can get exclusive access to discounts, newsletters, and great free content in your inbox daily

Follow these simple steps to get the benefits:

1. Scan the QR code or visit the link below

https://packt.link/free-ebook/978-1-80512-510-5

2. Submit your proof of purchase

3. That's it! We'll send your free PDF and other benefits to your email directly

Part 1: Understanding Security Automation and Setting Up the Environment

Security automation is rapidly transforming how organizations manage their cybersecurity posture. By automating repetitive tasks such as vulnerability scanning, threat detection, and incident response, businesses can reduce human error, improve response times, and allocate resources more efficiently. This part introduces the core concepts of security automation and walks you through the initial steps of setting up the necessary environment to automate security workflows. From installing essential tools to configuring systems, this guide will help you lay the foundation for building effective security automation processes.

This part has the following chapters:

- *Chapter 1, Introduction to Security Automation with Python*
- *Chapter 2, Configuring Python - Setting Up Your Development Environment*
- *Chapter 3, Scripting Basics - Python Essentials for Security Tasks*

1

Introduction to Security Automation with Python

In today's rapidly evolving cybersecurity landscape, traditional manual methods to ensure security often fall short, especially when security teams are bombarded with thousands of alerts and logs daily. Imagine a scenario where an analyst has to manually review system logs to detect suspicious activity across hundreds of endpoints. This process is time-consuming, prone to human error, and often results in missed or delayed responses to critical threats. The sheer volume of data makes it nearly impossible to identify emerging patterns or rapidly respond to incidents, leaving organizations vulnerable to attacks. Manual processes simply can't scale with the growing sophistication of modern cyber threats.

This is where security automation becomes invaluable. Automation tools can sift through vast amounts of data in real time, flagging anomalies and suspicious activity within seconds – something that could take a human analyst hours or even days. By leveraging Python, organizations can automate tasks such as log analysis, threat detection, and incident response, ensuring faster, more accurate responses. Automation not only reduces the risk of oversight but also frees up security teams to focus on more strategic and complex challenges, enhancing the overall security posture and resilience.

We'll cover the following topics in this chapter:

- Python security automation overview
- Understanding security automation
- Python and its functionality
- Introducing automation security in an organization

Python security automation overview

Python is a powerful and flexible programming language that's well suited for security automation because of its simplicity and extensive library ecosystem make it ideal for automating routine security tasks such as log analysis, vulnerability scanning, incident response, and configuration management. Python's compatibility with security tools and APIs allows security professionals to automate workflows that would otherwise require manual, time-consuming efforts, thereby reducing human error and increasing operational efficiency.

In the realm of cybersecurity, the real-world impact of security incidents can be profound, affecting not only an organization's financial health but also its reputation and operational integrity. For example, consider a retail company that experiences a data breach due to a vulnerability in its payment processing system. Without the ability to swiftly automate threat detection and response using Python-based security tools, the organization might remain unaware of the breach for weeks. During this time, attackers could siphon off sensitive customer data, leading to significant financial losses and legal repercussions.

In the aftermath, the company faces not only the costs associated with remediation – such as forensic investigations, regulatory fines, and potential lawsuits – but also the erosion of customer trust. Customers may choose to take their business elsewhere, resulting in long-term revenue decline. By employing security automation, the organization could have detected the breach in real time, responded promptly to mitigate damage, and implemented automated safeguards to prevent future incidents. This proactive approach not only protects sensitive data but also preserves the organization's reputation and customer loyalty, illustrating the tangible benefits of investing in security automation technologies.

Understanding security automation

With the evolution of the cybersecurity landscape, organizations face an ever-growing number of threats that can compromise the integrity, confidentiality, and availability of their sensitive data and critical systems. Traditional approaches to cybersecurity, which rely heavily on manual processes and human intervention, are no longer sufficient to defend against these threats effectively. As a result, there has been a growing emphasis on security automation – the process of automating repetitive tasks, workflows, and processes in cybersecurity to improve efficiency, accuracy, and response times.

The need for security automation

The increasing complexity and volume of cyber threats, coupled with resource constraints and skill shortages, have made it challenging for organizations to keep pace with the evolving threat landscape using manual methods alone. Manual processes are often slow, error-prone, and labor-intensive, leading to delays in detecting and responding to security incidents. Additionally, human analysts may struggle to handle the sheer volume of security data generated by modern IT environments, leading to missed threats and false positives.

Security automation addresses these challenges by leveraging technology to automate routine tasks and workflows, enabling organizations to do the following:

- **Improve efficiency**: Automation allows organizations to perform security tasks more quickly and consistently than manual methods, freeing up valuable time and resources for more strategic activities. Tasks such as log analysis, vulnerability scanning, and incident response can be automated to reduce response times and minimize the risk of human error.

- **Enhance accuracy**: Automated security processes follow predefined rules and guidelines, reducing the likelihood of mistakes and ensuring consistent application of security measures across the organization. By eliminating human error, automation helps organizations improve the accuracy and effectiveness of their security operations.

- **Scale security operations**: As organizations grow and their digital footprint expands, manual security processes become increasingly difficult to manage. Automation provides scalability by enabling organizations to handle large volumes of security-related tasks and data without significantly increasing resource requirements. Automated workflows can adapt to changes in workload and demand, ensuring that security operations remain efficient and effective.

- **Augment human analysts**: Rather than replacing human analysts, security automation is designed to complement their skills and expertise. By automating repetitive and mundane tasks, automation allows analysts to focus their efforts on more strategic activities, such as threat hunting, incident investigation, and developing proactive security measures.

- **Improve threat detection and response**: Automation plays a crucial role in improving threat detection and response capabilities. Automated systems can analyze vast amounts of security data in real time, identify potential threats, and trigger predefined responses or remediation actions. By automating threat detection and response workflows, organizations can reduce the time it takes to detect and respond to security incidents, minimizing the impact of cyber threats on their operations.

In summary, the need for security automation is driven by the imperative to enhance efficiency, accuracy, and responsiveness in the face of evolving cyber threats, making it a critical component for maintaining a robust and proactive security posture.

Key components of security automation

Security automation encompasses a wide range of technologies, tools, and techniques, each serving a specific purpose in automating security tasks and processes. The following are some of the key components of security automation:

- **Scripting languages**: Scripting languages such as Python, PowerShell, and Bash are commonly used in security automation due to their flexibility, ease of use, and extensive libraries of prebuilt modules and tools. These languages allow security professionals to automate various tasks, including log analysis, vulnerability scanning, and incident response.

- **Orchestration platforms**: Orchestration platforms such as Ansible, Puppet, and Chef provide frameworks for automating and managing complex workflows and processes. These platforms enable organizations to define and automate security workflows, coordinate tasks across multiple systems, and enforce security policies consistently. The following is an example of a security orchestration workflow - the end-to-end process of defining policies, selecting tools, automating tasks, monitoring activities, and evaluating compliance outcomes:

```
A[Start Security Workflow] --> B[Define Security Policy]
B --> C[Select Orchestration Tool]
C --> D{Choose Task}
D -->|Configure Systems| E[Use Ansible/Puppet/Chef]
D -->|Deploy Security Updates| F[Deploy Updates Across
Systems]
D -->|Automate Compliance Checks| G[Perform Compliance
Scans]
D -->|Incident Response Automation| H[Trigger Incident
Response]
E --> I[Task Execution on Target Systems]
F --> I
G --> I
H --> I
I --> J[Monitor and Log Activities]
J --> K[Generate Reports and Alerts]
K --> L{Evaluate Results}
L -->|Policy Compliant| M[End Workflow]
L -->|Non-compliant| B
```

- **Security Information and Event Management (SIEM) systems**: SIEM systems collect, aggregate, and analyze security data from various sources, such as network devices, servers, and applications, to identify security threats and anomalies. Automation capabilities within SIEM systems allow organizations to automate threat detection, incident triage, and response workflows, enabling faster and more effective incident response.

- **Application programming interfaces (APIs)**: APIs allow different security tools and systems to communicate and exchange information, enabling seamless integration and interoperability between disparate security technologies. By leveraging APIs, organizations can automate workflows that span multiple security tools and systems, such as orchestrating vulnerability scans, deploying patches, and updating firewall rules.

- **Vulnerability management**: Automated vulnerability scanning tools can continuously scan networks, systems, and applications for known vulnerabilities. These tools can prioritize vulnerabilities based on severity, impact, and exploitability, enabling security teams to focus on patching critical vulnerabilities first.

The key components of security automation include automated threat detection and response, vulnerability management, compliance and auditing, incident response, and continuous security monitoring. By integrating these components, organizations can streamline their security operations, enhance their ability to detect and mitigate threats, and maintain a proactive security posture in an increasingly complex threat landscape.

Example of security automation using Python and NMAP

Here's a simple Python example demonstrating security automation for automating vulnerability scanning using the nmap library:

```
# Import the nmap library to utilize Nmap functionalities
import nmap
# Define a function to scan the network
def scan_network(target):

    # Initialize the Nmap PortScanner object to scan the target
    nm = nmap.PortScanner()

    # Perform a TCP SYN scan (-sS) on the target IP address
    nm.scan(target, arguments='-sS')

    # Check if the target host is up and responding
    if nm[target].state() == 'up':

        # Print confirmation that the host is up
        print(f"Host: {target} is up")

        # Iterate over all scanned hosts (though in this case, it's
just the target)
        for host in nm.all_hosts():

            # Print open ports for the target host
            print(f"Open Ports on {host}:")

            # Loop through each protocol (e.g., TCP or UDP) used in
the scan
            for proto in nm[host].all_protocols():

                # Get all scanned ports for the specific protocol
                ports = nm[host][proto].keys()
```

```
                    # Loop through each port and print its status (open/
closed/etc.)
                    for port in ports:
                        print(f"Port: {port} - State: {nm[host][proto]
[port]['state']}")
        else:
            # If the host is down, print that the target is not responding
            print(f"Host: {target} is down")

# Entry point of the script
if __name__ == "__main__":

    # Specify the target IP address or IP range to scan
    target_ip = "192.168.1.1"

    # Call the scan function to perform a vulnerability scan on the
target IP
    scan_network(target_ip)
```

This script demonstrates how to use the nmap library in Python to perform a network discovery scan (TCP SYN) on a specified target IP address. The script checks whether the target is up, then iterates over each scanned port and prints the results, including the port number and its state (open, closed, or filtered). You can see how Python can be used to automate security tasks such as vulnerability scanning, enabling security teams to identify potential security risks in their network infrastructure efficiently.

Now, let's say we've identified vulnerabilities in the environment and we want to create an automated script that will ensure all patch packages are available for deployment. Here's a Python example demonstrating a basic patch management automation script:

```
import os
import subprocess
def check_for_updates():
    # Check for available updates using the package manager
    if os.name == 'posix':  # For Unix-like systems (e.g., Linux)
        subprocess.run(['apt', 'update'])  # Update package lists
        return subprocess.run(['apt', 'list', '--upgradable'],
capture_output=True, text=True).stdout
    elif os.name == 'nt':  # For Windows systems
        return subprocess.run(['wmic', 'qfe', 'list', 'full'],
capture_output=True, text=True).stdout
    else:
        return "Unsupported operating system"
```

```python
def install_updates():
    # Install available updates using the package manager
    if os.name == 'posix':  # For Unix-like systems (e.g., Linux)
        subprocess.run(['apt', 'upgrade', '-y'])  # Upgrade packages
    elif os.name == 'nt':  # For Windows systems
        subprocess.run(['wuauclt', '/detectnow'])  # Force Windows
Update detection
    else:
        print("Unsupported operating system")


if __name__ == "__main__":
    print("Checking for available updates...")
    updates_available = check_for_updates()
    print(updates_available)

    if updates_available:
        print("Installing updates...")
        install_updates()
        print("Updates installed successfully.")
    else:
        print("No updates available.")
```

This script checks for available updates on the system using the appropriate package manager (apt for Linux-based systems and wmic for Windows) and then installs the updates if any are found. First, it checks the operating system's type to determine which commands to use for update checks and installations.

This example showcases how Python can be used to automate patch management tasks across different operating systems, allowing system administrators to keep their systems up to date with the latest security patches and software updates efficiently.

Understanding security automation is crucial in today's rapidly evolving digital landscape. As cyber threats become more sophisticated and frequent, traditional manual methods of security management are insufficient to keep pace. Security automation provides a scalable solution to these challenges, enabling continuous monitoring, rapid detection, and efficient response to security incidents. It allows organizations to optimize their resources, reduce human error, and maintain a consistent security posture across all systems and processes. By integrating automation into their cybersecurity strategies, organizations can not only enhance their resilience against attacks but also ensure compliance with industry standards and regulations. A deep understanding of security automation empowers organizations to safeguard their assets, protect sensitive data, and maintain trust with their stakeholders in an increasingly interconnected world. The following diagram shows the different areas Python can be used in:

PYTHON LANGUAGE

Major Uses of the Python Programming Language

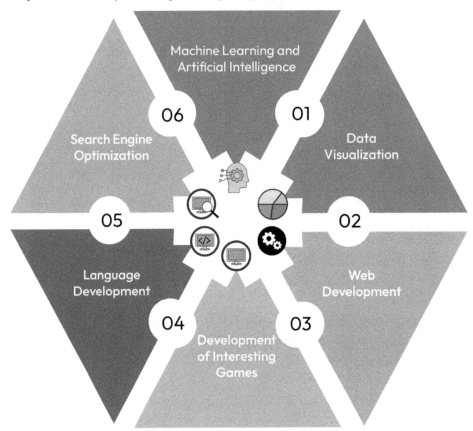

Figure 1.1 – Python and its functionality

Let's delve into the vast functionality that Python offers, and understand why it continues to captivate developers worldwide:

- **Python's clean and readable syntax**: Python's syntax is renowned for its cleanliness and readability. With its use of indentation to denote block structures and its minimalist approach to punctuation, Python code is intuitive and elegant. This simplicity not only makes Python an ideal language for beginners to learn but also enhances the productivity of seasoned developers, enabling them to focus on problem-solving rather than wrestling with syntax intricacies.

- **Versatility in application**: Python's versatility knows no bounds, spanning a wide spectrum of domains. In web development, frameworks such as Django and Flask empower developers to build scalable and feature-rich applications with ease. For data analysis and scientific computing, libraries such as NumPy, pandas, and Matplotlib offer powerful tools for processing, analyzing, and visualizing data. In the realm of machine learning and artificial intelligence, libraries such as TensorFlow and PyTorch provide the building blocks for developing cutting-edge models for tasks such as image recognition, natural language processing, and predictive analytics.

- **Extensive standard library**: Python's standard library is a treasure trove of functionality that encompasses modules and packages for a myriad of tasks. Whether it's file manipulation, network communication, database interaction, or mathematical computations, Python's standard library offers robust solutions out of the box. This rich collection of built-in modules minimizes the need for external dependencies, streamlining development and ensuring cross-platform compatibility.

- **Strong community support**: Python boasts a vibrant and supportive community of developers, educators, and enthusiasts. Online forums, such as Stack Overflow and Reddit, serve as hubs for knowledge-sharing and problem-solving. Additionally, Python's extensive documentation and plethora of tutorials cater to learners of all levels, providing a wealth of resources to aid in skill development and project implementation. The strength of Python's community fosters collaboration, innovation, and continuous improvement within the ecosystem.

- **Cross-platform compatibility**: Code written in Python can run seamlessly on various operating systems, including Windows, macOS, and Linux, without the need for modification. This inherent portability simplifies deployment and maintenance, enabling developers to focus on delivering robust solutions rather than grappling with platform-specific intricacies.

Building automated code using Python typically involves several steps, which can vary depending on the specific task or project requirements. Here's a general path to build automated code using Python:

1. **Identify the task**: Clearly define the task or process that you want to automate. This could be anything from data processing and analysis to system administration tasks.

2. **Research and plan**: Research existing solutions and best practices for automating similar tasks. Determine the tools, libraries, and frameworks that will be most suitable for your project. Create a plan outlining the steps needed to achieve automation.

3. **Set up a development environment**: Install Python and any necessary dependencies or libraries for your project. Set up a development environment using an **integrated development environment (IDE)** or a text editor.

4. **Write code**: Start writing code to automate the identified task. Break down the task into smaller, manageable steps and write Python code to perform each step. Use appropriate data structures, functions, and modules to organize your code effectively.

5. **Testing**: Test your code thoroughly to ensure it functions as expected. Write unit tests to verify the behavior of individual components. Use automated testing frameworks such as `unittest` or `pytest` to automate the testing process.

6. **Error handling and logging**: Implement error handling mechanisms to handle exceptions and unexpected errors gracefully. Incorporate logging functionality to track the execution of your automated code and troubleshoot issues.

7. **Integration and deployment**: Integrate your automated code into the target environment or workflow. Deploy the code to production or staging environments as needed. Set up scheduled tasks or triggers to execute the code automatically at specified intervals or in response to events.

8. **Monitoring and maintenance**: Monitor the performance and behavior of your automated code in production. Implement monitoring solutions to detect and alert on any issues or failures. Regularly review and update the code to accommodate changes in requirements or environments.

9. **Documentation**: Document your automated code thoroughly, including its purpose, functionality, usage instructions, and configuration settings. Provide clear documentation for other developers or team members who may need to maintain or extend the code in the future.

10. **Continuous improvement**: Continuously seek opportunities to optimize and improve your automated code. Collect feedback from users and stakeholders to identify areas for enhancement. Refactor the code to improve readability, performance, and maintainability over time.

By following these steps, you can build automated code effectively using Python to streamline processes, increase efficiency, and reduce manual effort in various domains and industries.

Here's an example of a simple Python script for automating security tasks related to password management:

```python
import random
import string

def generate_password(length=12):
    """Generate a random password."""
    characters = string.ascii_letters + string.digits + string.
punctuation
    password = ''.join(random.choice(characters) for _ in
range(length))
    return password

def save_password(username, password):
    """Save the generated password to a file."""
    with open('passwords.txt', 'a') as f:
        f.write(f'{username}: {password}\n')
    print(f'Password for {username} saved successfully.')

def main():
    username = input('Enter username: ')
    password = generate_password()
    save_password(username, password)
```

```
if __name__ == "__main__":
    main()
```

This script performs the following tasks:

- **Generates a password**: The `generate_password` function generates a random password of a specified length using a combination of uppercase letters, lowercase letters, digits, and punctuation characters.

- **Saves the password**: The `save_password` function saves the generated password alongside the corresponding username to a text file named `passwords.txt`.

- **Utilizes the main function**: The `main` function prompts the user to enter a username, generates a password using the `generate_password` function, and then saves the username-password pair using the `save_password` function.

When run, this script prompts the user to enter a username, generates a random password, saves the username-password pair to a file, and prints a success message.

This is a basic example, but you can extend it so that it includes additional functionality, such as encryption, password strength validation, integration with password managers, or automation of password rotation processes. Additionally, you can incorporate error handling, logging, and other best practices to enhance the reliability and security of the script.

Here's an advanced example of automated security using Python for network monitoring and intrusion detection:

```
import time
import socket

def monitor_network_traffic():
    """Monitor network traffic for suspicious activity."""
    print("Monitoring network traffic...")
    while True:
        try:
            # Create a socket to listen for incoming network traffic
            with socket.socket(socket.AF_INET, socket.SOCK_RAW,
socket.IPPROTO_TCP) as s:
                s.bind(('0.0.0.0', 0))
                s.setsockopt(socket.IPPROTO_IP, socket.IP_HDRINCL, 1)
                # Capture packets and analyze them
                data, addr = s.recvfrom(65536)
                print(f"Received packet from {addr}: {data}")
                # Implement custom logic to detect suspicious activity
                # For example, check for patterns indicative of an
attack
```

```
                    if "malicious_pattern" in data:
                        print("Suspicious activity detected! Initiating
response...")
                        # Take appropriate action such as blocking IP
addresses, alerting security teams, etc.
            except Exception as e:
                print(f"Error: {e}")
            time.sleep(1)

if __name__ == "__main__":
    monitor_network_traffic()
```

Let's try and understand the preceding script:

- **Monitor network traffic**: The `monitor_network_traffic` function continuously listens for incoming network traffic using a raw socket. It captures packets and analyzes their content.

- **Detect suspicious activity**: Within the packet data, the script implements custom logic to detect suspicious activity. This could involve pattern matching, anomaly detection, or other methods to identify potential security threats.

- **Take action**: If suspicious activity is detected (for example, a malicious pattern is found in the packet data), the script initiates a response. This could include blocking IP addresses, sending alerts to security teams, logging events, or other appropriate actions based on the security policy.

- **Error handling**: The script includes error handling to gracefully handle exceptions that may occur during network monitoring.

- **Continuous monitoring**: The script runs indefinitely, continuously monitoring network traffic in real time.

This example demonstrates how Python can be used to build an advanced automated security solution for real-time network monitoring and intrusion detection. Depending on specific requirements and use cases, additional features such as machine-learning-based anomaly detection, integration with SIEM systems, and automated incident response workflows can be incorporated to enhance the effectiveness of the security solution.

Introducing automation security in an organization

While introducing automation into an organization's security operations is a powerful way to enhance efficiency, it also brings new challenges that require careful planning. One of the primary concerns is access control – who or what systems have the authority to automate certain tasks. Without proper access controls, unauthorized individuals could gain the ability to execute critical actions, leading to significant vulnerabilities. Automating sensitive tasks such as system updates, backups, or vulnerability scanning without strict safeguards can lead to unintended consequences, including configuration errors or security lapses.

Security automation needs to be implemented with robust oversight mechanisms, ensuring that automated systems adhere to the organization's security policies and standards. This includes ensuring proper logging and auditing so that any actions that are taken by automation scripts are fully tracked and can be reviewed. Moreover, the automation of sensitive tasks should be limited to trusted environments, with appropriate permissions and authentication methods in place to minimize risk. By focusing on these concerns, an organization can balance the efficiency gained through automation with the need to maintain a secure and controlled environment.

Here's a breakdown of the key aspects when introducing automation security:

- **Understanding the need**: Begin by assessing the current security landscape and identifying areas where automation can bring significant benefits. This may include repetitive tasks such as vulnerability scanning, log analysis, patch management, incident response, and compliance checks.

- **Defining objectives**: Clearly define the objectives of automation security initiatives. These objectives may vary depending on organizational goals, but common objectives include improving incident response times, reducing human error, enhancing compliance, and enabling security teams to focus on strategic initiatives.

- **Selecting automation tools**: Choose appropriate automation tools and platforms that align with organizational requirements and security objectives. This may involve leveraging specialized security automation frameworks, orchestration platforms, and scripting languages such as Python, as well as integrating with existing security tools and technologies.

- **Designing workflows**: Develop comprehensive workflows that outline the sequence of automated tasks, decision points, and escalation procedures. Workflows should be designed to handle various security scenarios, from routine tasks to critical incident response.

- **Implementing security controls**: Implement security controls to ensure the integrity, confidentiality, and availability of automated processes and data. This includes access controls, encryption, secure coding practices, and auditing mechanisms to track and monitor automation activities.

- **Testing and validation**: Thoroughly test automated workflows in a controlled environment to identify and address any potential issues or vulnerabilities. Validate the effectiveness of automation solutions through simulated scenarios and real-world testing before deploying them in production environments.

- **Monitoring and optimization**: Continuously monitor automated processes to ensure they operate as intended and remain resilient to evolving threats. Regularly review and optimize automation workflows based on feedback, performance metrics, and changes in the threat landscape.

- **Training and skill development**: Provide training and skill development opportunities for security teams to leverage automation tools and technologies effectively. Foster a culture of automation security awareness and collaboration across the organization.

By introducing automation security, organizations can streamline security operations, improve incident response capabilities, and strengthen overall cyber resilience in an increasingly complex and dynamic threat landscape. Automation serves as a force multiplier for security teams, enabling them to identify and mitigate risks proactively while adapting to emerging threats more efficiently.

Security automation reduces risk in the following ways:

- **Consistency and accuracy**: Automated processes ensure that security tasks are executed consistently and accurately every time, reducing the likelihood of human error. This consistency helps maintain compliance with security policies and standards, thereby reducing the risk of non-compliance penalties or security breaches due to misconfigurations.

- **Faster response times**: Automation enables rapid detection and response to security incidents by automatically triggering predefined actions based on predefined criteria or alerts. This swift response minimizes the window of opportunity for attackers, reducing the impact and scope of security incidents.

- **Scalability**: Automation allows security teams to scale their operations more efficiently to handle growing volumes of security-related tasks, alerts, and incidents. By automating repetitive tasks, security professionals can focus their efforts on more strategic initiatives, such as threat hunting, risk analysis, and security strategy development.

- **Continuous monitoring and compliance**: Automated monitoring tools can continuously scan and assess the security posture of IT infrastructure, applications, and networks. By automatically identifying vulnerabilities, misconfigurations, and compliance violations in real time, organizations can proactively address security risks before they escalate into full-blown incidents.

- **Streamlined incident response**: Automation streamlines the incident response process by orchestrating the actions of various security tools and technologies in a coordinated manner. Automated incident response workflows can prioritize and remediate security incidents based on their severity, impact, and relevance to the organization's risk profile.

- **Improved visibility and reporting**: Automated security solutions provide greater visibility into security events, trends, and vulnerabilities across the organization's IT environment. This enhanced visibility enables security teams to make data-driven decisions, prioritize remediation efforts, and generate comprehensive reports for stakeholders, auditors, and regulatory bodies.

- **Adaptability to the changing threat landscape**: Automation allows security teams to quickly adapt to evolving threats by updating and refining automated workflows, detection rules, and response mechanisms. This agility enables organizations to stay ahead of emerging threats and mitigate risks proactively before they can exploit vulnerabilities.

Overall, security automation plays a critical role in reducing risk by enhancing the efficiency, effectiveness, and agility of security operations, enabling organizations to better protect their assets, data, and reputation in an increasingly complex and dynamic threat landscape.

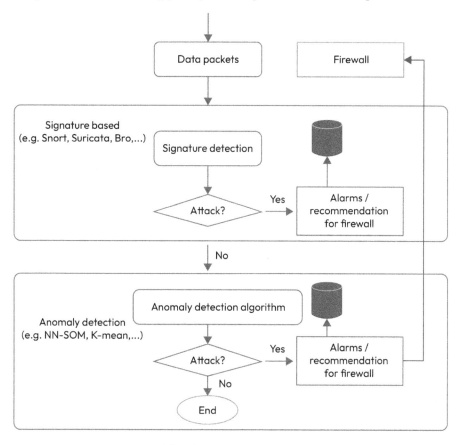

Figure 1.2 – Workflow for an intrusion detection system (IDS)

Let's consider an example of security automation using a SIEM system.

Scenario: An organization wants to automate the response to detected security incidents related to unauthorized access attempts to critical servers:

- **Detection**: The SIEM system monitors logs from various sources, including firewalls, **intrusion detection systems (IDSs)**, and authentication servers. It detects multiple failed login attempts to critical servers within a short time frame, triggering a security incident.

- **Automated response workflow:**

Figure 1.3 – Workflow for risk assessment

Let's take a closer look:

- **Trigger**: The SIEM sends an alert to a designated security automation platform (for example, **Security Orchestration, Automation, and Response** (**SOAR**) upon detecting unauthorized access attempts.

- **Investigation**: The automation platform automatically retrieves additional contextual information about the incident, such as the source IP address, user account, and affected server.

- **Risk assessment**: The automation platform assesses the risk associated with the incident based on predefined criteria, such as the number of failed login attempts and the sensitivity of the server.

- **Response decision**: Based on the risk assessment, the automation platform determines the appropriate response action.

- **Response actions**:

  - **If the risk is deemed low**: The automation platform automatically adds the source IP address to a temporary blocklist on the firewall to prevent further login attempts for a predefined period.

- **If the risk is high**: The automation platform escalates the incident to the **security operations center (SOC)** for manual investigation and response.

- **Notification**: The automation platform sends notifications to relevant stakeholders, such as IT administrators and security analysts, informing them of the detected incident and the automated response taken.

- **Execution**:

  - The automation platform executes the predefined response workflow without human intervention, ensuring a timely and consistent response to security incidents.

  - The response actions are logged and documented for audit and compliance purposes, providing a record of automated security responses.

- **Monitoring and feedback**:

  - The automation platform continuously monitors the effectiveness of automated response actions and adjusts response strategies based on feedback and performance metrics.

  - Security analysts review and analyze automated response activities to identify any false positives, optimization opportunities, or gaps in the automation workflow.

By automating the response to security incidents using a SIEM and security automation platform, organizations can reduce response times, mitigate risks, and improve the overall security posture by proactively addressing threats in real-time.

Setting up an automated environment using Python involves several steps to ensure seamless execution of scripts and processes. Here's a general guide to get started:

1. **Install Python**: Ensure Python is installed on your system. You can download the latest version of Python from the official website and follow the installation instructions.

   As of July 2024, the latest stable version of Python is Python 3.11.4. You can download it from the official Python website. Here's the direct link to the downloads page, where you can find the latest version and installation instructions for various operating systems: `https://www.python.org/downloads/`.

2. **Virtual environments**: It's recommended to use virtual environments to isolate project dependencies. Use `virtualenv` or `venv` to create a virtual environment for your project:

   ```
   python3 -m venv myenv
   source myenv/bin/activate   # Activate the virtual environment
   ```

3. **Dependency management**: Use `pip` to install project dependencies within the virtual environment:

   ```
   pip install package-name
   ```

4. **Code editor/IDE**: Choose a code editor or IDE for writing and editing Python scripts. Popular options include VS Code, PyCharm, and Sublime Text.

5. **Version control**: Set up version control using Git to manage your project's code base. Initialize a Git repository in your project directory:

    ```
    git init
    ```

6. **Project structure**: Organize your project directory with a clear structure. Common directories include `src` for source code, `tests` for testing scripts, and `docs` for documentation.

7. **Environment variables**: Utilize environment variables for sensitive information such as API keys and passwords. You can use the `dotenv` library to load environment variables from a `.env` file.

8. **Configuration files**: Create configuration files (for example, JSON, YAML, and so on) to store settings and parameters used by your scripts. Use libraries such as `configparser` and `yaml` to parse configuration files.

9. **Script execution**: Write Python scripts to automate tasks such as data processing, file manipulation, or system monitoring. Ensure scripts are well-documented and follow best practices for readability and maintainability.

10. **Testing and debugging**: Implement unit tests using frameworks such as `unittest` and `pytest` to ensure script functionality. Use logging libraries (`logging`, `loguru`, and so on) for effective debugging and error handling.

11. **Automation tools**: Explore automation tools such as **cron** (Unix) and **Task Scheduler** (Windows) to schedule script execution at specific intervals or events.

12. **Continuous integration/continuous deployment (CI/CD)**: Integrate your project with CI/CD pipelines to automate testing, code linting, and deployment processes. Tools such as Jenkins, Travis CI, and GitHub Actions can facilitate CI/CD workflows.

By following these steps, you can establish a robust automated environment using Python, enabling you to streamline workflows, increase productivity, and maintain a secure and efficient development process.

Summary

Security automation is a critical component of modern cybersecurity practices that allows organizations to enhance their defense mechanisms, streamline processes, and respond effectively to threats. Throughout this chapter, we've explored the fundamentals of security automation using Python by covering the following topics:

- **Introduction to security automation**: We provided an overview of the importance and benefits of automation in cybersecurity, highlighting Python's role in building automated solutions.

- **Setting up a Python environment**: We specified the steps for installing Python, creating virtual environments, and managing dependencies for security automation.

- **Python scripting basics**: We covered the core Python programming concepts that are necessary for automating security tasks.

- **Automating vulnerability scanning**: We covered building automated solutions for vulnerability scanning using Python to detect and address security risks.

- **Automation in incident response**: We learned how to use Python to automate incident response processes, improving reaction times and efficiency.

- **Integrating with security tools**: We leveraged Python to interact with security tools and platforms for seamless automation.

- **Conclusion and empowerment**: We reflected on how security automation enhances cybersecurity, boosts team efficiency, and reduces risks.

By mastering Python-based security automation, you can streamline processes, improve detection and response times, and stay ahead of cyber threats in today's evolving landscape.

To further enrich this summary and prepare you for the challenges ahead, it's essential to consider the complexities that come with security automation, such as managing false positives and balancing automation with human oversight. While automation can significantly enhance efficiency, there are inherent trade-offs. For instance, automated systems may occasionally flag legitimate activities as threats (false positives), or they may fail to catch subtle anomalies that human intuition might identify. As we move forward, understanding these challenges is crucial in designing robust and effective automated security systems.

In the next chapter, we'll focus on setting up your Python environment specifically for security automation. This includes not just technical configurations, but also strategies to minimize errors and security risks in your automation workflows. By the end of the next chapter, you'll have a solid foundation so that you can begin automating security tasks with confidence while staying mindful of the potential pitfalls and trade-offs that come with relying heavily on automation.

2

Configuring Python – Setting Up Your Development Environment

Before diving into the world of security automation with Python, it's crucial to establish a well-configured development environment. A properly set up environment ensures that you can efficiently write, test, and deploy Python scripts for various security tasks. This chapter will guide you through the process of configuring Python on your system, setting up essential tools, and creating a solid foundation for effective development.

Python is widely regarded as a top choice for security automation due to its simplicity, readability, and extensive libraries that cater specifically to security needs. Its versatility allows for the rapid development of scripts that can automate tedious tasks, interact with APIs, and analyze data efficiently, making it an invaluable tool for security professionals.

We will walk through installing Python, managing dependencies using virtual environments, and utilizing **integrated development environments** (**IDEs**) for an optimized workflow. Whether you're working on Windows, macOS, or Linux, this chapter will provide step-by-step instructions to get your Python environment up and running. By the end, you'll be equipped with the right tools and configurations to begin automating security tasks with Python seamlessly.

In this chapter, we'll cover the following:

- Setting up and using Python virtual environments
- Security best practices
- Learning resources
- Installing essential libraries—tools for security automation
- Best practices for security automation and customization
- Best practices and customization—optimizing your Python setup

Technical requirements

Configuring Python for development or security automation requires several technical components to ensure smooth operation and compatibility with various tools and libraries. Here is an overview of the essential technical requirements:

- **Python installation**:
  - **Python version**: Ensure the latest stable version of Python is installed, typically Python 3.x. Older versions (such as Python 2.x) are deprecated and lack support for many modern libraries.
  - **Cross-platform support**: Python runs on Windows, macOS, and Linux, so ensure your system meets the **operating system (OS)** requirements for Python installation.
  - **Installation package**: Use the official Python installer from `https://www.python.org/downloads/` or package managers such as `brew` (for macOS), `apt` (for Linux), or `choco` (for Windows) to install Python.

- **Development environment**:
  - **IDE or text editor**: Set up a Python-friendly IDE such as PyCharm, **Visual Studio Code (VS Code)**, or Sublime Text. These editors often come with syntax highlighting, debugging tools, and linting to streamline development.
  - **Virtual environment setup**: It's essential to create isolated Python environments using tools such as `venv` or `virtualenv` to manage dependencies for each project independently and avoid conflicts between libraries.

- **Package management**:
  - **pip (Python package installer)**: Ensure `pip` is installed to handle Python libraries and dependencies. The `pip` package installer comes bundled with Python in most distributions, but you can verify it by running `pip --version`.
  - **Package repositories**: For security automation, you may need to install specific packages such as `requests`, `scapy`, or `paramiko`. You can find and install these from the **Python Package Index (PyPI)** using `pip install <package-name>`.

System dependencies

OS-specific dependencies refer to software libraries or components that are tailored to work with a particular OS. Different OSs—such as Windows, macOS, and Linux—have distinct architectures, filesystems, and methods for handling system calls and resources. Consequently, certain libraries or tools may function optimally or only on specific OS platforms:

- **OS-specific libraries**: Some Python libraries may require OS-specific dependencies. For example, `libpcap` is required for packet sniffing with `scapy`, and `libssl-dev` is often needed for cryptography packages.

- **Python path configuration**: Ensure that Python and `pip` are properly added to your system's environment variables so they can be accessed from the command line.

By ensuring these technical requirements are met, you will be ready to configure Python for development or security automation, with full access to its rich ecosystem of tools and libraries.

Setting up and using Python virtual environments

Setting up Python in a **virtual environment** is a best practice that offers several significant advantages, particularly when working on multiple projects or using various libraries and dependencies. The following subsections explain why setting up Python in a virtual environment is important.

Dependency isolation

A virtual environment creates an isolated space where project-specific libraries and dependencies are installed. This ensures that dependencies for one project do not conflict with those of another. Without a virtual environment, installing packages globally can lead to version conflicts, especially when different projects require different versions of the same package.

For example, Project A might require **Django 3.1**, while Project B requires **Django 2.2**. Without a virtual environment, managing both versions simultaneously would be difficult.

> **What is Django?**
> Django is a high-level web framework for building web applications using the Python programming language. It follows the **Model-View-Template** (**MVT**) architectural pattern and is designed to promote rapid development, clean design, and the creation of scalable and secure web applications.

Reproducibility

Virtual environments make it easy to replicate the exact setup of a project, ensuring that others working on the same project or moving the project to a different system can run it without issues. By using a virtual environment and a `requirements.txt` file (which lists all the installed packages and their versions), you can easily recreate the environment by running the following:

```bash
pip install -r requirements.txt
```

This leads to consistent development environments across different machines and reduces the likelihood of "*it works on my machine*" issues.

Avoiding polluting the global Python installation

Installing libraries and dependencies directly into the global Python environment can lead to unnecessary clutter and potential system conflicts. A virtual environment keeps the global Python installation clean and untouched. This also reduces the risk of accidentally breaking system-wide applications that rely on specific Python packages.

For instance, system tools or applications on Linux that depend on a particular version of `requests` might break if you install or upgrade a package globally without knowing its impact.

Flexibility in experimentation

Virtual environments allow you to experiment with different libraries, versions, and configurations without risking your primary setup. You can create and discard virtual environments as needed, providing a safe space for testing new tools, libraries, or frameworks.

Using a virtual environment in Python development is critical for dependency management, project reproducibility, and preventing conflicts between projects. It ensures cleaner project organization and greater flexibility, making it a vital part of Python development workflows.

Common pitfalls to avoid

While virtual environments offer significant advantages, there are some common pitfalls that developers should be aware of:

- **Failing to activate the environment**: One of the most frequent mistakes is forgetting to activate the virtual environment before running a script or installing packages. This can lead to installing packages in the global environment rather than the intended virtual environment, resulting in unexpected behavior.

- **Mismatched dependencies**: If you create multiple virtual environments for different projects, ensure that you keep track of the required dependencies for each one. Inconsistent dependencies across environments can lead to confusion and errors when switching between projects.

- **Not updating the requirements.txt file**: After installing new packages, it's essential to update your `requirements.txt` file to reflect these changes. Failing to do so can make it challenging to replicate the environment later.

By being mindful of these potential pitfalls and actively managing your virtual environments, you can enjoy the full benefits they offer while minimizing issues that could disrupt your development workflow.

Installing Python

To install Python, simply download the latest version from the official Python website, run the installer, and ensure you check the box to add Python to your system's PATH environment variable for easy access. Instructions for the different platforms are provided next:

- **Windows**:

    I.   Download Python:

    - Go to the official Python website (`https://www.python.org/downloads/`).

    - Download the latest version of Python for Windows.

    II.   Run the installer:

    - Run the downloaded installer.

    - Make sure to check the box that says **Add Python to PATH**.

    III.   Choose **Install Now** or **Customize installation** for more options (such as setting the installation location or enabling/disabling optional features).

- **macOS**:

    I.   Download Python:

    - Go to the official Python website (`https://www.python.org/downloads/`).

    - Download the latest version of Python for macOS.

    II.   Run the installer: Run the downloaded installer and follow the instructions.

    III.   Using Homebrew (alternative method):

    - Install Homebrew from `brew.sh` (`https://brew.sh/`).

    - Open a terminal and run `brew install python`.

- **Linux**:

    I.   Using a package manager:

    - **Debian-based (Ubuntu)**: Run `sudo apt-get update` and `sudo apt-get install python3`

    - **Red Hat-based (Fedora)**: Run `sudo dnf install python3`

    - **Arch-based**: Run `sudo pacman -S python`

By following the installation steps and properly configuring your system, including adding Python to your PATH environment variable and setting up virtual environments, you'll be ready to start coding efficiently and manage projects seamlessly.

Setting up a virtual environment

Let us learn how to create and configure a Python virtual environment to isolate project-specific dependencies. We'll explore how virtual environments help manage different library versions and prevent conflicts across multiple projects.

Follow these steps to set up a virtual environment:

1. Install venv (if not already installed):

    I.   Run pip install virtualenv (for Python 2).

    II. For Python 3, venv is included in the standard library.

2. Create a virtual environment:

    I.   Navigate to your project directory.

    II. Run python -m venv env (where env is the name of your virtual environment).

3. Activate the virtual environment:

    I.   Windows: .\env\Scripts\activate.

    II. macOS/Linux: source env/bin/activate.

4. Deactivate the virtual environment:

    I.   Run deactivate.

In conclusion, setting up a Python virtual environment is crucial for managing dependencies and ensuring project isolation. By using virtual environments, you create a more organized and conflict-free development process, allowing for smoother and more flexible project management.

Installing an IDE

Choosing an IDE depends on your preference. Here are some popular ones:

-   **VS Code**:

    I.   Download and install:

        •   Download VS Code from the VS Code website (https://code.visualstudio.com/).
        •   Install the downloaded file.

II.   Install the Python extension:

  • Open VS Code.

  • Go to **Extensions** (*Ctrl + Shift + X*).

  • Search for `Python` and install the Microsoft extension.

III.   Configure the Python interpreter:

  • Open the Command Palette (*Ctrl + Shift + P*).

  • Type `Python: Select Interpreter`.

  • Choose your virtual environment's interpreter.

- **PyCharm**:

I.   Download and install:

  • Download PyCharm from the JetBrains website (`https://www.jetbrains.com/pycharm/`).

  • Install the downloaded file.

II.   Configure the project interpreter:

  • Open PyCharm.

  • Create a new project or open an existing one.

  • Go to **File | Settings | Project: <Project Name> | Project Interpreter**.

  • Add your virtual environment's interpreter.

- **Other IDEs**:

  • **Jupyter Notebook**: For data science projects. Install via `pip install notebook` and run with `jupyter notebook`.

  • **Sublime Text**: Lightweight editor with Python support via plugins.

  • **Atom**: Another lightweight editor with Python support via plugins.

With features such as code completion, debugging tools, and project management capabilities, an IDE simplifies development, allowing you to focus on writing efficient and error-free code while managing projects more effectively.

Choosing an IDE for security automation

Selecting the right IDE can significantly impact your workflow when writing Python scripts for security automation. Here are some popular IDEs within the security community, along with what makes them particularly suited for security tasks:

- **PyCharm**: PyCharm, developed by JetBrains, is highly favored in the security community for its robust features and comprehensive support for Python. Its features (such as code analysis, an integrated debugger, and support for virtual environments) make it ideal for complex security scripts. PyCharm Professional even has dedicated tools for database integration and scientific libraries, which are useful for advanced security analysis.

- **VS Code**: Known for its versatility and customization options, VS Code is a popular choice for security professionals. Its rich extension ecosystem includes plugins for Python, Docker, remote development, and even security-specific tools such as code linters and vulnerability checkers. It's lightweight but powerful, making it suitable for developers who want a highly customizable environment without sacrificing performance.

- **Jupyter Notebook**: Although not a traditional IDE, Jupyter Notebook is widely used in the security field for data analysis, exploratory scripting, and rapid prototyping. Its cell-based format is excellent for testing security scripts, analyzing data, and presenting results step by step. It's particularly useful for security professionals who need to perform vulnerability assessments or automate report generation interactively.

- **Atom**: Atom is an open source editor that offers Python support through plugins. Its flexibility and strong community support make it a good option for those looking for a lightweight and customizable editor. Atom's **Teletype** feature also allows for live collaboration, which can be helpful when working with security teams.

- **Sublime Text**: Lightweight and fast, Sublime Text is ideal for quick edits and script development on the go. While it lacks some built-in debugging tools, it's highly customizable and can be extended to support Python development with packages such as Anaconda. Many security professionals appreciate Sublime Text for its minimalism and efficiency.

While either of these IDEs will work for security automation, choosing the right one depends on your personal preferences, specific project needs, and whether you prioritize features such as debugging, collaboration, or lightweight speed. Experimenting with a few can help you find the best fit for your development style.

Installing essential Python packages

When using `pip` to install packages, the commands work across all major OSs (Windows, macOS, and Linux) but are entered in different **command-line interfaces** (**CLIs**) depending on the OS:

- **Windows**: You'd typically use **Command Prompt** (**CMD**) or **PowerShell**. The command to install packages is the following:

    ```cmd
    pip install package_name
    ```

- **macOS and Linux**: The installation happens in **Terminal**. The command is the same as on Windows:

    ```bash
    pip install package_name
    ```

If Python was installed recently, `pip` should work right from these command-line tools on all three OSs. But it's worth noting a couple of key points:

- **Python environment setup**: On some systems, especially macOS and Linux, you may need to use `pip3` instead of `pip` if both Python 2 and Python 3 are installed. In such cases, the command would look like this:

    ```bash
    pip3 install package_name
    ```

- **Virtual environments**: If working within a virtual environment, make sure the environment is activated first. This ensures the packages are installed within the environment rather than system-wide.

Let's summarize what we've just learned:

- **Command Prompt or PowerShell** is generally used on Windows.

- **Terminal** is used on macOS and Linux.

- **Virtual environments** should be activated before running any `pip` installation to manage dependencies specific to the project.

Using `pip`, you can install the necessary packages in the following way:

1. Upgrade `pip`:

    *   Run `pip install --upgrade pip`.

2. Install packages. Commonly used packages include the following (the command to install each package follows the package name):

    *   `numpy`: `pip install numpy`
    *   `pandas`: `pip install pandas`
    *   `requests`: `pip install requests`
    *   `matplotlib`: `pip install matplotlib`
    *   `scipy`: `pip install scipy`
    *   `scikit-learn`: `pip install scikit-learn`

3. Freeze requirements:

    *   To create a `requirements.txt` file listing your dependencies, run `pip freeze > requirements.txt`.
    *   To install dependencies from a `requirements.txt` file, run `pip install -r requirements.txt`.

By leveraging tools such as `pip` to install libraries, you can easily integrate powerful features into your projects, streamline workflows, and access a vast ecosystem of pre-built modules, ensuring efficient and flexible coding across various applications.

Additional tool – virtualenvwrapper

For those looking to streamline their virtual environment management, `virtualenvwrapper` is a valuable tool that extends the capabilities of `virtualenv`. It provides additional commands and features that can enhance productivity, especially for users managing multiple projects or frequently switching between environments.

Some advantages of `virtualenvwrapper` include the following:

*   **Centralized location**: By default, `virtualenvwrapper` keeps all virtual environments in a single directory, making them easy to find and manage.

*   **Convenient commands**: It adds commands such as `mkvirtualenv` (for creating environments), `workon` (for activating environments), and `rmvirtualenv` (for removing environments), which simplify workflows and reduce the need to remember paths.

- **Automatic activation**: With `workon`, you can switch environments seamlessly without needing to navigate to the environment directory manually.

To get started with `virtualenvwrapper`, you can install it with `pip`:

```
pip install virtualenvwrapper
```

On macOS and Linux, you'll need to add the following to your shell's startup file (for example, `.bashrc` or `.zshrc`):

```
export WORKON_HOME=$HOME/.virtualenvs
source /usr/local/bin/virtualenvwrapper.sh
```

On Windows, you can use `virtualenvwrapper-win` instead:

```
pip install virtualenvwrapper-win
```

With `virtualenvwrapper`, managing multiple environments becomes easier, making it an excellent addition for those advancing in their Python and security automation work.

Version control with Git

Using Git for version control is essential for managing your code base. Follow the next steps to get started with Git:

1. Install Git: Download and install Git (`https://git-scm.com/`).

2. Configure Git: Set your username and email:

    - `git config --global user.name "Your Name"`
    - `git config --global user.email "you@example.com"`

3. Initialize a repository:

    I.   Navigate to your project directory.
    II. Run `git init`.

4. Create a `.gitignore` file: Specify files and directories to ignore (for example, `env/` for the virtual environment, and `*.pyc` for compiled Python files).

5. Commit changes:

   - Add files to the staging area by running `git add`.

   - Commit changes by running `git commit -m "Initial commit"`.

6. Push to a remote repository:

   - Create a repository on GitHub, GitLab, or Bitbucket.

   - Link the local repository to the remote one:

     - `git remote add origin <repository_url>`

     - `git push -u origin master`

Additional tools and best practices

Tools such as vulnerability scanners, **security information and event management** (**SIEM**) systems, and patch management software work in tandem to enhance detection, remediation, and monitoring processes. Best practices such as regularly updating software, using automation for repetitive tasks, and maintaining a robust incident response plan further help in strengthening security posture. Leveraging these tools and practices ensures that organizations stay proactive in managing security risks while maximizing operational efficiency:

- **Linters and formatters** (the commands to install them follow):

  I.   **Flake8**: `pip install flake8`

  II.   **Black**: `pip install black`

  III. **Pylint**: `pip install pylint`

- **Debugging**:

  I.   Use the built-in debugger in your IDE

  II.   For the command line, use the `pdb` module

- **Documentation**:

  I.   Write docstrings for your functions and classes

  II.   Use tools such as **Sphinx** (`pip install sphinx`) for generating documentation

- **Testing**:

  I.   Use **unittest** (built-in) or **pytest** (`pip install pytest`) for writing tests

  II.   Run tests frequently to catch bugs early

- **Continuous integration and continuous deployment (CI/CD):**

    I.   Set up CI/CD pipelines with tools such as GitHub Actions, Travis CI, or Jenkins

Environment management tools

Environment management tools allow teams to efficiently manage development, testing, and production environments, reducing the likelihood of conflicts and errors. By maintaining isolated environments, these tools enable developers and security professionals to configure, replicate, and scale environments quickly and securely. Popular tools in this category include **Docker** for containerization, **Vagrant** for virtual machine management, and **Terraform** for infrastructure-as-code automation, all of which help streamline security operations while ensuring compatibility across different platforms and environments.

- **pipenv**: Combines `pip` and `virtualenv` for better dependency management:

    I.   Install `pipenv`:

    - Run `pip install pipenv`.

    II.   Create a virtual environment and install dependencies:

    - Navigate to your project directory.
    - Run `pipenv install <package_name>` to install a package.
    - Run `pipenv install` to install all packages from `Pipfile`.

    III.   Activate the virtual environment:

    - Run `pipenv shell`.

    IV.   Generate `Pipfile.lock`:

    - Run `pipenv lock`.

- **conda**: An environment manager popular in data science:

    I.   Install `conda`:

    - Download and install Anaconda or Miniconda.

    II.   Create a virtual environment:

    - Run `conda create --name myenv`.

III.   Activate the environment:

- Run `conda activate myenv`.

IV.   Install packages:

- Run `conda install <package_name>`.

V.   Export the environment:

- Run `conda env export > environment.yml`.

VI.   Create an environment from the YAML file:

- Run `conda env create -f environment.yml`.

By leveraging the above tools, developers can easily manage complex workflows and maintain clean, conflict-free environments for seamless development and deployment.

Code quality and automation

Code quality and automation are critical aspects of modern software development, ensuring that code is not only functional but also efficient, maintainable, and free from bugs. Code quality refers to readable, scalable, and reliable code that is a result of adhering to best practices and standards. It involves practices such as writing clean, well-documented code, following design patterns, and using static analysis tools to catch potential errors early. High-quality code leads to fewer bugs, easier maintenance, and better collaboration across development teams.

Automation plays a key role in maintaining code quality by integrating CI and CD pipelines. Automated testing, linting, and code reviews ensure that code meets predefined quality standards before it is merged or deployed. Tools such as **Jenkins**, **GitLab CI**, and **CircleCI** can automate tasks such as running unit tests, checking for code style violations, and deploying to production. Automated processes not only reduce human error but also improve efficiency, allowing developers to focus on innovation rather than repetitive manual tasks.

Incorporating both code quality practices and automation into development workflows enhances overall software reliability, accelerates the release cycle, and promotes consistency, making them essential components of any robust development strategy. Let's take a closer look at this:

- **Automated testing**:

  - **Unit tests**:

    i.   Create tests for your functions and methods to ensure they work as expected.

    ii.   Use `unittest` or `pytest` to write and run tests.

- **CI**:

    i.　Automate your testing with CI tools such as GitHub Actions, Travis CI, CircleCI, or Jenkins.

    ii.　Configure your CI pipeline to run tests on every commit or pull request.

- **Code quality tools**: While IDEs provide many useful tools for coding, they often aren't enough for comprehensive code quality checks. Here's why relying solely on an IDE for code quality can fall short and why additional tools are beneficial:

    - **Limited linting capabilities**: Most IDEs have basic linting capabilities, which help catch obvious syntax errors, unused variables, or missing imports. However, they may not fully enforce coding standards or detect more nuanced issues, such as complex logic that's difficult to maintain or non-standard patterns. External linters such as **Pylint** or **Flake8** enforce coding standards in a way that goes beyond the basic checks most IDEs offer.

    - **Static analysis for security and performance**: IDEs don't typically perform in-depth static analysis, which can identify potential security vulnerabilities or performance bottlenecks. Specialized tools such as **Bandit** (for Python) analyze code for security vulnerabilities such as injection flaws, insecure file handling, or hardcoded secrets, offering much more rigorous scrutiny than IDEs alone.

    - **Complexity and code quality metrics**: Measuring code complexity, such as cyclomatic complexity or code duplication, requires more advanced analysis tools than IDEs usually provide. Tools such as **Radon** (for complexity) or **SonarQube** (for broader quality metrics) offer insights into maintainability, test coverage, and areas of high complexity that IDEs can't typically address on their own.

    - **Automated testing integration**: While some IDEs offer testing frameworks, they're often limited in scope and don't cover automated testing strategies fully. Testing frameworks such as `pytest` or `unittest` allow you to create, manage, and run comprehensive test suites, often integrating with CI pipelines for automated testing that catches issues early and continuously—something an IDE alone may not manage effectively.

    - **Consistency and automation across teams**: IDEs vary in the quality and configuration of their code quality tools. External code quality tools, however, can be integrated into CI/CD pipelines, ensuring that the same quality checks run regardless of the IDE or setup each developer is using. This consistency across teams helps avoid IDE-specific dependencies and improves code quality across the board.

    - **CI/CD integration**: Tools that assess code quality, style, and security can be automated to run on each commit or pull request through CI/CD pipelines. This ensures code quality is checked continuously and consistently before deployment, something an IDE isn't equipped to handle on its own.

While IDEs provide valuable real-time feedback and are essential for productivity, they aren't a substitute for comprehensive code quality tools. By using additional tools for code quality, security, testing, and complexity analysis, developers can ensure that their code is robust, maintainable, and secure across projects and teams. Let's take a look at some of these:

- **Flake8**:

  - Linter for Python to check for code style violations

  - Run `flake8 your_script.py`

- **Black**:

  - Formatter for Python code to ensure a consistent style

  - Run `black your_script.py`

- **Pylint**:

  - Code analysis tool for Python to check for errors and enforce a coding standard

  - Run `pylint your_script.py`

- **Documentation**: Using the following ways can enhance documentation:

  - **Docstrings**:

    - Write docstrings for functions, classes, and modules to explain their purpose and usage

    - Follow conventions such as Google style (`https://sphinxcontrib-napoleon.readthedocs.io/en/latest/example_google.html`) or NumPy style (`https://numpydoc.readthedocs.io/en/latest/format.html`)

  - **Sphinx**:

    - Documentation generator that converts `reStructuredText` files into HTML websites and PDFs

    - Install Sphinx by running `pip install sphinx`

    - Initialize Sphinx in your project by running `sphinx-quickstart`

    - Generate HTML documentation by running `make html` (Linux/macOS) or `make.bat html` (Windows)

Setting up and using Python virtual environments is crucial for maintaining clean and organized development workflows. A virtual environment allows you to isolate project-specific dependencies, ensuring that different projects do not interfere with one another. This prevents version conflicts between libraries and helps keep your global Python installation clean. Virtual environments also make it easy to replicate the same setup across different machines or for team members, ensuring consistency in project configurations. By using virtual environments, developers can work more efficiently, avoid dependency issues, and ensure that each project operates in a controlled, isolated space.

In addition to preventing conflicts, virtual environments improve collaboration and project portability. When working in teams, virtual environments enable each developer to have the same dependencies and package versions, ensuring that code works consistently across all systems. The use of a `requirements.txt` file makes it easy to share project dependencies and quickly set up new environments, reducing setup time and minimizing errors when onboarding new team members.

Furthermore, virtual environments help with long-term project maintenance. As projects evolve, dependencies may need to be updated or changed. Using virtual environments ensures that these updates don't affect other projects relying on different versions of the same libraries, providing more flexibility to manage updates and rollbacks as needed. Setting up and using virtual environments is a best practice for organized, scalable, and conflict-free Python development.

Security best practices

Implementing strong security protocols ensures the protection of sensitive information, reduces the risk of breaches, and helps organizations comply with regulations. Core principles include regular software updates, which address known vulnerabilities, and the use of strong authentication mechanisms such as **multi-factor authentication** (**MFA**) to protect accounts and systems from unauthorized access.

Other key practices include encryption to protect data both in transit and at rest, and access control to limit who can interact with certain resources. Security measures should also extend to regular monitoring and auditing of systems for suspicious activity, as well as consistent backup strategies to protect against data loss or ransomware attacks. Finally, promoting security awareness training ensures that employees are equipped to recognize and respond to potential threats such as phishing and social engineering attacks.

Effective dependency management is crucial for maintaining secure, reliable, and efficient code, especially in security automation where outdated or vulnerable libraries can introduce significant risks. Managing dependencies ensures that all necessary packages are up to date, compatible, and free of known vulnerabilities, helping to mitigate security gaps and maintain a stable development environment.

By implementing tools such as `pip`, virtual environments, and dependency checkers, developers can streamline updates and reduce the risk of conflicts, making their automation solutions resilient and easier to maintain. Here are some best practices:

1. **Dependency management**: Dependency management is a crucial aspect of security best practices, as vulnerabilities in third-party libraries or outdated packages can expose applications to security risks. Proper dependency management ensures that all external libraries and frameworks integrated into a project are up to date, secure, and reliable. Here are some key best practices for managing dependencies with security in mind:

   - **Check for vulnerabilities**:

     - Use tools such as `safety` to check for known vulnerabilities in your dependencies

     - Run `pip install safety` and `safety check`

2. **Secure coding practices**:

   - **Input validation**: Always validate and sanitize user inputs to prevent injection attacks

   - **Secrets management**:

     - Avoid hardcoding secrets (such as API keys) in your code

     - Use environment variables or secret management services

Advanced dependency management with automation tools

For more advanced dependency management, automated tools such as **Dependabot** and GitHub Security Alerts can help keep your code secure and up to date by identifying outdated libraries and potential vulnerabilities in real time. Let's look at how they work and why they're useful.

Dependabot

Dependabot is a GitHub-integrated tool that automatically checks for outdated dependencies in your project. When it finds outdated libraries or dependencies with known security vulnerabilities, it creates a pull request with the recommended updates. Dependabot supports a range of programming languages and package managers, including Python's `pip` and `pipenv`:

- **How it works**: Dependabot scans your dependency files (such as `requirements.txt` or `Pipfile`) and compares them against the latest versions available. If updates are available, it generates a pull request with the required version changes.

- **Advantages**: Automates dependency updates, reduces security risk by ensuring the latest versions are used, and integrates directly into GitHub, making it easy to review and merge updates.

GitHub Security Alerts

GitHub Security Alerts (part of GitHub's dependency graph) is a feature that scans your project for dependencies with known vulnerabilities. When it detects a security issue, it generates an alert in your GitHub repository and often suggests a version upgrade to address the vulnerability:

- **How it works**: GitHub uses a database of known vulnerabilities to analyze your dependencies. When vulnerabilities are detected, it alerts repository administrators and provides relevant details, including potential upgrade paths or patches.

- **Advantages**: Adds an extra layer of security, alerts you of vulnerabilities even without direct action, and integrates with GitHub, allowing you to monitor dependencies alongside code changes.

Integration into CI/CD pipelines

Both Dependabot and GitHub Security Alerts can be integrated into your CI/CD pipelines. By combining them with CI/CD tools (such as **GitHub Actions** or **Jenkins**), you can automatically test dependencies, ensuring that updates or vulnerability patches won't disrupt your code base.

Benefits of automated dependency management

Automated dependency management has the following primary benefits:

- **Security**: Automated tools help ensure that you're using the latest, most secure versions of dependencies.

- **Reduced technical debt**: By regularly updating dependencies, you prevent the accumulation of technical debt and avoid the risks of outdated or unsupported libraries.

- **Time savings**: Automated tools reduce the time spent on manual updates, allowing your team to focus on development rather than maintenance.

Performance optimization

In today's digital landscape, performance optimization is critical for delivering fast, responsive applications that provide a seamless user experience and make efficient use of resources. Whether you're building web applications, mobile apps, or backend systems, optimizing performance not only improves speed and responsiveness but also enhances scalability, reduces costs, and keeps users engaged. Let's look at some ways this can be achieved:

1. **Profiling**:

    - `cProfile`:

        - Built-in module for profiling Python programs

        - Run `python -m cProfile your_script.py`

- `line_profiler`:

  - Line-by-line profiling to see which lines of code are taking the most time

  - Install it by running `pip install line_profiler`

  - Add the `@profile` decorator to the functions you want to profile and run with `kernprof -l -v your_script.py`

2. **Optimization techniques**:

   - **Algorithmic improvements**: Optimize the algorithm to reduce time complexity.

   - **Use built-in functions**: Utilize Python's built-in functions and libraries that are implemented in C and optimized for performance.

   - **Parallelism**: Parallelism is a technique in computing where multiple tasks or processes are executed simultaneously, taking advantage of multi-core processors and distributed computing resources to perform operations faster. By splitting a task into smaller parts that can run concurrently, parallelism reduces the overall execution time, which is particularly beneficial for tasks that involve heavy computations or processing large datasets.

In conclusion, following security best practices is essential for protecting systems, applications, and data from potential cyber threats. By regularly updating software, implementing strong authentication methods, encrypting sensitive data, and managing access controls, organizations can significantly reduce the risk of breaches. Additionally, proactive measures such as dependency management, monitoring, auditing, and security awareness training further strengthen defenses. Prioritizing these best practices ensures a more secure, resilient, and compliant environment, safeguarding both the organization and its users from evolving security challenges.

Concurrency in security automation with asyncio

In security automation, many tasks involve waiting on I/O-bound operations, such as querying servers, scanning networks, or fetching data from multiple sources. Using concurrency techniques such as **asyncio** can significantly improve the efficiency of these processes by allowing multiple operations to run "concurrently" rather than waiting for each to complete sequentially.

Key tools and techniques

To perform security automation with `asyncio`, we use the following tools:

- **asyncio**: This Python library enables asynchronous programming by allowing you to execute multiple I/O-bound tasks simultaneously, using the `async` and `await` keywords. This is especially useful in security automation where tasks such as API calls or port scans can happen simultaneously, dramatically reducing waiting time.

- **Threading and multiprocessing**: While `asyncio` is great for I/O-bound tasks, threading and multiprocessing libraries in Python are more suitable for CPU-bound tasks. For example, multiprocessing can distribute cryptographic computations across multiple CPU cores.

Example scenarios in security automation

We typically have the following scenarios to deal with in security automation:

- **Parallel network scanning**: The `asyncio` library can handle multiple network ports concurrently, making network scanning faster and more efficient.

- **Automated API requests**: For tools that interact with vulnerability databases or other resources, using `asyncio` allows multiple API requests to run in parallel, speeding up data retrieval for larger assessments.

These techniques allow you to increase performance in security automation tasks without needing additional hardware resources, making them a cost-effective way to scale your automation workflows.

Learning resources

There are many learning resources available to learn how to utilize Python for different aspects in security. Some of them are as follows:

- **Python for Cybersecurity Specialization (Coursera)**: This specialization focuses on using Python for various security applications, including penetration testing, malware analysis, and security tool development. It provides hands-on labs and exercises tailored for cybersecurity professionals.

- **Python for Offensive Security (Udemy)**: This course is ideal for those interested in offensive security, focusing specifically on using Python for penetration testing. Topics include network scanning, exploiting vulnerabilities, and creating custom hacking tools.

- **Python for Pentesters (INE)**: INE's course offers comprehensive coverage on using Python for penetration testing and ethical hacking, with a focus on scripting for network scanning, exploitation, and automating common pentesting tasks.

- **Black Hat Python: Python Programming for Hackers and Pentesters (book and course)**: Based on the popular book *Black Hat Python*, this course covers Python tools and techniques for penetration testing, including creating reverse shells, network sniffers, and keyloggers. It's a practical, code-driven course that's widely respected in the security community.

- **SANS SEC573: Automating Information Security with Python (SANS Institute)**: This course offers an in-depth curriculum for security automation using Python, covering topics such as data processing, network automation, and penetration testing. Though intensive, it's highly regarded for its applicability in professional security settings.

Online tutorials and courses

The following are some online tutorials and courses you can look into:

- **Official Python documentation**: `https://www.python.org/doc/`
- **Real Python**: `https://realpython.com/`
- **Coursera**: Python courses from various universities
- **edX**: Python courses from various institutions
- **Udemy**: Various Python courses from different instructors

Communities

Following are some great communities you can be a part of:

- **Stack Overflow**: Ask and answer questions
- **Reddit (r/learnpython)**: Community of Python learners
- **Python Discord**: Chat with other Python developers

By following this guide, you will have a well-configured Python development environment that is efficient, secure, and conducive to producing high-quality code.

Installing essential libraries – tools for security automation

Security automation involves using tools and scripts to automate the detection and remediation of security issues. Here are some essential libraries and tools for security automation in Python:

- **Bandit**: Bandit is a tool designed to find common security issues in Python code:
  - **Install Bandit**: Run `pip install bandit`
  - **Usage**:
    - To scan a single file, run `bandit your_script.py`
    - To scan an entire directory, run `bandit -r your_directory/`
  - **Configuration**: You can configure Bandit using a `.bandit` configuration file to specify custom settings, such as excluding certain tests or paths.
- **Safety**: Safety-check your installed dependencies for known security vulnerabilities:
  - **Install Safety**: Run `pip install safety`

- **Usage**:

  - To check installed packages, run `safety check`

  - To check a `requirements.txt` file, run `safety check -r requirements.txt`

- **Pylint**: Pylint is a static code analysis tool that can help identify code errors, enforce coding standards, and detect code smells, including some security issues:

  - **Install Pylint**: Run `pip install pylint`

  - **Usage**:

    - To analyze a file, run `pylint your_script.py`

    - To analyze a directory, run `pylint your_directory/`

  - **Configuration**: Customize Pylint behavior using a `.pylintrc` configuration file.

- **YARA-Python**: YARA is a tool aimed at helping malware researchers identify and classify malware samples. YARA-Python allows using YARA's pattern-matching capabilities from Python scripts:

  - **Install YARA-Python**: Run `pip install yara-python`

  - **Usage**:

    - Import YARA in your Python script: `import yara`.

    - Compile and match YARA rules within your Python code.

- **Requests**: The Requests library is not inherently a security tool, but it's crucial for security automation scripts that need to interact with web services, REST APIs, or download content:

  - **Install Requests**: Run `pip install requests`

  - **Usage**:

    - Import Requests in your script: `import requests`

    - Perform HTTP requests: `response = requests.get('https://example.com')`

- **Paramiko**: Paramiko is a Python implementation of SSHv2. It provides both client and server functionalities, making it ideal for automating secure file transfers and remote command execution:

  - **Install Paramiko**: Run `pip install paramiko`

  - **Usage**:

    - Import Paramiko in your script by running `import paramiko`.

    - Connect to an SSH server and execute commands or transfer files.

- **Scapy**: Scapy is a powerful Python library for network packet manipulation. It's widely used in security testing for creating, sending, sniffing, and dissecting network packets:

  - **Install Scapy**: Run `pip install scapy`

  - **Usage**:

    - Import Scapy in your script: `from scapy.all import *`.

    - Create and send packets: `send(IP(dst="1.2.3.4")/ICMP())`.

- **Nmap**: Nmap is a powerful network scanning tool. The `python-nmap` Python library provides an interface to Nmap from Python:

  - **Install Nmap and python-nmap**:

    - Ensure Nmap is installed on your system. For installation instructions, visit `nmap.org`.

    - Install `python-nmap` by running `pip install python-nmap`.

  - **Usage**:

    - Import `python-nmap` in your script by running `import nmap`.

    - Create an Nmap scanner instance and perform scans.

- **SQLMap**: SQLMap is an open source penetration testing tool that automates the process of detecting and exploiting SQL injection flaws. The `sqlmapapi` Python library allows integration with SQLMap:

  - **Install SQLMap and sqlmapapi**:

    - Ensure SQLMap is installed on your system. For installation instructions, visit `sqlmap.org`.

    - The API is part of the SQLMap installation; no separate installation is needed.

  - **Usage**:

    - Start the SQLMap API server by running `python sqlmapapi.py -s`.

    - Use the API to send commands to the SQLMap engine.

- **Cryptography**: The Cryptography library provides cryptographic recipes and primitives to help you secure your applications:

  - **Install Cryptography**: Run `pip install cryptography`

  - **Usage**:

    - Import `cryptography` in your script by running:
      `from cryptography.fernet import Fernet`.

    - Generate keys, and encrypt and decrypt data.

- **Python-OpenStackClient**: For managing OpenStack security settings and automating cloud security tasks:

  - **Install Python-OpenStackClient**: Run `pip install python-openstackclient`
  - **Usage**:

    - Import the OpenStack client in your script by running `from openstack import connection`.
    - Use the client to manage OpenStack resources securely.

- **Pexpect**: Pexpect allows you to spawn child applications and control them automatically. It is used for automating interactive applications such as SSH, FTP, `passwd`, and others:

  - **Install Pexpect**: Run `pip install pexpect`
  - **Usage**:

    - Import Pexpect in your script: `import pexpect`.
    - Automate interactions with command-line applications.

Best practices for security automation

Implementing security automation can greatly enhance your organization's security posture, but it must be done thoughtfully to avoid potential pitfalls. Here are key best practices to follow:

- **Define clear objectives**: Before implementing automation, clearly define the goals you want to achieve. This could include automating vulnerability scanning, **incident response** (**IR**), or compliance checks. Having well-defined objectives helps focus efforts and measure success.

- **Start small and scale up**: Begin with automating small, repeatable tasks to understand the process and tools involved. Once you've successfully implemented automation in these areas, gradually scale up to more complex tasks, ensuring that your automation processes are robust and effective.

- **Maintain visibility and control**: Ensure that automated processes have clear logging and monitoring. This visibility allows you to track actions taken by automated systems, identify potential issues, and maintain control over your security posture.

- **Regularly review and update automation scripts**: Security threats evolve constantly, and your automation scripts must keep pace. Regularly review and update scripts to incorporate new **threat intelligence** (**TI**), adjust to changes in infrastructure, and refine processes based on lessons learned.

- **Implement version control**: Use **version control systems** (**VCSs**) (such as Git) to manage automation scripts. This allows for better collaboration, tracking changes over time, and rolling back to previous versions if issues arise.

- **Integrate with existing security tools**: Ensure that your automation efforts are compatible with existing security tools and platforms. Integration can streamline processes and enhance overall security effectiveness, enabling information sharing between systems.

- **Test thoroughly before deployment**: Before deploying any automated scripts, conduct thorough testing in a controlled environment. This helps ensure that scripts function as intended without introducing unintended vulnerabilities or issues into your systems.

- **Prioritize security by design**: When developing automation scripts, prioritize security best practices, such as secure coding techniques and minimizing permissions. Ensure that sensitive information is handled securely and that scripts do not expose vulnerabilities.

- **Provide training and documentation**: Ensure that team members involved in security automation are adequately trained on the tools and processes being used. Additionally, maintain up-to-date documentation for automation scripts and workflows to facilitate understanding and continuity.

- **Adopt a feedback loop**: Establish a feedback loop to gather input from security analysts and stakeholders on the effectiveness of automation processes. Use this feedback to improve and refine your automation strategies continuously.

By following these best practices, organizations can maximize the effectiveness of their security automation efforts while minimizing risks and ensuring robust security operations. This structured approach helps in maintaining a secure, efficient, and responsive security environment.

Using environment variables for sensitive data, such as API keys and passwords, enhances security by keeping confidential information outside of your source code, reducing the risk of accidental exposure. Storing sensitive data in environment variables ensures that it's only accessible within the runtime environment, minimizing the chances of it being checked into version control or accessible by unauthorized users. This approach is essential for secure and scalable applications, as it simplifies sensitive data management across development, testing, and production environments:

1. **Use environment variables for sensitive data**:

   - Store API keys, passwords, and other sensitive information in environment variables.

   - Access these variables in your Python script using the `os` module: `import os` and `os.getenv('MY_SECRET_KEY')`.

2. **Keep dependencies updated**:

   - Regularly update your dependencies to ensure you have the latest security patches.

   - Use tools such as `pip-review` to check for updates: `pip install pip-review` and `pip-review --auto`.

3. **Use version control**:

   - Keep your code in a VCS such as Git.

   - Regularly commit changes and use branches for new features or fixes.

4. **Implement logging**:

   - Use the `logging` module to log important events and errors.

   - Ensure logs are stored securely and monitored for suspicious activities.

5. **Write tests**:

   - Write unit tests for your security automation scripts to ensure they work as expected.

   - Use the `pytest` or `unittest` frameworks for writing and running tests.

6. **Monitoring and alerting**: Automate monitoring and alerting to detect and respond to security incidents in real time.

Prometheus and Grafana

Prometheus and **Grafana** are powerful tools commonly used together for monitoring and visualizing system performance and metrics. Their combined capabilities enable organizations to gain insights into application behavior, resource utilization, and overall system health.

Prometheus and Grafana provide a powerful solution for real-time monitoring and visualization of system metrics, allowing you to track performance, detect anomalies, and gain insights into your infrastructure's health. Prometheus serves as a metrics collection and alerting toolkit, while Grafana offers a flexible interface for visualizing the data collected by Prometheus, creating detailed dashboards and alerts. Together, they form a robust foundation for proactive system monitoring and resource management:

1. **Install Prometheus and Grafana**: Follow the installation instructions on the Prometheus website and the Grafana website.

2. **Configure Prometheus**: Set up Prometheus to scrape metrics from your applications and infrastructure.

3. **Create Grafana dashboards**: Connect Grafana to Prometheus and create dashboards to visualize your metrics.

4. **Set up alerts**: Configure alerting rules in Prometheus to notify you of any anomalies or incidents.

ELK Stack (Elasticsearch, Logstash, Kibana)

The ELK Stack is used for centralized logging and monitoring. The following are the steps for setting up and utilizing the ELK Stack:

1. **Install ELK Stack**: Follow the installation instructions at `https://www.elastic.co/guide/en/elastic-stack/current/installing-elastic-stack.html`.

2. **Collect logs**: Use Logstash to collect and process logs from various sources.

3. **Store logs**: Store logs in Elasticsearch for easy searching and analysis.

4. **Visualize logs**: Use Kibana to create visualizations and dashboards for your logs.

5. **Set up alerts**: Configure Kibana or use **ElastAlert** to set up alerts based on log data.

IR automation

Python plays a significant role in the automation of tasks related to monitoring and visualization tools. Here's how:

- **Data collection**:

  - Python can be used to write scripts that collect and prepare data for Prometheus. You can create custom exporters that expose metrics from your application or environment, making them available for Prometheus to scrape.

  - *Example*: A Python script could monitor the health of a web service and expose metrics such as response times and error rates via an HTTP endpoint. Prometheus would scrape this endpoint periodically to collect the metrics.

- **Integration with APIs**:

  - Many monitoring tools, including Grafana, offer APIs that allow developers to automate tasks such as creating dashboards, managing alerts, or fetching metrics programmatically. Python's rich set of libraries, such as `requests`, makes it easy to interact with these APIs.

  - *Example*: You could write a Python script that uses the Grafana API to dynamically create dashboards based on specific metrics that you are monitoring. This allows you to adjust visualizations based on changing requirements without manual intervention.

- **Custom dashboards and visualizations**:

  - While Grafana provides built-in visualization capabilities, you can extend its functionality using Python to process data or create custom visualizations that better suit your needs.

  - *Example*: You could develop a custom Grafana panel plugin using JavaScript, but you could use Python to preprocess or aggregate data that is then visualized in Grafana. This might involve using Python to perform complex calculations or data transformations before sending the results to Grafana.

- **Automation of alerts and notifications**:

  - Using Python, you can create scripts that integrate with monitoring tools to automate responses to alerts. For example, when Prometheus triggers an alert based on a metric threshold, a Python script can be invoked to perform specific actions, such as restarting a service or sending notifications.

- *Example*: A Python script could be set up to respond to alerts from Prometheus, checking the status of a service and automatically restarting it if it is down, or sending an email alert with the relevant logs.

- **Scheduling and orchestration**:

  - Python can be used in conjunction with task schedulers (such as **cron** on Unix-based systems or **Task Scheduler** on Windows) or orchestration tools (such as **Airflow**) to automate regular monitoring tasks.

  - *Example*: A Python script that collects and processes logs daily can be scheduled using `cron`. The results can be sent to Prometheus for monitoring and later visualized in Grafana.

Customization of tools

Many of the tools discussed can be customized to suit specific needs, enhancing their capabilities in the following ways:

- **Prometheus custom exporters**:

  - You can create custom exporters in Python that collect specific metrics from your applications, databases, or systems. This allows you to monitor application-specific metrics that are not covered by default exporters.

  - *Example*: A Python exporter could expose metrics about application-level performance, such as cache hits/misses or database query execution times.

- **Grafana dashboard automation**:

  - Using the Grafana API, you can automate the creation and management of dashboards programmatically. Python scripts can be developed to generate dashboards based on specific monitoring needs or user preferences.

  - *Example*: A Python script could dynamically generate a Grafana dashboard for a new microservice, pulling in the necessary metrics and visualizations based on the current application architecture.

- **Custom alerts with Python**:

  - You can write custom alerting logic using Python, allowing for more sophisticated alert conditions based on the metrics collected by Prometheus.

  - *Example*: Instead of relying solely on Prometheus' built-in alerting rules, a Python script could analyze historical data trends and set alerts based on predicted future values, making the monitoring system more proactive.

By integrating Python with tools such as Prometheus and Grafana, organizations can build a highly customized and automated monitoring environment that enhances visibility, responsiveness, and efficiency in managing their applications and infrastructure.

Security orchestration, automation, and response platforms

Security orchestration, automation, and response (SOAR) platforms such as Splunk Phantom and IBM Resilient automate the entire IR life cycle:

1. **Install a SOAR platform**: Choose a SOAR platform and follow the installation instructions provided by the vendor.

2. **Create playbooks**: Define playbooks to automate common IR tasks, such as data collection, analysis, and remediation.

3. **Integrate with your environment**: Integrate the SOAR platform with your existing security tools and infrastructure.

4. **Automate responses**: Use the playbooks to automate IR actions and reduce response times.

Custom IR scripts

Use Python to create custom scripts for automating specific IR tasks:

1. **Collect evidence**: Automate evidence collection using libraries such as `requests` for API calls, `paramiko` for SSH, and `os` for system commands.

2. **Analyze data**: Use libraries such as `pandas` for data analysis and `scapy` for network traffic analysis.

3. **Take action**: Automate remediation actions such as isolating affected systems, blocking IP addresses, or revoking access.

TI automation

Automate the collection and analysis of TI to stay ahead of emerging threats. The following platforms can be used for this.

OpenCTI

OpenCTI is a powerful platform designed for managing and analyzing TI data. By integrating OpenCTI with various TI feeds, organizations can centralize their threat data, enabling better detection, visualization, and automation of threat responses. The following steps outline how to leverage OpenCTI for optimizing TI workflows:

1. **Install OpenCTI**: Begin by following the official installation instructions to set up OpenCTI in your environment. This step ensures that the platform is configured properly and ready for use.

2. **Integrate TI feeds**: OpenCTI supports the integration of multiple TI feeds, allowing security teams to enrich their data with up-to-date information about emerging threats, attack patterns, and vulnerabilities. Integrating these feeds enables proactive monitoring and detection of potential threats.

3. **Analyze threat data**: Once the data is collected, use OpenCTI's powerful analysis and visualization tools to identify patterns, assess risks, and gain actionable insights into security threats.

4. **Automate threat detection**: By creating custom rules and alerts within OpenCTI, you can automate the detection of certain types of threats, reducing manual effort and enabling faster response times. This helps organizations stay ahead of attackers by reacting to threats as they emerge, based on intelligence data.

By following these steps, organizations can integrate OpenCTI into their security infrastructure, improving their ability to detect, analyze, and respond to threats quickly and accurately.

Malware Information Sharing Platform

Malware Information Sharing Platform (**MISP**) is an open source tool designed to facilitate the sharing, storing, and correlation of TI data. By centralizing this information, MISP helps organizations detect and respond to emerging cyber threats more effectively. The following are the key steps to integrate MISP into your TI workflow:

1. **Install MISP**: Begin by following the installation guide provided on the official MISP website. This will ensure the proper setup of the platform within your environment.

2. **Integrate TI feeds**: MISP supports integration with various external TI feeds, allowing you to enrich the platform with up-to-date threat data. By connecting these feeds, you can gain insights into **indicators of compromise** (**IOCs**), attack techniques, and more, enhancing your threat detection capabilities.

3. **Share and analyze threat data**: Use MISP to collaborate with trusted partners, sharing threat data across organizations to enhance collective defense. In addition, MISP offers tools to analyze incoming threat data, helping you identify attack patterns and assess potential risks to your network.

4. **Automate threat detection**: By creating custom scripts and workflows, you can automate the processing of TI data within MISP. These automated processes can help quickly identify and respond to threats, improving your organization's overall security posture and minimizing manual intervention.

By implementing MISP in this way, organizations can enhance their ability to share, analyze, and act on TI data, fostering stronger collaboration and faster threat mitigation.

Vulnerability management automation

Automate the process of detecting, prioritizing, and remediating vulnerabilities. The following platforms can be used for this.

OpenVAS

OpenVAS is a widely used, open source vulnerability scanning tool designed to identify and manage security risks within your network and applications. By automating the scanning and vulnerability management process, OpenVAS enhances your organization's ability to proactively detect security issues and mitigate potential threats. Here's how you can implement OpenVAS effectively:

1. **Install OpenVAS**: Start by following the installation guide on the OpenVAS website – `https://www.openvas.org/`. This will set up the necessary components on your system, ensuring that OpenVAS is ready for use in scanning your network and systems.

2. **Configure scans**: After installation, configure vulnerability scans to target your network, servers, and applications. This step ensures that OpenVAS is set up to detect known vulnerabilities, misconfigurations, and security risks based on the specific assets in your environment.

3. **Automate scanning**: To maintain regular vulnerability assessments, automate the scanning process by scheduling scans at predefined intervals. You can also set up automatic reporting so that scan results are promptly delivered to the security team for analysis and action.

4. **Integrate with ticketing systems**: For streamlined vulnerability management, integrate OpenVAS with ticketing systems such as Jira. This integration automatically creates tickets for detected vulnerabilities, allowing the security team to track remediation efforts, prioritize issues, and ensure that vulnerabilities are addressed efficiently.

By integrating OpenVAS in this way, you can automate key aspects of vulnerability management, enhance your organization's security posture, and improve response times to detected threats.

Nessus

Nessus, a leading commercial vulnerability scanner, is widely known for its rich set of features and flexible API, making it an ideal tool for automating vulnerability management workflows. By integrating Nessus into your security automation process, you can improve your ability to detect and address vulnerabilities across your infrastructure. Here's how to effectively use Nessus in your automation workflow:

1. **Install Nessus**: Start by following the installation instructions available on the Tenable website. This will guide you through setting up the Nessus scanner on your system, ensuring that it's properly configured to start scanning your network and assets.

2. **Configure scans**: Once Nessus is installed, set up vulnerability scans tailored to your network, applications, and specific security needs. Customizing scan configurations helps ensure that you detect all potential security risks in your environment.

3. **Automate scanning with the API**: Nessus offers a robust API that allows you to automate scanning tasks, such as initiating scans and generating reports. This integration can be achieved by referring to the Nessus API documentation to set up automated processes for regular scans and vulnerability assessments, reducing manual intervention and improving efficiency.

4. **Remediation automation**: To take your automation further, Nessus can be integrated with configuration management tools such as Ansible or Puppet. This integration allows you to automatically apply remediation measures, such as patching or system reconfigurations, based on the vulnerabilities identified in the scan results. This streamlines the vulnerability management process, ensuring quicker response times and minimizing the impact of security risks.

By leveraging Nessus and its API, you can automate scanning, reporting, and remediation tasks, helping to improve the security posture of your organization through proactive and efficient vulnerability management.

Compliance automation

Automate compliance checks to ensure your systems meet regulatory requirements and internal policies. The following platforms can be used for this:

AWS Config

AWS Config continuously monitors and records **Amazon Web Services** (**AWS**).

AWS Config is a powerful tool that continuously monitors and records the configuration of AWS resources, providing a real-time view of compliance and security. By automating compliance checks and remediation, AWS Config helps ensure that resources comply with internal policies and external regulations, significantly reducing manual oversight and risk. The following is a breakdown of how to leverage AWS Config effectively:

1. **Enable AWS Config**: To get started, you need to enable AWS Config by following the official AWS Config documentation – `https://aws.amazon.com/config/`. This will set up AWS Config to start recording resource configurations and track any changes across your AWS environment. Enabling AWS Config is the first step in establishing an automated framework for compliance and monitoring.

2. **Define compliance rules**: Once AWS Config is enabled, you can define compliance rules tailored to your organization's needs. These rules allow you to specify which configurations should be tracked and what constitutes non-compliance. AWS Config provides a set of predefined rules, but you can also create custom rules to monitor specific configurations, such as ensuring that security groups or IAM policies align with your security standards.

3. **Automate remediation**: The key advantage of using AWS Config is its ability to automatically remediate non-compliant resources. When a resource deviates from the defined rules, AWS Config can trigger automated actions to correct the issue—such as reverting a configuration change, applying a patch, or enforcing a policy update. This reduces the manual effort required for remediation and ensures that non-compliance issues are addressed swiftly.

The integration of these steps with AWS Config provides a comprehensive solution for ensuring consistent resource configurations, improving security, and automating compliance across your AWS infrastructure. By leveraging AWS Config, organizations can streamline their security and compliance efforts, ensuring that their AWS environment remains secure, compliant, and free of configuration drift.

CIS-CAT

Center for Internet Security Configuration Assessment Tool (CIS-CAT) is a widely used tool for assessing system configurations against CIS benchmarks, helping organizations maintain security best practices and compliance. By automating the configuration assessment process, CIS-CAT ensures that your systems are continuously aligned with the recommended security configurations. Here's how to effectively use CIS-CAT to automate your security posture:

1.   **Download and install CIS-CAT**: The first step is to download CIS-CAT from the CIS website. Installing CIS-CAT provides access to the configuration assessment tool that is crucial for evaluating system configurations against CIS's security benchmarks. The installation process ensures you have the necessary toolset for regular assessments.

2.   **Run assessments**: Once CIS-CAT is installed, you can begin running assessments on your systems. These assessments compare the configuration of your infrastructure (servers, networks, and applications) against predefined security benchmarks provided by CIS. Running these assessments helps identify any gaps in compliance and highlights areas requiring improvement to meet security standards.

3.   **Automate reporting**: Automating assessments is a powerful way to ensure that your environment is continuously monitored for security compliance. With CIS-CAT, you can schedule assessments at regular intervals and automatically generate compliance reports. These reports can be used for auditing purposes, making it easier to demonstrate compliance with industry standards and regulatory requirements.

The integration of these steps ensures that your system configurations are secure and compliant with CIS benchmarks. Automating this process reduces the manual overhead of configuration checks and enhances the overall security posture of your organization. By utilizing CIS-CAT, you gain a structured approach to aligning your infrastructure with best practices, reducing vulnerabilities, and improving audit readiness.

Security policy enforcement

Automate the enforcement of security policies across your environment using **Open Policy Agent (OPA)**. OPA is a general-purpose policy engine that can enforce policies across various systems. Follow these steps:

1.   **Install OPA**: Follow the installation instructions at `https://www.openpolicyagent.org/`.

2.   **Define policies**: Write policies in Rego, OPA's policy language.

3.   **Integrate OPA**: Integrate OPA with your applications and infrastructure to enforce policies.

4.   **Automate policy enforcement**: Use OPA to continuously enforce security policies.

Data loss prevention automation

Automate the detection and prevention of data leaks and unauthorized data access. The following platforms can be used for this.

Google DLP API

Google Cloud's **Data Loss Prevention** (**DLP**) API helps organizations automate the discovery, classification, and protection of sensitive data. It enables the scanning of your data across various storage locations to identify and manage sensitive information such as personal identifiers or financial data. The following are the steps to integrate and automate data protection using the Google DLP API:

1. **Enable the Google DLP API**: To get started, you must first enable the DLP API within the Google Cloud Console. Enabling the API is the foundation for using the Google DLP features within your environment, allowing access to the DLP services for scanning and classifying data across Google Cloud services.

2. **Install the Google Cloud SDK**: Once the API is enabled, the next step is installing the Google Cloud SDK. The SDK provides the necessary tools and libraries to interact with Google Cloud services from your local machine or development environment. You can follow the installation instructions on the Google Cloud SDK website. This step is crucial for setting up your development environment to work with the DLP API.

3. **Use the DLP API**: With the API enabled and the SDK installed, you can now write Python scripts to automate data classification and protection tasks. By interacting with the DLP API, you can scan text, files, or other data for sensitive information, apply redaction or masking techniques, and even enforce compliance by ensuring data is properly protected according to your organization's security policies.

These steps outline the core actions needed to integrate Google DLP into your automated security processes. By automating data discovery, classification, and protection, organizations can enhance their data security posture, ensuring that sensitive information is identified and appropriately safeguarded without manual intervention. The ability to schedule and automate these tasks provides consistency and scalability in securing sensitive data across cloud environments.

OpenDLP

OpenDLP is an open source tool designed to scan data at rest for sensitive information, providing an essential solution for automating data protection across your systems. It helps organizations ensure that sensitive data such as personal identifiers, credit card numbers, and other private information is properly protected. The following steps explain how to use OpenDLP to automate your data protection efforts:

1. **Install OpenDLP**: The first step to using OpenDLP is installing the tool. You can follow the installation instructions provided on the OpenDLP GitHub page – `https://github.com/ezarko/opendlp` or `https://github.com/cloudsecuritylabs/openDLP`.

This installation process sets up the necessary components to enable data scanning in your environment. By installing OpenDLP, you're preparing your infrastructure for automated data discovery and protection, which is a key step in preventing data breaches.

2. **Configure scans**: Once installed, you need to configure data scans to target the areas where sensitive data might reside (e.g., databases and filesystems). Configuring scans involves specifying the locations to search, selecting the types of sensitive data to detect, and adjusting parameters such as the scan frequency and data handling actions. This step is essential for customizing the scanning process to meet your specific needs, ensuring that OpenDLP checks relevant data sources.

3. **Automate data protection**: With OpenDLP configured, you can set it up to automatically detect and protect sensitive data. This can involve actions such as redacting, masking, or flagging sensitive information upon detection. Automating these tasks reduces the reliance on manual oversight, ensuring consistent and continuous data protection. With automation, you ensure that sensitive data is managed in real time, reducing the chances of exposure or unauthorized access.

These steps provide a comprehensive approach to using OpenDLP for automating the discovery and protection of sensitive information. By configuring automated scans and protection actions, OpenDLP helps organizations stay compliant with data protection regulations while minimizing the risk of data breaches. Automating this process is a proactive step toward securing sensitive data and ensuring privacy, which is a core requirement in today's data-driven environment.

API security automation

Automate the security testing and monitoring of APIs to ensure they are secure. The following platforms can be used for this.

OWASP ZAP

OWASP ZAP (**Zed Attack Proxy**) is an open source web application security scanner designed to help with finding vulnerabilities in web applications. The following is a detailed explanation of the key steps for integrating OWASP ZAP into your security workflow:

1. **Install OWASP ZAP**: To begin using ZAP, you'll need to install it on your system. Installation instructions can be found on the official OWASP ZAP website (`zaproxy.org`). Once installed, ZAP provides a user-friendly interface for both manual and automated penetration testing of web applications.

2. **Automate security tests**:

   - The ZAP API allows for automating security testing on your web applications and APIs. This integration enables you to run security scans on demand, which can be particularly useful when testing different environments or making regular security checks part of your development process. Automating security testing ensures that vulnerabilities are detected early, preventing potential security risks from reaching production.

   - *Example*: Use Python or other scripting languages to interface with the ZAP API and trigger scans automatically after every code commit or in response to specific events.

3. **Integrate with CI/CD**:

   - Integrating OWASP ZAP into your CI/CD pipeline is essential for maintaining consistent security across your development cycle. This ensures that every time a developer pushes code changes to the repository, ZAP automatically scans the new API or web application for vulnerabilities. This integration is particularly useful for preventing security issues from making it into production by catching them early in the development life cycle.

   - *Example*: Add a step in your Jenkins, GitLab, or CircleCI pipeline that triggers an OWASP ZAP scan every time a new build is deployed to a test environment. This could include checking for common vulnerabilities such as SQL injection, XSS, and authentication issues.

By automating security testing and integrating it into your CI/CD pipeline, you ensure that security is an ongoing part of the development process. This proactive approach helps identify and mitigate vulnerabilities faster, reducing the risk of a successful attack.

The main benefit of these steps is that they make security testing a regular, automated part of your workflow, allowing your development and security teams to focus on other high-priority tasks while still ensuring that your web applications and APIs are secure.

Postman

Postman is widely recognized as an essential tool for API development and testing, including security testing. Here's how you can leverage Postman to secure your APIs and integrate security testing into your CI/CD pipeline:

1. **Install Postman**: Begin by downloading and installing Postman from the official website – https://www.postman.com/. It's available for various OSs, including Windows, macOS, and Linux. Once installed, you can start creating and testing APIs directly through Postman's user-friendly interface.

2. **Create security tests**: After setting up Postman, you can write and save security-specific tests for your APIs. This might include checking for vulnerabilities such as improper authentication, insecure data transmission, or broken access control. Postman allows you to create pre-request scripts and tests in JavaScript to automate these checks, ensuring that each API request is thoroughly validated for potential security risks.

3. **Automate with Newman**:

    *   To integrate your Postman tests into your CI/CD pipeline, you can use **Newman**, Postman's command-line tool. Newman allows you to run your saved Postman collections and tests as part of your CI/CD workflows, ensuring that each deployment is tested for security vulnerabilities automatically.

    *   **Installation**: Install Newman globally using npm:

        ```
        npm install -g newman
        ```

    Once installed, you can run your Postman tests from the command line, making it easy to integrate them into your automated deployment pipeline (e.g., Jenkins, CircleCI, or GitLab CI). This allows your security tests to run with each new code deployment, helping to catch vulnerabilities early and continuously monitor API security.

By using Postman in combination with Newman, you can effectively automate the security testing of your APIs, ensuring that security is always a part of your development and deployment processes. This proactive approach reduces the chances of vulnerabilities slipping into production.

Best practices and customization – optimizing your Python setup

Optimizing your Python development environment involves best practices, customizing your tools, and streamlining workflows to improve productivity, code quality, and security. Here's a structured approach to set up your project:

1. **Project structure and organization**:

    Organizing your files consistently from the start makes your project easier to manage. A standard project layout can help with scalability and maintainability. Here's a common structure:

    ```
    project_name/
    ├── docs/              # Documentation
    ├── project_name/      # Main package
    │   ├── __init__.py
    │   ├── module1.py
    │   ├── module2.py
    ├── tests/             # Test suite
    │   ├── __init__.py
    ```

```
|     ├── test_module1.py
|     ├── test_module2.py
├── .gitignore          # Git ignore file
├── requirements.txt    # Dependencies
├── setup.py            # Installation script
└── README.md           # Project description
```

- **Using README.md**: After establishing the project structure, write a detailed README.md file to provide essential information about your project. Include the following:

  - Project description

  - Installation instructions

  - Usage examples

  - Contribution guidelines

- **Using .gitignore**: Next, ensure that your .gitignore file is properly configured to ignore unnecessary files. Here's an example of files to exclude:

```
__pycache__/
*.py[cod]
*.egg-info/
.env
```

2. **Dependency management**:

   Use pip and virtualenv to manage dependencies in isolated environments. This ensures that your project has a consistent set of dependencies that won't interfere with other projects:

   I.   Create a virtual environment:

   ```
   python -m venv venv
   ```

   II.   Activate the virtual environment:

   i.   On Windows: venv\Scripts\activate

   ii. On macOS/Linux: source venv/bin/activate

   III. Install dependencies:

   ```
   pip install -r requirements.txt
   ```

3. **Using pip-tools for dependency management**: For more advanced dependency management, install `pip-tools` to manage direct and transitive dependencies more effectively:

I. Install `pip-tools`:

```
pip install pip-tools
```

II. Create a `requirements.in` file: List your direct dependencies here.

III. Compile dependencies:

```
pip-compile
```

IV. Synchronize the installed packages:

```
pip-sync
```

This order provides clarity by first establishing the project structure with README and `.gitignore`, then managing dependencies, and further enhancing with tools such as `pip-tools`. This helps create a solid foundation before proceeding with other optimizations.

4. **Project structure and organization**: Follow a standard project layout, organizing your project files and directories in a consistent manner. Here's a common structure:

```
project_name/
├── docs/              # Documentation
├── project_name/      # Main package
│   ├── __init__.py
│   ├── module1.py
│   ├── module2.py
├── tests/             # Test suite
│   ├── __init__.py
│   ├── test_module1.py
│   ├── test_module2.py
├── .gitignore         # Git ignore file
├── requirements.txt   # Dependencies
├── setup.py           # Installation script
└── README.md          # Project description
```

Write a detailed `README.md` file with the following defined:

*   Project description
*   Installation instructions
*   Usage examples
*   Contribution guidelines

Use `.gitignore` to specify files and directories to be ignored by Git. Here's some example content:

```
__pycache__/
*.py[cod]
*.egg-info/
.env
```

5.   **Dependency management**: Use `pip` and `virtualenv`:

I.   Create a virtual environment:

```
python -m venv venv
```

II.   Activate the virtual environment:

- On Windows, run `venv\Scripts\activate`
- On macOS/Linux, run `source venv/bin/activate`

III. Install dependencies:

```
pip install -r requirements.txt
```

Use `pip-tools` for dependency management:

- Install `pip-tools`:

```
pip install pip-tools
```

- Create a `requirements.in` file: List your direct dependencies in `requirements.in`.
- Compile dependencies:

```
pip-compile
```

- Install dependencies:

```
pip-sync
```

6. **Coding standards**: Follow PEP 8. PEP 8 is the style guide for Python code. Use linters to enforce coding standards:

   I.   Install Flake8 as follows:

   ```
   pip install flake8
   flake8 your_project/
   ```

   II.   Install Black (code formatter) as follows:

   ```
   pip install black
   black your_project/
   ```

7. **Use type annotations**: Type annotations help with code readability and can be checked with tools such as mypy:

   ```
   def greet(name: str) -> str:
       return f"Hello, {name}
   ```

   Check types:

   ```
   pip install mypy
   mypy your_project/
   ```

8. **Automated testing**: Use `unittest` or `pytest`:

   - `unittest` is a built-in testing framework. Import it as follows:

   ```python
   import unittest

   class TestMath(unittest.TestCase):
       def test_add(self):
           self.assertEqual(1 + 1, 2)

   if __name__ == '__main__':
       unittest.main()
   ```

   - `pytest` is a popular testing framework. Install it as follows:

   ```bash
   pip install pytest
   ```

   ```python
   def test_add():
       assert 1 + 1 == 2
   ```

9. **Automate testing with CI/CD**: Integrate testing with CI/CD pipelines using tools such as GitHub Actions, Travis CI, or CircleCI:

```yaml
# .github/workflows/python-app.yml for GitHub Actions
name: Python application

on: [push]

jobs:
  build:

    runs-on: ubuntu-latest

    steps:
    - uses: actions/checkout@v2
    - name: Set up Python
      uses: actions/setup-python@v2
      with:
        python-version: '3.x'
    - name: Install dependencies
      run: |
        python -m pip install --upgrade pip
        pip install flake8 pytest
    - name: Lint with flake8
      run: |
        flake8 your_project/
    - name: Test with pytest
      run: |
        pytest
```

10. **Version control**: Use Git for version control:

I.   Initialize a Git repository:

```bash
git init
```

II. Commit changes:

```
git add .
git commit -m "Initial commit"
```

III.   Use branches:

```
git checkout -b feature_branch
```

Follow Git best practices:

- Commit often with meaningful messages

- Use pull requests for code reviews

- Tag releases with version numbers

11. **Documentation**: Write docstrings:

Use docstrings to document your code. Follow conventions such as Google style or NumPy style:

```python
def add(a: int, b: int) -> int:
    """
    Add two integers.

    Args:
        a (int): First integer.
        b (int): Second integer.

    Returns:
        int: Sum of a and b.
    """
    return a + b
```

Generate documentation with Sphinx:

- Install Sphinx:

```bash
pip install sphinx
```

- Initialize Sphinx:

```
sphinx-quickstart
```

- Generate HTML documentation:

```
make html
```

12. **Logging and monitoring**: Use the `logging` module.

    Set up logging to track application behavior and errors:

    ```python
    import logging
    logging.basicConfig(level=logging.INFO)
    logger = logging.getLogger(__name__)

    logger.info('This is an info message')
    ```

    Log to external services:

    - Use logging libraries such as `loguru` or `structlog` for advanced logging features

    - Integrate with external logging services such as ELK Stack, Splunk, or Google Cloud Logging

13. **Security best practices**: Handle secrets securely:

    - Use environment variables for sensitive information

    - Use libraries such as `python-dotenv` to load environment variables from a `.env` file:

    ```
    import os
    from dotenv import load_dotenv

    load_dotenv()
    api_key = os.getenv('API_KEY')
    ```

    - Keep dependencies updated:

        - Regularly update dependencies to ensure you have the latest security patches

        - Use tools such as `safety` to check for vulnerabilities:

        ```bash
        pip install safety
        safety check
        ```

    - Secure coding practices:

        - Validate and sanitize user inputs

        - Use secure libraries and frameworks

        - Avoid using `exec` or `eval` with untrusted inputs

14. **Performance optimization**: Profile and optimize code.

Use cProfile to profile your code:

```
python -m cProfile -o profile.out your_script.py
```

Analyze the profile using pstats or visualization tools such as SnakeViz.

Use efficient data structures:

- Use built-in data structures such as lists, sets, and dictionaries effectively.

- Consider using libraries such as numpy for numerical computations and pandas for data manipulation.

15. **Development workflow customization**: Customize your editor/IDE:

- Use extensions and plugins for code linting, formatting, and autocompletion.

- Popular editors/IDEs include VS Code, PyCharm, and Sublime Text.

Automate repetitive tasks: Use task runners such as Invoke or Make to automate repetitive tasks:

```makefile
# Makefile
install:
    pip install -r requirements.txt
test:
    pytest

lint:
    flake8
```

- Use pre-commit hooks to run linters and tests before committing code:

```yaml
# .pre-commit-config.yaml
repos:
- repo: https://github.com/pre-commit/pre-commit-hooks
  rev: v3.4.0
  hooks:
  - id: trailing-whitespace
  - id: end-of-file-fixer
- repo: https://github.com/psf/black
  rev: 21.6b0
  hooks:
  - id: black
```

By following these best practices and customizing your development environment, you can create a more efficient, secure, and maintainable Python setup. This will help you focus on writing high-quality code and reduce the overhead of managing your development workflow.

Summary

This chapter provided a comprehensive guide to setting up a Python development environment, essential for effective and efficient programming. We began with the installation of Python, covering the latest version and ensuring that Python is added to your system's PATH environment variable for easy access. The chapter then explored the importance of using virtual environments to isolate project dependencies, manage different library versions, and avoid conflicts between projects.

In this chapter, we covered the following:

- **Python installation**: Successfully installed Python on your OS, ensuring compatibility for future development.

- **Virtual environments**: Gained an understanding of virtual environments and how to use them to manage dependencies and isolate projects effectively.

- **Choosing the right tools**: Explored different IDEs and text editors, selecting the right one based on your workflow preferences and needs.

- **Dependency management**: Learned how to install, manage, and track Python libraries using `pip` and `requirements.txt` files for streamlined project management.

- **Environment verification**: Confirmed that your Python development environment is set up correctly, enabling you to begin scripting for security automation.

With your development environment configured, you're now ready to embark on automating security tasks with Python confidently and efficiently. The next chapter will provide a comprehensive introduction to the fundamental concepts of Python scripting tailored specifically for security professionals.

3

Scripting Basics – Python Essentials for Security Tasks

The ability to automate security tasks is an indispensable skill for cybersecurity professionals. With the ever-growing number of threats and vulnerabilities, manual intervention alone is no longer sufficient to ensure robust and timely defense mechanisms. This is where scripting languages such as Python, come into play. Python's simplicity, readability, and vast array of libraries make it an ideal choice for automating repetitive tasks, performing data analysis, and integrating various security tools.

This chapter aims to provide a comprehensive introduction to the fundamental concepts of Python scripting tailored specifically for security professionals. Whether you're new to programming or looking to enhance your skill set, this guide will equip you with the knowledge and tools necessary to streamline and enhance your security operations.

We'll begin with the basics of Python, covering essential concepts such as variables, data types, control structures, and functions. These building blocks will form the foundation upon which more advanced scripting techniques are built. Understanding these basics is crucial as they enable you to write scripts that can automate mundane and repetitive security tasks, thereby freeing up your time to focus on more complex and strategic initiatives.

As we delve deeper, we'll explore how to leverage Python libraries that are particularly useful in the realm of cybersecurity. Libraries such as `requests` for web interactions, `scapy` for network packet manipulation, and `BeautifulSoup` for web scraping will be covered in detail. Practical examples and exercises will demonstrate how these tools can be used to perform tasks such as scanning for open ports, analyzing network traffic, and extracting useful information from web pages.

By the end of this chapter, you'll not only have a solid understanding of Python basics but also possess the practical skills to apply Python scripting to real-world security scenarios. Whether it's automating vulnerability scans, parsing log files, or integrating with security APIs, Python will become a powerful addition to your cybersecurity toolkit, enabling you to respond more effectively to threats and enhance your overall security posture.

As such, we'll cover the following main topics in the chapter:

- Automating security in Python

- Exploring Python syntax and data types for security scripts

- Understanding control structures and functions in Python security automation

Technical requirements

To successfully automate tasks using Python, you need to ensure that your development environment has been set up correctly and that you have the necessary tools and libraries at your disposal. Let's look at the key technical requirements for automating tasks with Python.

Python installation

You'll need the following:

- **Python Interpreter**: Ensure that Python is installed on your system. The latest version of Python can be downloaded from `https://www.python.org/downloads/`.

- **Version**: Python 3.6 or higher is recommended for compatibility with the latest libraries and features.

Development environment

Here's what you'll need:

- **Integrated development environment (IDE)**: Use an IDE or code editor that supports Python development. The following are some popular choices:

  - **PyCharm**

  - **Visual Studio Code**

  - **Atom**

  - **Sublime Text**

- **Text editor**: For lighter scripting tasks, a text editor such as Notepad++ or Vim can also be used.

Package management

You'll need the following:

- `pip`: Ensure `pip`, the Python package installer, is installed and updated. It's typically included with Python installations.

- `virtualenv`: Use `virtualenv` to create isolated Python environments, which helps with managing dependencies and avoiding conflicts.

Essential libraries

You can install the essential libraries using `pip`. Here are some common libraries that are used in automation:

- `requests`: For making HTTP requests:

  `pip install requests`

- `BeautifulSoup`: For web scraping:

  `pip install beautifulsoup4`

- `lxml`: For parsing XML and HTML:

  `pip install lxml`

- `pandas`: For data manipulation and analysis:

  `pip install pandas`

- `selenium`: For automating web browser interaction:

  `pip install selenium`

- `paramiko`: For SSH connectivity:

  `pip install paramiko`

- `scapy`: For network packet manipulation:

  `pip install scapy`

System dependencies

Ensure that any system dependencies required by Python libraries are installed. For example, `lxml` may require `libxml2` and `libxslt` on Linux.

API access

Ensure you have the following:

- **API keys**: If your environment is automating tasks that interact with external services, ensure you have the necessary API keys and credentials.
- **Environment variables**: To boost security, store sensitive information such as API keys in environment variables.

Automation tools

You'll require the following:

- **Task scheduling**: Use tools such as cron (Linux/macOS) or Task Scheduler (Windows) to schedule your Python scripts.
- **Continuous integration/continuous deployment (CI/CD) integration**: Integrate Python CI/CD pipelines using a tool such as Jenkins, GitLab CI, or GitHub Actions.

Source control

You'll need the following:

- **Version control system**: Use Git for version control to manage your code base.
- **Repository hosting**: Host your code on a platform such as GitHub, GitLab, or Bitbucket.

Documentation

- `Docstrings`: Include docstrings in your scripts for better documentation.
- `README`: Maintain a README file in your project directory so that you can provide an overview and instructions for your scripts.

Testing

You'll require unit testing so that you can write unit tests for your scripts. You can do this using libraries such as `unittest` and `pytest`:

```
pip install pytest
```

By adhering to these technical requirements, you can create a robust Python development environment that facilitates security automation efficiently.

Automating security in Python

Automating security tasks in Python can significantly enhance your security operations by making repetitive tasks more efficient and reducing the risk of human error. Let's look at some common security automation tasks you can implement with Python:

- Vulnerability scanning
- Log analysis
- Threat intelligence integration
- Incident response
- Compliance checking
- Patch management

Example – automating vulnerability scanning with Nessus

Nessus, a popular vulnerability scanning tool, provides a comprehensive API that allows users to automate various security tasks, enabling more efficient vulnerability management workflows. Python, with its rich libraries and ease of use, is a perfect language for interacting with the Nessus API to streamline scanning, data extraction, and report generation. Here's a list of specific Nessus API functionalities that can be automated using Python:

- **Session management**:
  - **API endpoint**: `/session`.
  - **Description**: This API is used to authenticate and create a session. A valid session is required to access other Nessus API endpoints.
  - **Python automation**: Automate the login process by sending a `POST` request with credentials. Handle session tokens in your scripts to maintain authenticated sessions without having to enter login information repeatedly.
- **Scanning and policy management**:
  - **Scan creation**:
    - **API endpoint**: `/scans`.
    - **Description**: This API lets users create, configure, and launch new scans. You can specify targets, scan policies, and schedules.
    - **Python automation**: With Python, you can write scripts to define custom scan policies, select specific targets, and launch scans based on dynamic criteria. For instance, you might automate scans on newly discovered hosts.

- **Scan status check:**

  - **API endpoint:** `/scans/{scan_id}`.

  - **Description:** Check the status of ongoing or scheduled scans, view scan history, or retrieve scan details.

  - **Python automation:** Scripts can be set to periodically check scan progress, send notifications, or trigger additional tasks based on scan status.

- **Report and export management:**

  - **Report generation:**

    - **API endpoint:** `/scans/{scan_id}/export`.

    - **Description:** Export scan results in various formats, such as HTML, CSV, or Nessus proprietary format.

    - **Python automation:** Automate the process of exporting scan reports as soon as scans are completed, allowing for immediate distribution or further processing. You can customize exports based on the recipient's needs (for example, a detailed CSV for technical teams or a summarized PDF for management).

  - **Export download:**

    - **API endpoint:** `/scans/{scan_id}/export/{file_id}/download`.

    - **Description:** Download generated reports.

    - **Python automation:** Automate report downloads and storage, or integrate report files into other security systems and dashboards.

- **Vulnerability data extraction:**

  - **API endpoint:** `/scans/{scan_id}/vulnerabilities`.

  - **Description:** Extract detailed vulnerability data from completed scans, including affected hosts, CVSS scores, and vulnerability details.

  - **Python automation:** Use Python to fetch and parse vulnerability data, then integrate it with other systems (for example, ticketing systems or dashboards) or analyze trends and common vulnerabilities to refine security measures.

- **Policy and plugin management:**

  - **Plugin details:**

    - **API endpoint:** `/plugins/plugin/{plugin_id}`.

- **Description**: Retrieve detailed information about individual plugins, such as descriptions and recommendations.

- **Python automation**: Automate the process of fetching information on specific plugins to understand which vulnerabilities or configurations they check for, helping prioritize scans or reports based on plugin data.

- **Policy management**:

  - **API endpoint**: `/policies`.

  - **Description**: Manage scan policies, including creation, modification, and deletion.

  - **Python automation**: Automate policy updates or create custom policies dynamically based on current needs, adjusting scan configurations so that they match specific compliance or security requirements.

- **User and role management**:

  - **API endpoint**: `/users`.

  - **Description**: Add, remove, or modify user accounts and assign permissions for different security roles.

  - **Python automation**: Python can automate the process of onboarding and offboarding users in Nessus, manage access rights, and create periodic role reviews for audit and compliance.

- **Asset tagging and management**:

  - **API endpoint**: `/tags`.

  - **Description**: Organize assets by applying tags to scanned hosts, enabling better categorization and prioritization of scan results.

  - **Python automation**: Scripts can automate the process of tagging new assets based on a network segment or business unit, making it easier to prioritize remediation efforts based on asset criticality.

Example code snippet for automated scanning in Python

Here's a Python code snippet that demonstrates how to use the Nessus API to automate scan creation and status monitoring:

```
import requests
import time

# Configure Nessus API credentials and URL
api_url = "https://your-nessus-server:8834"
username = "your_username"
```

```python
password = "your_password"

# Create a session to authenticate
session = requests.Session()
login_payload = {"username": username, "password": password}
response = session.post(f"{api_url}/session", json=login_payload)
token = response.json()["token"]
headers = {"X-Cookie": f"token={token}"}

# Create and launch a scan
scan_payload = {
    "uuid": "YOUR_SCAN_TEMPLATE_UUID",
    "settings": {
        "name": "Automated Scan",
        "text_targets": "192.168.1.1,192.168.1.2",
    }
}
scan_response = session.post(f"{api_url}/scans", headers=headers,
json=scan_payload)
scan_id = scan_response.json()["scan"]["id"]

# Check scan status and download report once completed
while True:
    scan_status = session.get(f"{api_url}/scans/{scan_id}",
headers=headers).json()["info"]["status"]
    if scan_status == "completed":
        print("Scan completed. Downloading report...")
        # Export and download the report
        export_payload = {"format": "csv"}
        export_response = session.post(f"{api_url}/scans/{scan_id}/
export", headers=headers, json=export_payload)
        file_id = export_response.json()["file"]

        download_response = session.get(f"{api_url}/scans/{scan_id}/
export/{file_id}/download", headers=headers)
        with open("scan_report.csv", "wb") as file:
            file.write(download_response.content)
        print("Report downloaded.")
        break
    else:
        print(f"Scan in progress: {scan_status}")
    time.sleep(10)
```

```
# Logout
session.delete(f"{api_url}/session", headers=headers)
```

This script authenticates with Nessus, initiates a scan, monitors the scan's status, and downloads the report when the scan completes. With such automated workflows, you can streamline Nessus operations and manage security tasks more efficiently.

By leveraging the Nessus API with Python, security teams can automate their vulnerability management processes, freeing up time and resources for more complex security tasks.

Let's explore a complete Python script that automates the process of creating a scan, launching it, monitoring its progress, and downloading the report from a Nessus server. You'll need the following prerequisites to run the script:

- The Nessus server installed and configured
- API keys for authentication
- Python installed, along with the `requests` library

Let's see what's being done in the provided Python code execution.

Overview

The code is designed to parse a log file (in this case, `security.log`) and search for lines containing a specific keyword (for example, ERROR). It utilizes a function to read the log file, check each line for the keyword, and process any lines that match. Additionally, a decorator is employed to add logging functionality to the parsing process.

Code execution breakdown

Let's take a closer look:

1. **Function definition**: `parse_logs(file_path, keyword)`.

   Purpose: This function takes in a file path and a keyword, reads the specified log file, and looks for lines containing the keyword.

   File handling:
   ```
   with open(file_path, 'r') as file:
   ```

   This line opens the file in read mode. The `with` statement ensures the file is closed properly after its suite finishes, even if an error is raised.

Line iteration:

```
for line in file:
```

This loop iterates over each line in the log file.

Keyword check:

```
if keyword in line:
```

For each line, it checks if the specified keyword exists. If it does, it calls the `process_log_line(line)` function to process the matching line.

2. **Function definition:** `process_log_line(line)`.

    Purpose: This function processes a log line when the keyword is found.

    Here's its output:

    ```
    print(f"Keyword found: {line.strip()}")
    ```

    It prints the log line that contains the keyword, removing any leading or trailing whitespace using `.strip()`.

3. **Decorator definition:** `log_decorator(func)`.

    Purpose: This function acts as a decorator, adding pre and post-processing behavior to the `parse_logs` function.

    Wrapper function:

    ```
    def wrapper(*args, **kwargs):
    ```

    The `wrapper` function takes any arguments and keyword arguments that have been passed to the decorated function.

    Logging start:

    ```
    print(f"Parsing logs with keyword: {args[1]}")
    ```

    Before calling the original `parse_logs` function, it logs the keyword that will be parsed.

    Function call:

    ```
    result = func(*args, **kwargs)
    ```

    It calls the original function (in this case, `parse_logs`) with the provided arguments and stores its result.

4. **Logging completion:**

    ```
    print("Log parsing complete")
    ```

After the original function finishes executing, it logs that the log parsing is complete.

Return value:

```
return result
```

It returns the result of the original function.

5. **Applying the decorator**:

```
@log_decorator
def parse_logs(file_path, keyword):
```

This line applies `log_decorator` to the `parse_logs` function, meaning that every time `parse_logs` is called, the additional logging functionality is executed as well.

6. **Setting variables and initiating parsing**:

```
log_file = "security.log"
keyword = "ERROR"
parse_logs(log_file, keyword)
```

Let's take a closer look:

- `log_file`: This specifies the name of the log file to be parsed.

- `keyword`: This defines the keyword to search for within the log file.

- `parse_logs(log_file, keyword)`: This is called to start the log parsing process, triggering the entire sequence of operations defined previously.

This code automates the process of parsing a log file for specific keywords, enhancing monitoring and alerting capabilities. By utilizing functions and decorators, it allows for a clean, organized structure that can be easily maintained and extended for additional functionality. For the complete script and further details, you're encouraged to refer to this book's GitHub repository.

In this section, we explored the power of automating vulnerability scanning using Nessus and Python, streamlining the process of identifying potential security risks. By integrating Python scripts with the Nessus API, we can automatically initiate scans, retrieve detailed reports, and even prioritize vulnerabilities based on severity.

The following are the key takeaways from this section:

- **API integration**: We can leverage Nessus's API to automate scan initiation and report extraction

- **Efficiency gains**: Automation significantly reduces the manual overhead involved in vulnerability scanning

- **Customization**: Python allows us to customize scan parameters and automated reporting, allowing for tailored scanning processes

- **Scalability**: Automating with Nessus makes vulnerability management scalable across large environments, ensuring continuous security

With these automation techniques, security teams can optimize their vulnerability scanning processes, allowing them to focus on remediating risks more effectively and quickly.

Additional security automation examples

As security automation continues to evolve, its applications extend far beyond traditional use cases. In this section, we'll explore additional examples of how automation can streamline various security tasks, from compliance monitoring to threat intelligence enrichment. These examples highlight the versatility and power of automation tools, providing security professionals with efficient ways to enhance their operations, reduce manual efforts, and respond more swiftly to emerging threats. Whether it's addressing network security or incident response, these automation solutions offer a glimpse into the future of security management.

Integrating threat intelligence

Integrating threat intelligence into your security operations offers several key benefits:

- **Proactive defense**: Threat intelligence provides real-time insights into emerging threats, allowing security teams to act proactively and defend against potential attacks before they occur.

- **Improved incident response**: By enriching security data with threat intelligence, organizations can better understand the context and scope of attacks, leading to faster and more effective incident response.

- **Prioritization of threats**: This helps in distinguishing between high-priority and low-priority threats, enabling security teams to allocate resources more efficiently to the most critical vulnerabilities.

- **Enhanced decision-making**: Threat intelligence provides valuable context, helping security professionals make informed decisions about how to mitigate risks and strengthen their defenses against known adversaries and attack vectors.

Integrating threat intelligence strengthens the overall security posture by making it more proactive, contextual, and focused on the most relevant threats.

Using Python code for threat intelligence serves several important purposes:

- **Automation**: Python can automate the process of collecting, processing, and analyzing threat intelligence data from multiple sources, saving time and reducing manual effort.

- **Customizable data integration**: Python allows security teams to integrate threat intelligence feeds (for example, IP blacklists and malware indicators) into their existing security systems, ensuring seamless and real-time updates.

- **Efficient data parsing and analysis**: Python's powerful libraries, such as `pandas` for data manipulation and `requests` for API interaction, make it easy to parse large datasets, identify patterns, and correlate intelligence with ongoing security events.

- **Scalability**: Python scripts can handle large volumes of threat data and can be scaled to fit the evolving needs of organizations, allowing for more comprehensive threat detection and analysis.

Integrating threat intelligence with Python involves automating the process of collecting, processing, and utilizing threat intelligence feeds to enhance security operations. The code generally connects to external threat intelligence sources, processes data (such as IP addresses, domain names, or hashes), and integrates this information into the organization's security systems. Here is an example script:

```
import requests

api_url = 'https://api.threatintelligenceplatform.com/v1/lookup'
api_key = 'your-api-key'
domain = 'example.com'

params = {
    'apiKey': api_key,
    'domain': domain
}

response = requests.get(api_url, params=params)
if response.status_code == 200:
    threat_data = response.json()
    print(json.dumps(threat_data, indent=4))
else:
    print(f"Failed to retrieve threat data: {response.status_code}")
```

Best practices for integrating threat intelligence

Integrating threat intelligence into your security framework is crucial for staying ahead of emerging threats and enhancing your organization's defense mechanisms. Effective integration allows security teams to leverage real-time data on malicious IPs, domains, and attack patterns, helping to automate threat detection and response. This section outlines best practices for incorporating threat intelligence into your security operations, ensuring that the information is actionable, timely, and seamlessly integrated into existing tools such as SIEMs and firewalls to mitigate risks proactively:

- **Secure your API keys**: Store API keys securely using environment variables or secret management tools

- **Error handling:** Implement comprehensive error handling to make your automation scripts robust

- **Logging**: Use logging to keep track of actions, successes, and failures
- **Regular updates**: Keep your dependencies and scripts updated to mitigate security vulnerabilities
- **Testing**: Regularly test your automation scripts in a controlled environment before deploying them in production

Detailed example – log analysis with Python

In this example, we'll explore the following scenario:

You want to automate the process of monitoring log files for specific security-related keywords or patterns. If any suspicious activity is detected, the script should alert you or take predefined actions.

Prerequisites

Before diving into log analysis with Python, it's important to ensure that you have a solid understanding of the necessary prerequisites so that you can leverage Python's capabilities for automating and enhancing log analysis tasks:

- **Python installed**: Ensure you have Python installed on your system
- **Logs directory**: Identify the directory where your log files are stored – for example, `/var/log/security`

Script breakdown

To fully grasp how Python can be utilized for automating tasks, it's essential to break down the script step by step. This will allow us to understand each component and how it contributes to the overall functionality. Let's walk through the Python script to see how it works in practice:

1. **Import the necessary libraries**: We'll use the `os` and `re` libraries for directory traversal and pattern matching, respectively.
2. **Define patterns to search**: Create a list of keywords or regular expressions that signify suspicious activities.
3. **Traverse log files**: Go through the specified log directory recursively and read each log file.
4. **Pattern matching**: Search for the defined patterns in each log file.
5. **Alerting**: Print alerts to the console or send notifications if patterns are matched.

Script

The script to carry out the scenario we discussed above is as follows:

```python
import os
import re
import smtplib
from email.mime.text import MIMEText

# Configuration
log_directory = '/var/log/security'
alert_keywords = ['unauthorized', 'failed login', 'error']
email_alert = True  # Set to True to enable email alerts
email_config = {
    'smtp_server': 'smtp.example.com',
    'smtp_port': 587,
    'from_email': 'alert@example.com',
    'to_email': 'admin@example.com',
    'username': 'smtp_user',
    'password': 'smtp_password'
}

def send_email_alert(message):
    if not email_alert:
        return

    msg = MIMEText(message)
    msg['Subject'] = 'Security Alert'
    msg['From'] = email_config['from_email']
    msg['To'] = email_config['to_email']

    try:
        with smtplib.SMTP(email_config['smtp_server'], email_
config['smtp_port']) as server:
            server.starttls()
            server.login(email_config['username'], email_
config['password'])
            server.send_message(msg)
        print("Alert email sent successfully.")
    except Exception as e:
        print(f"Failed to send email alert: {e}")

def analyze_logs(directory):
```

```
        alert_patterns = [re.compile(keyword, re.IGNORECASE) for keyword
in alert_keywords]

    for root, _, files in os.walk(directory):
        for file in files:
            file_path = os.path.join(root, file)
            with open(file_path, 'r') as f:
                for line in f:
                    for pattern in alert_patterns:
                        if pattern.search(line):
                            alert_message = f'Alert: {line.strip()} in
file {file_path}'

                            print(alert_message)
                            send_email_alert(alert_message)

if __name__ == "__main__":
    analyze_logs(log_directory)
```

Script explanation

Now that we've walked through the components of the script, let's dive deeper into how each section of the Python code works and how it contributes to the overall functionality of the task at hand:

- **Import the necessary libraries**: Here, os and re are used for file handling and pattern matching. Additionally, smtplib and email.mime.text are used for sending email alerts.

- **Configuration**:

  - log_directory: Path to the directory containing log files.

  - alert_keywords: List of keywords that you want to search for in the logs.

  - email_alert and email_config: Email alert configuration (SMTP server details, sender and receiver email addresses, and so on).

- **The send_email_alert function**: Sends an email alert using the provided SMTP server details if email_alert is set to True.

- **The analyze_logs function**:

  - Compiles the alert keywords into regular expression patterns.

  - Traverses the log directory and reads each file.

  - Searches for patterns in each line of the log files.

  - Prints alerts and sends email notifications if a pattern is matched.

- **The main block**: Calls `analyze_logs` with the specified log directory.

Running the script

With the script thoroughly understood, we can run the Python code. This will allow us to see its practical application and observe the results in real time:

1. **Save the script**: Save the script as `log_analysis.py`.
2. **Run the script**: Execute the script using Python.

   ```
   python log_analysis.py
   ```

Extending the script

Having successfully executed the initial script, we can now explore ways to extend its functionality, adding features or enhancements that will increase its effectiveness and adaptability for various use cases:

- **Additional notification methods**: Integrate with other notification systems, such as Slack or SMS.
- **Enhanced pattern matching**: Use more complex regular expressions to detect a wider range of suspicious activities.
- **Log rotation handling**: Implement logic to handle rotated log files (for example, `.log.1` and `.log.2.gz`).
- **Dashboard integration**: Send alerts to a centralized monitoring dashboard for a comprehensive view.

To practice explaining scripts and improve your understanding of Python code, you can use several online platforms that provide interactive coding environments, detailed explanations, and code challenges. Here are a few references you can explore:

- **Real Python** (`https://realpython.com/`): Real Python offers in-depth tutorials and examples with explanations of Python scripts. It's a great resource for practicing and understanding Python code in areas such as automation, web scraping, and security.
- **Exercism.io** (`https://exercism.io/`): Exercism provides interactive challenges in Python (and other languages), along with real-world examples. You can practice solving problems, write scripts, and receive feedback from mentors.
- **Codecademy** (`www.codeacademy.com`): Codecademy offers interactive lessons on Python, where you can practice writing and explaining scripts. They provide step-by-step guidance, making it easier to understand what the code does.
- **HackerRank** (`www.hackerrank.com`): HackerRank is excellent for practicing Python through coding challenges and competitions. You can solve real-world problems and analyze other users' solutions to understand their code explanations.

- **GitHub repositories**: You can browse open source Python projects on GitHub and practice explaining the code to yourself or others. Look for repositories tagged with topics such as "automation" and "threat intelligence" to explore practical examples.

- **W3Schools** (`www.w3schools.com`): W3Schools provides beginner-friendly Python tutorials and examples that are great for practicing script explanations. They break down the code with explanations for each part, making it easy to follow.

These platforms will help you gain a deeper understanding of Python code while improving your ability to explain scripts effectively.

By automating the process of collecting and processing threat data, security teams can proactively identify and mitigate risks before they materialize. As we've explored, following best practices ensures that threat intelligence is utilized effectively to enhance detection, response, and overall security posture. In the next section, we'll delve deeper into how this integration works in real-world environments, showcasing its impact through case studies.

Exploring Python syntax and data types for security scripts

When writing security scripts in Python, it's essential to have a solid understanding of Python syntax and data types. This knowledge allows you to automate tasks, analyze data, and interact with security tools and APIs effectively. This section will provide an overview of Python syntax and key data types relevant to security scripting.

Basic Python syntax

Here are the components of a basic Python syntax:

- **Comments**:
  - Use # for single-line comments
  - Use triple quotes (`'''` or `"""`) for multi-line comments or docstrings

  Here's an example showing the usage of single-line and multi-line comments:

  ```python
  # This is a single-line comment
  """
  This is a multi-line comment or docstring.
  Useful for documenting your scripts.
  """
  ```

- **Variables**: Variables are used to store data and don't require explicit declaration of data types:

```
hostname = "localhost"
port = 8080
```

- **Control structures**:

  - `if-else` statements:

```
if port == 8080:
    print("Default port")
else:
    print("Custom port")
```

  - Loops:

```
# For loop
for i in range(5):
    print(i)

# While loop
count = 0
while count < 5:
    print(count)
    count += 1
```

- **Functions**: Define reusable blocks of code with `def`:

```
def scan_port(host, port):
    # Code to scan port
    return result

result = scan_port(hostname, port)
```

Data types

In Python, data types are fundamental concepts that define the kind of values a variable can hold, and are critical to in how we manipulate and store data within our security scripts. Understanding these data types is essential for implementing logic effectively and ensuring the accuracy of our code in various security applications:

- **Numeric types**: In programming, numeric types refer to data types that are used to represent numbers. Integers and floats are used for numerical operations:

```
ip_octet = 192
response_time = 0.254
```

- **Strings**: Strings are a data type that's used to represent sequences of characters, such as letters, numbers, symbols, or spaces. In most programming languages, strings are typically enclosed in quotes (either single, double, or triple quotes, depending on the language):

  - Use single, double, or triple quotes for strings:

    ```
    ip_address = "192.168.1.1"
    log_message = "Connection established"
    ```

  - String operations:

    ```
    concatenated_string = ip_address + " " + log_message
    formatted_string = f"IP: {ip_address}, Message: {log_message}"
    ```

- **Lists**: A list is a data type that's used to store a collection of items in a specific order. Lists are mutable, meaning their elements can be changed, added, or removed after the list is created. In most programming languages, lists can contain different data types, such as integers, strings, or even other lists. Ordered, mutable collections:

  ```
  ip_addresses = ["192.168.1.1", "192.168.1.2", "192.168.1.3"]
  ip_addresses.append("192.168.1.4")
  print(ip_addresses[0])
  ```

- **Tuples**: In Python, tuples are immutable, ordered collections of elements, similar to lists but with the key difference being that their values can't be changed after creation. Tuples are defined by placing elements inside parentheses (( )), and they can store a mix of data types (for example, integers, strings, and other tuples). Since tuples are immutable, they're ideal for representing fixed collections of related data where modification isn't needed, such as coordinates, configuration settings, or database records. Additionally, tuples offer a performance advantage over lists in certain cases due to their immutability. Ordered, immutable collections:

  ```
  port_range = (20, 21, 22, 23, 80, 443)
  print(port_range[1])
  ```

- **Dictionaries**: A dictionary is a data type that stores collections of key-value pairs, where each key is unique and maps to a specific value. In most programming languages, dictionaries are also known as hash maps or associative arrays. They allow for fast data retrieval based on keys rather than indexing by position, making them useful for scenarios where data lookup and association are needed. Here's an example of using key-value pairs to store related data:

  ```
  vulnerability = {
      "id": "CVE-2021-1234",
      "severity": "High",
      "description": "Buffer overflow in XYZ"
  }
  print(vulnerability["severity"])
  ```

- **Sets**: A set is a data type that represents an unordered collection of unique elements. Sets are typically used when you need to store multiple items and ensure that no duplicates exist. Unlike lists or tuples, sets don't maintain any particular order, and elements can't be accessed by index. The following is an example of an unordered collection of unique elements:

```
unique_ports = {22, 80, 443, 22}  # Duplicates will be removed
print(unique_ports)
```

Working with files

Working with files in Python involves reading from, writing to, and manipulating data stored in various formats, which is essential for tasks such as log analysis, data processing, and security automation. By mastering file handling techniques, we can manage and analyze the data that drives our security operations efficiently. Here is the syntax for reading and writing files:

- **Reading files**:

```
with open('log.txt', 'r') as file:
    logs = file.readlines()
    for line in logs:
        print(line.strip())
```

- **Writing files**:

```
with open('output.txt', 'w') as file:
    file.write("Scan results\n")
```

Libraries for security scripting

Libraries are essential in Python security scripting as they provide pre-built functions and tools that simplify complex tasks, enabling security professionals to focus on automating and enhancing their security processes rather than writing code from scratch. By leveraging libraries specifically designed for security applications – such as `requests` for network interactions, `pandas` for data manipulation, and `scikit-learn` for machine learning – developers can quickly implement robust security solutions, streamline workflows, and improve overall efficiency in threat detection, incident response, and data analysis.

Here's an example of using `requests` for HTTP requests:

```
import requests

response = requests.get('https://api.example.com/data')
print(response.json())
```

Here's an example of using os and subprocess for system commands:

```
import os
import subprocess

# Using os
os.system('ping -c 4 localhost')

# Using subprocess
result = subprocess.run(['ping', '-c', '4', 'localhost'], capture_
output=True, text=True)
print(result.stdout)
```

Here's an example of using socket for network operations:

```
import socket
s = socket.socket(socket.AF_INET, socket.SOCK_STREAM)
s.connect(('localhost', 8080))
s.sendall(b'Hello, world')
data = s.recv(1024)
print('Received', repr(data))
s.close()
```

Example – Simple Port Scanner

The following Simple Port Scanner script demonstrates the use of variables, loops, and the socket library:

```
import socket

def scan_port(host, port):
    s = socket.socket(socket.AF_INET, socket.SOCK_STREAM)
    s.settimeout(1)
    try:
        s.connect((host, port))
        s.shutdown(socket.SHUT_RDWR)
        return True
    except:
        return False
    finally:
        s.close()

host = 'localhost'
ports = [21, 22, 23, 80, 443]
```

```
for port in ports:
    if scan_port(host, port):
        print(f"Port {port} is open on {host}")
    else:
        print(f"Port {port} is closed on {host}")
```

Understanding Python syntax and data types is crucial for creating effective security scripts. Mastering these basics allows you to automate tasks, analyze data, and interact with various security tools and systems. By leveraging Python's simplicity and powerful libraries, you can enhance your ability to manage and respond to security threats efficiently.

This Simple Port Scanner script is designed to check the availability of specified ports on a target host, allowing users to identify open and closed ports. By sending connection requests to a range of ports, the script evaluates the response from each port, providing valuable information about the target's network services and potential vulnerabilities. This tool is particularly useful for security professionals conducting assessments of network security and identifying potential entry points for unauthorized access.

Understanding control structures and functions in Python security automation

Control structures and **functions** are fundamental aspects of Python programming that play a crucial role in automating security tasks. These constructs allow you to manage the flow of your scripts and encapsulate reusable code, making your security automation more efficient and maintainable.

Control structures

Control structures in Python are essential for directing the flow of execution within a script, enabling us to implement logic that dictates how our code responds to different conditions and scenarios. By mastering these structures, such as conditionals and loops, we can create more dynamic and responsive security scripts tailored to specific requirements and situations:

- `if-else`: An `if-else` statement allows you to execute code conditionally, which is essential for making decisions based on specific criteria in your security scripts:

  ```
  # Example: Checking if a port is open or closed
  port = 80
  if port == 80:
      print("HTTP port")
  elif port == 443:
  ```

```
        print("HTTPS port")
    else:
        print("Other port")
```

- **for**: A `for` loop is used to iterate over a sequence (such as a list or a range), which is useful for tasks such as scanning multiple IP addresses or ports:

```
# Example: Scanning a list of IP addresses
ip_addresses = ["192.168.1.1", "192.168.1.2", "192.168.1.3"]
for ip in ip_addresses:
    print(f"Scanning {ip}")
```

- **while**: A `while` loop executes so long as a condition is true. They're useful for repetitive tasks that need to run until a certain condition is met:

```
# Example: Retrying a connection until successful or max
attempts reached
attempts = 0
max_attempts = 5
while attempts < max_attempts:
    print(f"Attempt {attempts + 1}")
    attempts += 1
```

- **try-except**: A `try-except` block can be used to handle exceptions and errors gracefully, which is crucial in security automation to ensure your scripts can handle unexpected issues:

```
# Example: Handling connection errors
import socket

def connect_to_host(host, port):
    try:
        s = socket.socket(socket.AF_INET, socket.SOCK_STREAM)
        s.connect((host, port))
        print("Connection successful")
    except socket.error as e:
        print(f"Connection failed: {e}")
    finally:
        s.close()

connect_to_host("localhost", 80)
```

Advanced control structures

Advanced control structures in Python, such as nested loops, list comprehensions, and exception handling, provide powerful tools for creating more complex and efficient scripts that can handle a variety of scenarios in security automation. By leveraging these advanced constructs, we can enhance our code's functionality, improve readability, and streamline the decision-making processes within our security applications:

- **List comprehensions**: List comprehensions provide a concise way to create lists. They're useful for generating lists based on existing lists with specific conditions:

  ```
  # Example: List of open ports from a list of port scans
  ports = [21, 22, 23, 80, 443, 8080]
  open_ports = [port for port in ports if scan_port('localhost',
  port)]
  print(f"Open ports: {open_ports}")
  ```

- **Dictionary comprehensions**: These are similar to list comprehensions, but they're for creating dictionaries:

  ```
  # Example: Creating a dictionary with port statuses
  ports = [21, 22, 23, 80, 443, 8080]
  port_statuses = {port: scan_port('localhost', port) for port in
  ports}
  print(port_statuses)
  ```

- **Nested loops**: Nested loops allow you to perform complex iterations, such as scanning multiple hosts across multiple ports:

  ```
  # Example: Scanning multiple hosts on multiple ports
  hosts = ["192.168.1.1", "192.168.1.2"]
  ports = [22, 80, 443]

  for host in hosts:
      for port in ports:
          if scan_port(host, port):
              print(f"Port {port} is open on {host}")
          else:
              print(f"Port {port} is closed on {host}")
  ```

Functions

Functions encapsulate code into reusable blocks, which is particularly useful in security automation for tasks that are performed repeatedly.

They are essential building blocks that allow us to encapsulate reusable pieces of code, promoting modularity and efficiency in our security scripts. By defining functions, we can organize our code into logical segments, making it easier to manage, test, and maintain while enhancing the overall clarity of our security automation processes. Let's look at the most common operations when it comes to functions:

- **Defining functions**: Use the `def` keyword to define a function:

```python
# Example: Defining a function to scan a port
def scan_port(host, port):
    s = socket.socket(socket.AF_INET, socket.SOCK_STREAM)
    s.settimeout(1)
    try:
        s.connect((host, port))
        s.shutdown(socket.SHUT_RDWR)
        return True
    except:
        return False
    finally:
        s.close()
```

- **Calling functions**: Call functions by their name, followed by parentheses:

```python
# Example: Calling the scan_port function
host = "localhost"
ports = [21, 22, 23, 80, 443]

for port in ports:
    if scan_port(host, port):
        print(f"Port {port} is open on {host}")
    else:
        print(f"Port {port} is closed on {host}")
```

- **Functions with parameters and return values**: Functions can accept parameters and return values, allowing for flexible and reusable code:

```python
# Example: Checking if a service is vulnerable
def is_vulnerable(service_name):
    known_vulnerabilities = ["ftp", "telnet", "http"]
    return service_name in known_vulnerabilities
```

```
service = "ftp"
if is_vulnerable(service):
    print(f"{service} has known vulnerabilities")
else:
    print(f"{service} is secure")
```

- **Lambda functions**: Lambda functions are small anonymous functions that are defined using the `lambda` keyword, which is useful for short, throwaway functions:

```
# Example: Lambda function to check vulnerability
check_vulnerability = lambda service: service in ["ftp",
"telnet", "http"]
service = "ssh"
print(f"{service} is vulnerable: {check_
vulnerability(service)}")
```

Advanced function concepts

Advanced function concepts in Python, such as decorators, lambda functions, and higher-order functions, empower us to write more sophisticated and flexible code that can adapt to various requirements in security automation. By mastering these advanced techniques, we can enhance the functionality of our scripts, enabling more elegant solutions and efficient handling of complex tasks.

Let's go through some of these techniques as follows:

- **Functions as first-class objects**: In Python, functions can be assigned to variables, passed as arguments, and returned from other functions:

```
# Example: Passing a function as an argument
def check_vulnerability(service):
    return service in ["ftp", "telnet", "http"]

def perform_check(service, check_function):
    return check_function(service)

service = "ftp"
is_vulnerable = perform_check(service, check_vulnerability)
print(f"{service} is vulnerable: {is_vulnerable}")
```

- **Decorators**: Decorators are a powerful feature for modifying the behavior of functions or methods. They're useful for adding common functionality such as logging or timing to your functions:

```
# Example: Using a decorator to log function calls
def log_decorator(func):
    def wrapper(*args, **kwargs):
        print(f"Calling function: {func.__name__}")
        result = func(*args, **kwargs)
        print(f"Function {func.__name__} returned: {result}")
        return result
    return wrapper

@log_decorator
def scan_port(host, port):
    s = socket.socket(socket.AF_INET, socket.SOCK_STREAM)
    s.settimeout(1)
    try:
        s.connect((host, port))
        s.shutdown(socket.SHUT_RDWR)
        return True
    except:
        return False
    finally:
        s.close()

scan_port('localhost', 80)
```

- **Generators**: Generators are functions that return an iterator and allow you to iterate over data lazily. They're useful for handling large datasets or streams of data:

```
# Example: Using a generator to scan ports lazily
def port_scanner(host, ports):
    for port in ports:
        if scan_port(host, port):
            yield port

open_ports = list(port_scanner('localhost', range(20, 100)))
print(f"Open ports: {open_ports}")
```

By effectively combining control structures and functions in Python security automation, we can create more dynamic and reusable code that enhances the efficiency and adaptability of our security scripts, allowing for improved decision-making and streamlined processes.

Examples of control structures and functions in security automation

The following examples of control structures and functions in security automation illustrate how these programming constructs can be applied to real-world scenarios, enabling us to build more effective and efficient security scripts that respond intelligently to various conditions and inputs:

- **Port scanning with control structures**: Here, we're combining control structures and functions to create a comprehensive port scanning script:

```
import socket
def scan_ports(host, port_range):
    open_ports = []
    for port in port_range:
        if scan_port(host, port):
            open_ports.append(port)
    return open_ports

def scan_port(host, port):
    s = socket.socket(socket.AF_INET, socket.SOCK_STREAM)
    s.settimeout(1)
    try:
        s.connect((host, port))
        s.shutdown(socket.SHUT_RDWR)
        return True
    except:
        return False
    finally:
        s.close()

host = "localhost"
port_range = range(20, 100)
open_ports = scan_ports(host, port_range)
print(f"Open ports on {host}: {open_ports}")
```

- **Parsing logs with control structures and functions**: With this script, we can automate the process of analyzing log files to identify security events:

```
# Example: Parsing logs for a specific keyword
def parse_logs(file_path, keyword):
    with open(file_path, 'r') as file:
        for line in file:
            if keyword in line:
                process_log_line(line)
```

```
def process_log_line(line):
    print(f"Keyword found: {line.strip()}")


log_file = "security.log"
keyword = "ERROR"
parse_logs(log_file, keyword)
```

Integrating control structures and functions into security automation scripts

Control structures and functions are essential components of any automation script, enabling complex logic, decision-making, and code reuse. In security automation, these elements allow scripts to respond dynamically to various conditions, such as detecting anomalies, triggering alerts, or executing remediation actions based on defined criteria. By integrating control structures such as loops and conditional statements, alongside modular functions, effectively, security teams can create robust and scalable automation workflows that streamline operations, enhance threat detection, and improve incident response efficiency. This section explores how to leverage these tools to build smarter, more adaptive security scripts.

When integrating control structures and functions into security automation scripts, the code typically performs several key tasks that enhance decision-making, automation, and scalability in security operations.

Example 1 – Comprehensive Network Scanner

The Comprehensive Network Scanner script is a powerful tool that's designed to analyze a network by identifying active hosts, open ports, and the services running on those ports. This script typically operates by utilizing techniques such as ping sweeps to detect live devices and port scanning to gather information about the network services available on those devices.

The script systematically sends requests to a range of IP addresses within a specified subnet, checking for responses to determine which hosts are active. Once active hosts have been identified, it proceeds to scan specified ports for each host, gathering details about the services operating on those ports, such as HTTP, FTP, or SSH. This information is invaluable for security assessments as it helps identify potential vulnerabilities, unauthorized services, or misconfigured systems within the network.

The Comprehensive Network Scanner often includes features for outputting the collected data in a structured format, making it easier for security analysts to review their findings and take appropriate actions based on the results. By automating this process, the script significantly reduces the time and effort required for manual network assessments, enabling security teams to focus on analyzing results and implementing the necessary security measures.

Here's the script with explanations inserted between the lines. Remember to refer to GitHub for the full script:

```python
# Function to parse logs from a specified file.
def parse_logs(file_path, keyword):
    # Opens the specified file in read mode.
    with open(file_path, 'r') as file:
        # Iterates through each line in the file.
        for line in file:
            # Checks if the keyword exists in the current line.
            if keyword in line:
                # Processes the log line if the keyword is found.
                process_log_line(line)


# Function to process a log line when the keyword is found.
def process_log_line(line):
    # Prints the line that contains the keyword, stripped of leading/
trailing whitespace.
    print(f"Keyword found: {line.strip()}")


# A decorator function that adds logging functionality to other
functions.
def log_decorator(func):
    # Wrapper function to extend the behavior of the original
function.
    def wrapper(*args, **kwargs):
        # Logs the keyword being parsed.
        print(f"Parsing logs with keyword: {args[1]}")
        # Calls the original function and stores its result.
        result = func(*args, **kwargs)
        # Indicates that log parsing is complete.
        print("Log parsing complete")
        # Returns the result of the original function.
        return result
    return wrapper


# Applying the decorator to the parse_logs function.
@log_decorator
```

```
def parse_logs(file_path, keyword):
    # Reopens the specified file in read mode.
    with open(file_path, 'r') as file:
        # Iterates through each line in the file again.
        for line in file:
            # Checks if the keyword exists in the current line.
            if keyword in line:
                # Processes the log line if the keyword is found.
                process_log_line(line)


# Setting the log file name.
log_file = "security.log"

# Specifying the keyword to search for in the log file.
keyword = "ERROR"
# Initiating the log parsing process.
parse_logs(log_file, keyword)
```

For the full script and additional details, please refer to https://github.com/Packt Publishing/Security-Automation-with-Python/blob/main/chapter03/ comprehensive_network_scanner.py.

Example 2 – Log Analysis with Advanced Functions

The Log Analysis with Advanced Functions script is designed to automate the process of parsing and analyzing log files, enabling security professionals to extract meaningful insights from large volumes of data efficiently. This script utilizes advanced Python functions, such as higher-order functions and decorators, to enhance its functionality and streamline the analysis process. We won't be covering the entire script here as it is out of the scope of this book but the idea is to use it to utilize data efficiently.

Control structures and functions are essential tools in Python for creating robust, efficient, and reusable security automation scripts. By mastering advanced concepts such as list comprehensions, decorators, and generators, you can enhance the flexibility and power of your scripts. These techniques allow you to handle complex tasks, streamline workflows, and ensure your security operations are effective and responsive to threats.

Summary

This is a crucial chapter because it provides the foundational skills needed to automate and streamline security operations. By mastering Python's core concepts, you'll be equipped to write efficient scripts that handle tasks such as data parsing, log analysis, and vulnerability scanning, which are vital for enhancing security workflows.

In the next chapter, you'll learn how to automate vulnerability scanning using Python by focusing on integrating security tools and libraries to identify system weaknesses. You'll explore how to develop scripts that streamline the process of detecting vulnerabilities, enhancing your efficiency in network security assessments.

Part 2: Automation of the Security Practice

Automation in security practices is a game-changer, enabling organizations to streamline processes, improve efficiency, and strengthen their defense against emerging threats. By automating routine security tasks—such as patch management, vulnerability assessments, and incident response—security teams can focus on more strategic activities and reduce the risk of human error. This part delves into the key areas where automation enhances security operations, outlining how automated systems help to maintain a proactive and resilient security posture while reducing manual effort.

This part has the following chapters:

- *Chapter 4, Automating Vulnerability Scanning with Python*
- *Chapter 5, Network Security Automation with Python*
- *Chapter 6, Web Application Security Automation Using Python*

4

Automating Vulnerability Scanning with Python

In the ever-evolving landscape of cybersecurity, vulnerability scanning plays a critical role in identifying weaknesses within systems and networks. Manual scanning processes can be time-consuming and prone to errors, making automation essential for maintaining a proactive security posture. Python, with its extensive libraries and flexibility, is a powerful tool for automating vulnerability scanning tasks.

This chapter will introduce you to the fundamentals of automating vulnerability scanning with Python, covering key concepts, tools, and best practices. By leveraging Python, you can streamline your vulnerability scanning processes, ensuring that your systems are continuously monitored for potential risks.

You'll learn how to interact with popular vulnerability scanning tools such as Nessus, OpenVAS, and Qualys, integrate them into your Python scripts, and automate the scanning and reporting process. This chapter will also explore how to schedule automated scans, interpret results, and take action based on identified vulnerabilities.

By the end of this chapter, you will have a solid foundation in automating vulnerability scanning with Python, allowing you to enhance your organization's security posture, minimize manual effort, and ensure timely identification and remediation of security threats.

We'll cover the following topics in this chapter:

- Introduction to vulnerability scanning
- Building automated scanning scripts in Python
- Integrating vulnerability scanning into security workflows

Technical requirements

To effectively automate vulnerability scanning with Python, the following technical components are necessary:

- **Python environment**:
  - Python (preferably 3.x) installed on your system.
  - A virtual environment to manage dependencies, using `venv` or `virtualenv`.

- **Vulnerability scanning tools/platforms**:
  - Access to a vulnerability scanning tool or API such as Nessus, OpenVAS, Qualys, or Nmap.
  - Familiarity with APIs for these tools to automate scanning tasks.
  - API keys or authentication credentials to connect to the chosen tool.

- **Python libraries**:
  - `Requests` or `http.client`: For making HTTP requests to interact with vulnerability scanning APIs.
  - `Paramiko`: For automating SSH-based vulnerability scanning (if applicable).
  - `JSON` or XML parsing libraries: For handling the output of scans and processing the results.

- **Command-line tools (optional)**:
  - Integration with command-line vulnerability scanning tools (e.g., Nmap) using Python's `subprocess` library to automate execution and retrieve scan results.

- **Security credentials**:
  - Ensure you have proper access and permissions for performing vulnerability scans within your network.
  - Store API keys or credentials securely (using tools such as `Python-dotenv` or **AWS Secrets Manager**).

- **Network configuration**:
  - Ensure firewall and network settings allow communication with the target systems and vulnerability scanners.

What is vulnerability scanning?

In the context of cybersecurity, a vulnerability is a flaw or weakness in a system's design, implementation, or configuration that could be exploited to compromise security. Vulnerability scanning aims to address these weaknesses. Vulnerability scanning is a critical practice in cybersecurity that involves the automated identification of potential weaknesses in systems, networks, and applications. These vulnerabilities, if left unaddressed, can be exploited by attackers to compromise the confidentiality, integrity, and availability of information systems. As organizations grow and their infrastructure becomes more complex, maintaining a secure environment requires regular and systematic scanning for vulnerabilities.

Vulnerability scanning typically involves using specialized tools to probe systems for known vulnerabilities, misconfigurations, or outdated software. These tools assess the security posture of various components, such as operating systems, applications, network devices, and databases. They rely on vast databases of known vulnerabilities, often derived from sources such as the **Common Vulnerabilities and Exposures** (**CVE**) list, to identify potential security gaps.

To carry out vulnerability scanning, we can scan different aspects of the system, such as the following, to identify weaknesses:

- **Network scanning**: Focuses on identifying vulnerabilities in network devices and communication protocols. This type of scanning helps detect issues such as open ports, unsecured protocols, and misconfigured firewalls.

- **Web application scanning**: Targets web applications to find security flaws such as SQL injection, **cross-site scripting** (**XSS**), and insecure authentication mechanisms.

- **Host-based scanning**: Examines individual servers, workstations, or other devices for software vulnerabilities, missing patches, and misconfigurations.

- **Database scanning**: Evaluates databases for vulnerabilities related to access controls, encryption, and outdated software versions.

We will discuss the active and passive approach in vulnerability scanning later in the chapter. Basically, vulnerability scanning is not just about identifying flaws; it also helps to prioritize remediation efforts. By categorizing vulnerabilities based on their severity and potential impact, security teams can focus on addressing the most critical issues first.

However, vulnerability scanning is only one part of a comprehensive security strategy. While it can identify known issues, it does not guarantee that all potential threats are uncovered. As a result, vulnerability scanning is often used in conjunction with other security measures, such as penetration testing, code reviews, and security monitoring.

As cyber threats continue to evolve, organizations face a growing challenge in defending their systems against new and emerging vulnerabilities. Vulnerability scanners serve as an automated way to identify weaknesses before they can be exploited by attackers, allowing security teams to prioritize and remediate issues in a proactive manner.

Why is vulnerability scanning important in cybersecurity?

The weaknesses or vulnerabilities in a system can be found in software code, hardware components, network protocols, and user configurations. The impact of a successful exploitation can range from unauthorized access to sensitive data to complete system compromise.

The role of vulnerability scanning is to systematically search for these potential weak points across an organization's IT infrastructure. Vulnerability scanning tools automate this process by probing systems for known security issues and comparing them against regularly updated databases of vulnerabilities, such as the **National Vulnerability Database (NVD)**.

By identifying vulnerabilities, organizations can do the following:

- **Reduce the attack surface**: Scanning helps uncover areas where security controls are inadequate, allowing organizations to reduce their exposure to threats.

- **Prioritize remediation efforts**: Vulnerabilities are often ranked based on their severity and potential impact, allowing security teams to address the most critical issues first.

- **Ensure compliance**: Many industries have regulatory requirements (e.g., PCI-DSS, HIPAA, and the GDPR) that mandate regular vulnerability assessments. Scanning ensures organizations stay compliant with these standards.

- **Strengthen the security posture**: Regular vulnerability scanning is an integral part of maintaining a strong security posture, as it helps to continuously identify and address new vulnerabilities as they emerge.

Next, let's look at the types of vulnerability scans.

Types of vulnerability scans

There are several types of vulnerability scans, each designed to target specific areas of an infrastructure and provide insights into different types of security risks. These include **network scans**, which assess devices and services on a network for vulnerabilities, **web application scans**, which focus on identifying flaws in websites or web applications, and **database scans**, which evaluate the security of databases and their configurations. Understanding the various types of vulnerability scans and their purposes is crucial for maintaining a comprehensive security posture and ensuring all aspects of an organization's environment are properly protected.

Active and passive scanning are two essential techniques in cybersecurity using which different parts or aspects of the system can be checked. Both have distinct methods, purposes, and use cases.

Active scanning

Active scanning involves directly interacting with a network, system, or application to identify vulnerabilities, open ports, running services, and other potential security issues. It's a more hands-on approach that sends explicit requests to systems, collecting information through their responses.

Key characteristics of active scanning

Some of the key characteristics of active scanning are as follows:

- **Direct interaction**: Active scans initiate contact with the target systems, actively probing for responses.
- **Detectable**: Since active scans generate traffic to and from the system, they can be detected by monitoring tools or firewalls, potentially alerting network admins or intruders.
- **Detailed results:** Active scans can provide extensive and in-depth data such as service versions, OS details, and specific vulnerabilities.
- **Examples**: Tools such as Nmap, Nessus, and OpenVAS perform active scans, which are useful for in-depth vulnerability assessments.

Use cases for active scanning

Use cases for active scanning are as follows:

- **Vulnerability assessments**: Identify weaknesses in security infrastructure, such as unpatched software or misconfigured settings.
- **Penetration testing**: Proactively test and identify security gaps, simulating potential attacks.
- **Regulatory compliance audits**: Meet compliance standards by regularly scanning for and addressing vulnerabilities.

Passive scanning

Passive scanning, by contrast, involves monitoring network traffic to detect threats without directly interacting with the systems. It analyzes data that is already being transmitted to identify anomalies or indicators of compromise.

Key characteristics of passive scanning

Some of the key characteristics of passive scanning are as follows:

- **Non-intrusive**: Passive scans don't generate traffic or communicate directly with network devices, reducing detection risk.

- **Limited details**: Passive scans rely on observing existing data flows, which can sometimes limit the scope of information they uncover.

- **Continuous monitoring**: Passive scans can monitor network activity over time, detecting unusual patterns and behaviors as they occur.

- **Examples**: Tools such as Wireshark and **Network Intrusion Detection Systems** (**NIDS**) such as Snort are often used for passive scanning, as they analyze traffic data rather than engaging with the network.

Use cases for passive scanning

Use cases for passive scanning are as follows:

- **Threat detection and response**: Identify potential threats and suspicious activities in real time without alerting attackers.

- **Incident investigation**: Gather data on network behavior before, during, and after an event for forensics.

- **Network traffic analysis**: Monitor traffic patterns to detect unauthorized access or anomalies in user behavior.

Choosing between active and passive scanning

In most organizations, active and passive scanning complement each other. Active scanning can thoroughly examine the security posture during assessments, while passive scanning provides continuous monitoring and detection of emerging threats. Balancing both can offer a comprehensive view of network security, covering both proactive vulnerability identification and real-time threat detection. Let's take a look at the different ways in which active and passive scans can impact the security of an organization:

- **External versus internal scanning**: Understanding the distinction between external and internal scanning is essential for developing a comprehensive security strategy, as each type of scan targets different aspects of network defense. External scanning focuses on identifying vulnerabilities accessible from outside the network—typically from the perspective of an attacker—while internal scanning inspects potential threats and weaknesses within the network itself, often revealing issues an insider might exploit.

  - **External scanning**: This approach scans systems from an outsider's perspective, typically targeting the public-facing elements of an organization's infrastructure, such as web servers, firewalls, and email gateways. It helps assess how exposed the organization is to external attacks.

- **Internal scanning**: Conducted within an organization's network, this type of scanning identifies vulnerabilities that could be exploited by internal actors or if an attacker gains a foothold in the internal network.

- **Credentialed versus non-credentialed scanning**: Credentialed and non-credentialed scanning offer different levels of access and insight into system vulnerabilities, each serving a unique role in security assessments. Credentialed scans use authenticated access to probe deeper into systems, identifying issues such as misconfigurations or outdated software that are not visible externally. In contrast, non-credentialed scans assess vulnerabilities from an outsider's perspective, detecting weaknesses visible without privileged access and providing a more superficial but critical view of external exposure:

  - **Credentialed scanning**: In this approach, the scanner is given access to systems using credentials, allowing it to perform a more in-depth analysis. Credentialed scans can detect more detailed information, such as missing patches and configuration weaknesses.

  - **Non-credentialed scanning**: This type of scan does not use credentials and simulates an attack from an external attacker or an unprivileged user. It can identify vulnerabilities that are visible without authenticated access but may miss deeper issues.

The following table provides a brief overview of credentialed and non-credentialed approach in the context of different aspects:

Aspect	Credentialed Scan	Non-Credentialed Scan
Access Level	Uses login credentials to access system internals	Limited to surface-level, external observation
Scan Depth	Deep, detailed system and application-level scan	Limited to visible ports, services, and open vulnerabilities
Detection Accuracy	High, with reduced false positives	Lower, prone to higher false positives
Impact on System	Potentially higher impact due to resource usage	Lower system impact
Risk of Detection	Lower, as it mimics regular system access	Higher, often detectable as an external probing
Use Cases	Recommended for full system assessments, compliance audits	Quick vulnerability assessments, external exposure checks
Data Access	Can access detailed configuration files, software versions	Limited to publicly accessible data
Security Requirement	Requires secure handling of credentials	No credentials needed, lower security setup required

Table 4.1 – Credentialed versus non-credentialed scanning

- **Agent-based versus agentless scanning**:

  - **Agent-based scanning**: In this method, software agents are installed on the systems to be scanned, providing real-time vulnerability data directly from the host. This can be useful for devices that are frequently offline or outside the corporate network.

  - **Agentless scanning**: This traditional approach relies on network-based scanning tools that remotely probe systems. It is simpler to deploy but may not capture as much detail as agent-based scanning.

- **Continuous versus periodic scanning**:

  - **Continuous scanning**: With the rise of DevSecOps and Agile practices, continuous scanning helps ensure that new vulnerabilities are detected as soon as they appear, enabling quicker remediation.

  - **Periodic scanning**: Traditional periodic scanning involves scheduled scans, such as weekly or monthly, to identify vulnerabilities. This approach may miss vulnerabilities that emerge between scan cycles.

While vulnerability scanning is a vital security practice, it also comes with challenges.

Challenges in vulnerability scanning and what to keep in mind

One of the most common issues in vulnerability scanning is the high number of false positives, where a vulnerability is reported but does not actually exist. This can overwhelm security teams and divert resources from addressing real issues. Conversely, false negatives, where real vulnerabilities are not detected, can create a false sense of security.

Another challenge is keeping up with the volume of vulnerabilities. As new vulnerabilities are discovered daily, organizations may struggle to remediate them quickly enough, especially when combined with resource constraints.

Lastly, vulnerability scanning tools require careful configuration to avoid disrupting systems during scans. Some aggressive scanning techniques can inadvertently cause system outages, making it essential to balance thoroughness with caution.

Here are some common pitfalls to avoid when configuring automated scans, especially for newcomers in security automation:

- **Overlooking scope definition**: Failing to clearly define the scan's target scope can lead to scanning unintended systems, potentially causing disruptions and wasting resources.

- **Improper credential management**: For credentialed scans, using hard-coded or unsecured credentials poses a serious security risk. Store credentials securely, ideally in a vault, and ensure proper role-based access.

- **Ignoring exclusions**: Not excluding certain IPs or systems that should not be scanned can cause system instability. Mark critical servers or sensitive devices as `excluded` if they are not to be included in routine scans.

- **Setting high frequency on intensive scans**: Running high-frequency scans, especially deep credentialed scans, can overload networks and system resources. Schedule scans during off-hours to reduce operational impact.

- **Overlooking false positives and false negatives**: Automated scans can generate false positives or overlook subtle vulnerabilities. Always review scan results carefully and tune scanners for accuracy.

- **Neglecting scan report reviews**: Generating scan reports but not analyzing them can leave risks unaddressed. Establish a process for regular review, triage, and prioritization of vulnerabilities.

- **Inconsistent scan configurations**: Using inconsistent scan configurations across environments can lead to fragmented or incomplete coverage. Set standardized configurations to maintain consistency.

- **Failure to update scanners regularly**: Scanners need to be updated frequently to recognize the latest vulnerabilities. Keep your scanning tools and plugins current to ensure comprehensive coverage.

Keeping these in mind can help new practitioners maximize the value and effectiveness of their automated security scans. Let me know if you'd like me to expand on any of these areas!

Integrating vulnerability scanning into a broader security strategy

Integrating vulnerability scanning into a broader security strategy is essential for ensuring continuous, proactive defense against potential cyber threats. By incorporating regular scans into a comprehensive security approach, businesses can maintain up-to-date protection, reduce attack surfaces, and improve compliance with regulatory standards. Additionally, vulnerability scanning complements other security measures, such as patch management, incident response, and threat monitoring, creating a layered defense that strengthens the overall security posture.

Vulnerability scanning should be integrated into a broader security strategy in the following ways:

- **Patch management**: Scanning helps identify systems that require updates, but these vulnerabilities need to be addressed through timely patching and configuration management.

- **Penetration testing**: While vulnerability scanning focuses on identifying known issues, penetration testing involves simulating real-world attacks to uncover unknown vulnerabilities and assess overall security posture.

- **Security monitoring**: Continuous security monitoring can detect anomalous behavior and potential breaches in real time, complementing the proactive identification of vulnerabilities.

Integrating vulnerability scanning into broader security efforts is essential for several reasons:

- **Proactive risk management**: Vulnerability scanning helps identify weaknesses in systems before they can be exploited. Integrating it with other security measures ensures that vulnerabilities are addressed within a larger risk management framework, reducing the chances of successful attacks.

- **Improved incident response**: When integrated with threat intelligence, monitoring, and incident response tools, vulnerability scanning provides a real-time understanding of vulnerabilities, helping security teams prioritize responses based on actual risks.

- **Comprehensive security posture**: By aligning vulnerability scanning with patch management, network defense, and compliance efforts, organizations create a more holistic approach to securing their environment, addressing vulnerabilities as part of an overall strategy rather than in isolation.

- **Continuous monitoring and compliance**: Regular vulnerability scans integrated with broader security policies ensure that organizations maintain compliance with industry regulations and standards, while also continuously monitoring for new threats and vulnerabilities.

By identifying and prioritizing vulnerabilities, organizations can take proactive steps to reduce their risk of attack.

Now that we've explored the importance of vulnerability scanning, the next step is to streamline this process by building automated scanning scripts in Python. Automation not only reduces manual effort but also ensures that scans are conducted consistently and efficiently, helping to quickly identify vulnerabilities across systems and applications. Let's dive into how Python can be leveraged to create powerful, automated scanning solutions.

Building automated scanning scripts in Python

Automating vulnerability scanning using Python provides a powerful way to continuously monitor systems for security weaknesses, streamline the vulnerability assessment process, and reduce manual effort. Python, with its extensive libraries and modules, can interact with popular scanning tools, handle data processing, and automate tasks such as scheduling scans, parsing results, and triggering notifications.

This section will guide you through the steps required to build automated scanning scripts in Python, including setting up your environment, choosing the right tools, and writing the script logic.

Setting up your environment

Before you start writing Python scripts for automated vulnerability scanning, you need to set up your development environment with the necessary tools and libraries:

- **Python installation**: Ensure that **Python 3.x** is installed on your system. You can download it from the official Python website.

- **Package management**: Install pip, Python's package manager, to manage dependencies. You can install required libraries by running `pip install <package-name>`.

- **Virtual environment**: Create a virtual environment to isolate your project dependencies. This can be done using `venv` or `virtualenv`:

    ```bash
    python -m venv venv
    source venv/bin/activate  # On Windows, use venv\Scripts\
    activate
    ```

Choosing vulnerability scanning tools

Python scripts can automate the use of several popular vulnerability scanning tools. The choice of tool depends on your specific requirements, such as the scope of your scan (network, web application, or host-based) and the features provided by the scanning tool:

- **Nessus (Tenable)**: Nessus is a widely used vulnerability scanner that can be automated through Python using the `requests` library to interact with its API. Nessus can scan for various vulnerabilities, including network, operating system, and application flaws.

- **OpenVAS (Greenbone)**: OpenVAS is an open source vulnerability scanning tool that can be controlled using its API, which can also be accessed through Python scripts.

- **Qualys**: Qualys offers a cloud-based vulnerability management platform with APIs that allow integration with Python for scanning and reporting.

- **Nmap**: Nmap is a network scanner that can be automated using Python's `python-nmap` library. While not a full-fledged vulnerability scanner, Nmap can be used to gather information on open ports and services for further analysis.

Writing a basic Python script for scanning

We should follow a specific order when writing a basic Python script for scanning to ensure that the script is both functional and efficient:

1. Starting with *importing necessary libraries* provides access to essential tools and functionalities needed for scanning tasks, such as networking or HTTP requests.

2. Next, *defining the target scope* helps narrow down the specific systems, networks, or applications to be scanned, ensuring the script remains focused and efficient.

3. Then, by *implementing scanning logic*, you can incorporate the core functions of the scan, such as port checks or vulnerability detection.

4. Lastly, *outputting results and handling errors* ensures the script delivers clear, actionable insights and remains robust, even in cases of failures or unexpected inputs.

This structured approach makes the script logical, easy to troubleshoot, and effective for consistent scanning.

Adding common Python libraries for error handling is a great idea, especially to make scripts in security automation more reliable and beginner-friendly. Here's a quick guide to some essential libraries for error handling and logging.

try-except blocks with standard error types

In Python, error handling is essential for building robust and fault-tolerant applications, especially in security automation, where failures could have significant consequences. The `try-except` block allows you to handle exceptions gracefully and ensure that your program can recover from errors without crashing. When working with security automation scripts, it's important to not only catch generic errors but also handle specific exception types that might arise from common operations, such as network requests, file I/O, or API interactions.

Basic exception handling in Python is foundational for building robust and error-resilient applications. By using structured try-except blocks, developers can gracefully handle common errors without disrupting the execution flow. Let's see a use case below:

Use case: Basic exception handling:

```python
try:
    # Attempt to perform an action
except ExceptionType as e:
    print(f"Error occurred: {e}")
```

Standard types such as `FileNotFoundError`, `ValueError`, and `TimeoutError` are easy to use within `try-except` and are perfect for handling common errors

logging – detailed error logging

In any security automation script, having detailed error logging is crucial for diagnosing issues and tracking down the root causes of failures. Logging not only helps with debugging during development but is also essential for ongoing monitoring and post-deployment analysis. By including detailed error messages, you can identify where and why a failure occurred, making it easier to mitigate risks and improve your scripts over time. Let's take a look at the following example:

Use case: Logging errors and important info to a file or console, especially useful for scripts that may need review later.

An example is as follows:

```
import logging
# Set up basic logging configuration
logging.basicConfig(filename='app.log', filemode='w', level=logging.
ERROR)
try:
    # some risky code
except Exception as e:
    logging.error(f"An error occurred: {e}")
```

It helps track issues by writing errors to a log file, which is useful for security teams wanting a traceable record of script activities

traceback – detailed error information

When errors occur in a Python script, especially in security automation tasks, having access to detailed error information is crucial for diagnosing and resolving issues. The **traceback** provides a comprehensive view of the sequence of function calls that led to the error, making it easier to pinpoint exactly where things went wrong. This detailed error information is invaluable for troubleshooting and improving the robustness of your scripts. Let's understand this by the following example:

Use case: Retrieving a full traceback of an exception, which helps in debugging complex code.

An example is as follows:

```
import traceback
try:
    # risky code
except Exception as e:
    print(f"Error: {e}")
    traceback.print_exc()  # Prints a detailed traceback
```

When beginners encounter errors they don't fully understand, this module provides an expanded error context, making debugging easier.

retrying – automatic retries for resiliency

In the world of security automation, it's essential to design systems that can gracefully handle failures, particularly those caused by temporary issues such as network instability or brief downtime of external services. Automatic retries provide resiliency by allowing your scripts to attempt operations multiple times before failing completely. This ensures that transient problems don't cause unnecessary disruption in your security tasks, such as vulnerability scans or threat monitoring, by retrying the operation after a brief delay. Let's take a look at the following use case to understand this:

Use case:

```
from retrying import retry

@retry(stop_max_attempt_number=3)
def fetch_data():
    # code to fetch data that might fail
```

It's helpful for automation tasks where network calls or database queries might fail and need to be retried automatically

tenacity – robust retry mechanism with more control

In more complex security automation tasks, you may require a more sophisticated retry mechanism that offers greater control over how retries are handled. The **tenacity** library is a powerful tool for implementing advanced retry strategies in Python, allowing you to define the conditions under which retries occur, how many attempts are made, and how long to wait between each attempt. This level of control ensures that your automation scripts can handle failures more gracefully and efficiently. Let's take a look at the following use case:

Use case: Similar to `retrying`, but allows more customization.

Installation: `pip install tenacity`

An example is as follows:

```
from tenacity import retry, wait_fixed
@retry(wait=wait_fixed(2), stop=stop_after_attempt(3))
def secure_task():
    # potentially failing secure task
```

This library provides flexibility in configuring backoff strategies and retry limits, ideal for controlling repetitive errors in automation.

These libraries not only make scripts more beginner-friendly but also enhance robustness by catching, retrying, or logging failures appropriately. Including one or more of these libraries in examples can greatly improve reliability, making Python-based automation scripts easier to manage and debug.

Here's a basic example of a Python script to automate vulnerability scanning using the Nessus API. This example covers how to authenticate, launch a scan, and retrieve the scan results:

1. Install the required libraries:

    ```bash
    pip install requests
    ```

2. Write the script:

    ```python
    import requests
    import json
    import time

    # Nessus API details
    NESSUS_URL = "https://your-nessus-server:8834"
    USERNAME = "your_username"
    PASSWORD = "your_password"

    # Authentication function
    def authenticate():
        login_url = f"{NESSUS_URL}/session"
        login_data = {
            "username": USERNAME,
            "password": PASSWORD
        }
        response = requests.post(login_url, data=json.dumps(login_
    data), verify=False)
        if response.status_code == 200:
            return response.json()['token']
        else:
            raise Exception("Authentication failed!")

    # Function to launch a scan
    ```

```
def launch_scan(token, scan_id):
    headers = {
        "X-Cookie": f"token={token}",
        "Content-Type": "application/json"
    }
    launch_url = f"{NESSUS_URL}/scans/{scan_id}/launch"
    response = requests.post(launch_url, headers=headers,
verify=False)
    if response.status_code == 200:
        return response.json()['scan_uuid']
    else:
        raise Exception("Failed to launch scan!")

# Function to check scan status
def check_scan_status(token, scan_id):
    headers = {
        "X-Cookie": f"token={token}",
        "Content-Type": "application/json"
    Enhancing your script
```

Once you have the basic script working, you can enhance it with additional features such as the following. Enhancing your script when scanning is important for improving its effectiveness, efficiency, and reliability:

- **Error handling**: Add robust error handling to manage API failures, network issues, or other unexpected problems.

- **Logging**: Implement logging to track the progress and outcomes of your scans. Use Python's logging module to create detailed logs for troubleshooting and auditing purposes.

- **Scheduling**: Use the `schedule` library or cron jobs to automate the execution of your scripts at regular intervals, ensuring continuous monitoring of your environment.

- **Notifications**: Integrate with email or messaging services (e.g., Slack, Microsoft Teams) to send alerts when scans are complete or when vulnerabilities are detected.

- **Data parsing**: Enhance the script to parse and analyze the scan results automatically. You can use the `json` library to process the results and take actions based on the severity of the detected vulnerabilities.

Impact of security automation on system performance and resources

Automation in security provides enormous benefits, but it can also impact system resources and performance, especially when scanning, monitoring, or responding to threats at scale. Understanding these impacts helps in designing an efficient and balanced security automation strategy. Let's take a look at some commonly observed effects on the system performance and how to work around them:

- **CPU and memory utilization**:

  - Automated tasks such as vulnerability scans, file integrity monitoring, and threat hunting are resource-intensive. For instance, continuous scanning can consume significant CPU and memory, potentially slowing down other business-critical applications if not managed well.

  - *Enhancement*: Scheduling tasks during low-traffic periods or on dedicated systems can help mitigate these impacts. Additionally, configuring the frequency of scans based on asset criticality allows efficient resource use.

- **Network load**:

  - Network-based scans and automated data collection can put extra load on the network, especially when large volumes of data are sent to **security information and event management** (**SIEM**) systems or cloud services.

  - *Enhancement*: Using passive scanning techniques and optimizing the frequency of network traffic monitoring can balance the load without compromising coverage. Also, using tools that support incremental updates reduces data transfer sizes.

- **Storage requirements**:

  - Automated logging and data collection generate a significant amount of data, requiring scalable storage solutions. The longer data is stored for historical analysis, the greater the storage needs.

  - *Enhancement*: Implementing efficient data retention policies and using compression or cloud storage can help manage storage costs and improve accessibility for analysis.

- **Response time**:

  - Automated response measures/workflows, such as isolating compromised devices or blocking suspicious traffic, can speed up threat mitigation but may sometimes impact legitimate operations if not finely tuned.

  - *Enhancement*: Applying context-aware automation rules—such as allowing critical business systems to override certain responses—can prevent interruptions in legitimate activity while maintaining a strong security posture.

- **Cost efficiency versus resource demands:**

  - While automation reduces manual workload, configuring, maintaining, and updating automated systems come with infrastructure costs, especially in high-demand environments.

  - *Enhancement*: Using lightweight or serverless automation solutions for specific tasks, such as ephemeral scanning agents that activate only when needed, minimizes costs while maintaining security coverage.

These considerations allow organizations to gain a balanced view of how automation enhances both performance and security, making it easier to identify and address potential bottlenecks in resource use. This ensures that automation benefits—efficiency, scalability, and proactive threat management—are realized without overwhelming system resources.

Example – automating network scans with Nmap

For simpler use cases such as network port scanning, you can automate Nmap scans using Python's `python-nmap` library:

1. Install the required libraries:

    ```bash
    pip install python-nmap
    ```

2. Write the script:

    ```python
    import nmap

    def scan_network(target_ip):
        nm = nmap.PortScanner()
        nm.scan(target_ip, '20-1024')  # Scan ports 20-1024
        for host in nm.all_hosts():
            print(f"Host: {host}")
            for proto in nm[host].all_protocols():
                ports = nm[host][proto].keys()
                for port in ports:
                    print(f"Port {port}: {nm[host][proto][port]['state']}")

    if __name__ == "__main__":
        target_ip = '192.168.1.1/24'  # Replace with your target network
        scan_network(target_ip)
    ```

This script scans a network for open ports and displays the results. You can expand on this by automating the scan scheduling, logging results, and generating reports.

Integrating scripts with continuous monitoring and remediation

A powerful extension to automated vulnerability scanning scripts is integrating them with continuous monitoring and automated remediation solutions. Consider the following examples:

- **Continuous monitoring**: Set up your Python scripts to run continuously, checking for vulnerabilities on a regular basis. You can use tools such as cron (Linux) or Task Scheduler (Windows) to schedule the execution of your Python scripts at regular intervals.

- **Automated remediation**: Based on the scan results, you can trigger automated remediation actions, such as deploying patches or changing firewall rules, using Python automation libraries such as Ansible, or integrating with patch management tools via APIs.

Building automated scanning scripts in Python enables organizations to proactively monitor their systems and reduce the manual effort required to identify and mitigate vulnerabilities. By leveraging Python's capabilities and integrating it with existing vulnerability scanning tools, you can create scalable, efficient, and automated security solutions that enhance your organization's overall security posture. As your scripts evolve, consider adding features such as notifications, reporting, and integration with other security tools to create a comprehensive and automated vulnerability management workflow.

Integrating vulnerability scanning into security workflows

Integrating vulnerability scanning into security workflows is a critical step toward building a comprehensive and proactive security strategy. It enables organizations to continuously monitor their environments, prioritize remediation, and enhance their overall security posture. This integration not only automates vulnerability detection but also streamlines response and remediation processes, reducing the time needed/ taken to address security risks.

In this section, we'll explore how to effectively integrate vulnerability scanning into broader security workflows, covering key considerations, tools, and best practices.

Why we need to integrate vulnerability scanning in security workflows?

While vulnerability scanning is often seen as the first step in identifying potential security issues within an organization's infrastructure, its real value comes when it is fully integrated into security operations and incident response workflows. The goal is to move from simply identifying vulnerabilities to efficiently prioritizing and remediating them.

Integrating vulnerability scanning into security workflows can help your organization in the following ways:

- **Continuous monitoring**: Regular scans provide up-to-date information on vulnerabilities, allowing security teams to monitor their systems continuously and stay ahead of emerging threats.

- **Prioritization and risk management**: Scanning results can be integrated with risk management frameworks to prioritize vulnerabilities based on factors such as criticality, impact, and exploitability.

- **Automation of remediation**: Integrating scanning with automation tools enables immediate remediation actions, reducing the time taken between vulnerability detection and resolution.

- **Incident response**: Vulnerability scanning data can be used to enhance incident response efforts by providing detailed information on potential weaknesses that attackers might exploit.

The following diagram shows how the different phases in incident response actions and vulnerability management play out:

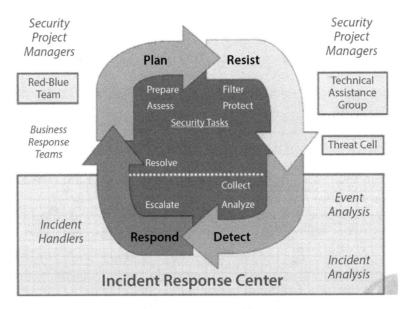

Figure 4.1 – A threat detection workflow diagram

Building a vulnerability management workflow

To integrate vulnerability scanning into your security workflows, consider building a comprehensive vulnerability management process that includes the following steps:

1. **Asset discovery**: Begin by identifying all the assets in your environment. This includes servers, endpoints, network devices, applications, and databases. Regular asset discovery ensures that your vulnerability scans cover all relevant systems.

2. **Vulnerability scanning**: Use automated vulnerability scanning tools to regularly scan your assets for security weaknesses. Schedule scans based on the criticality of the systems and the frequency of changes.

3. **Risk prioritization**: Not all vulnerabilities are created equal. Integrate your vulnerability scanning results with a risk prioritization framework that considers factors such as the following:

    - **Severity**: How critical is the vulnerability?

    - **Impact**: What would be the consequences of an exploit?

    - **Exploitability**: Is there an active exploit in the wild?

    - **Compliance requirements**: Are there any regulatory requirements that mandate remediation?

4. **Remediation planning**: Once vulnerabilities are prioritized, create a remediation plan that outlines the steps required to address each issue. This might involve deploying patches, reconfiguring systems, or applying workarounds.

5. **Automated remediation**: Integrate with automation tools such as Ansible (`https://access.redhat.com/blogs/2184921/posts/3064571`), Chef (`https://www.chef.io/ansible`), or Puppet to automate the deployment of patches, configuration changes, and other remediation action. This reduces manual effort and speeds up the response time.

6. **Verification and validation**: After remediation actions are taken, re-scan the affected systems to verify that the vulnerabilities have been successfully addressed. Continuous validation ensures that remediation efforts are effective.

7. **Reporting and metrics**: Generate reports that summarize the vulnerabilities identified, the remediation action taken, and the overall security posture. These reports can be used for compliance audits, executive reporting, and tracking progress over time.

8. **Continuous improvement**: Integrate feedback loops into your workflow to continuously improve your vulnerability management process. This includes regularly updating your scanning tools, fine-tuning your risk prioritization criteria, and improving your automation capabilities.

Tools for integrating vulnerability scanning

Several tools can help you integrate vulnerability scanning into your security workflows:

- **Vulnerability scanners**:

    - **Nessus/Tenable.io**: This offers comprehensive vulnerability scanning capabilities with APIs that allow integration into custom workflows.

    - **Qualys**: This provides cloud-based vulnerability management with extensive API support for automation and integration.

- **OpenVAS/Greenbone**: This is an open source scanner that can be integrated into workflows using its APIs.

- **Automation tools**:

  - **Ansible**: This can be used to automate patch deployment, configuration changes, and other remediation tasks based on vulnerability scan results.

  - **Puppet/Chef**: These are configuration management tools that can automate remediation actions, ensuring that systems stay compliant and vulnerabilities are addressed.

- **Orchestration and response platforms**:

  - **Security orchestration, automation, and response (SOAR) platforms**: Tools such as Splunk Phantom, Palo Alto Cortex XSOAR, and Demisto can orchestrate security workflows, automate responses, and integrate vulnerability scanning into incident response processes.

  - **SIEM**: Integrate vulnerability scanning results with SIEM platforms such as Splunk, IBM QRadar, and ArcSight to correlate vulnerabilities with other security events for better threat detection and response.

- **Patch management tools**:

  - **Windows Server Update Services (WSUS)**: This automates patching of Windows systems based on identified vulnerabilities.

  - **Tanium**: This provides real-time endpoint management and can be used to deploy patches and configuration updates in response to scan results.

- **Notification and reporting tools**:

  - **Slack/Microsoft Teams**: Use these communication platforms to send notifications to your security teams about vulnerabilities that need to be addressed.

  - **JIRA/ServiceNow**: Integrate vulnerability scanning results with ticketing systems to automatically create and track remediation tasks.

Example workflow – integrating Nessus with Ansible for automated patching

Integrating Nessus with Ansible enables an efficient workflow for automated vulnerability scanning and patching, helping security teams to quickly identify and remediate vulnerabilities. This workflow typically involves using Nessus to scan systems and report any detected vulnerabilities, then leveraging Ansible playbooks to automate the patching process based on Nessus's findings. With this setup, teams can streamline vulnerability management, ensuring that critical patches are applied promptly while reducing the need for manual intervention. This approach not only enhances security but also significantly improves operational efficiency.

Here's an example workflow for integrating Nessus with Ansible to automate patch management:

The process flow for an automated patch management solution is designed to ensure timely and efficient deployment of patches while minimizing risks and downtime. It typically follows a structured sequence of actions that streamline patch discovery, testing, approval, deployment, and validation across an organization's infrastructure:

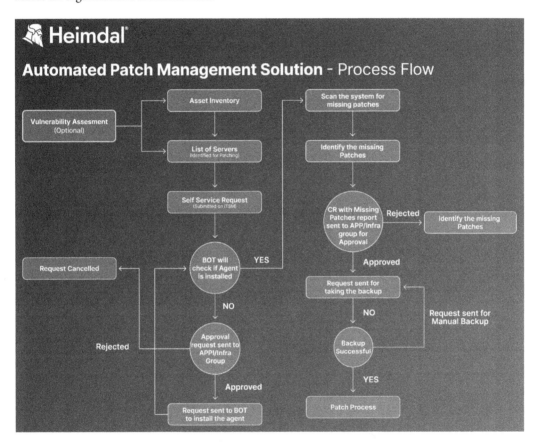

Figure 4.2 – A patch management process

1. **Scan with Nessus**: Use Nessus to scan your environment for vulnerabilities. Schedule regular scans for critical systems.

2. **Parse scan results**: Write a Python script to pull scan results from the Nessus API. Extract critical vulnerabilities that need to be patched.

3. **Create Ansible playbook**: Based on the scan results, generate an Ansible playbook that automates the deployment of patches. This playbook can be tailored to address specific vulnerabilities or apply patches to specific systems.

4. **Execute the playbook**: Run the Ansible playbook to automatically deploy the required patches across your environment.

5. **Re-scan for verification**: After patch deployment, trigger a re-scan with Nessus to verify that the vulnerabilities have been resolved.

6. **Reporting and notification**: Generate a report summarizing the vulnerabilities identified, the patches deployed, and the results of the verification scan. Send notifications to relevant stakeholders.

Best practices for integration

Here are some best practices to follow for integrating vulnerability scanning:

- **Start small and scale gradually**: Begin by integrating vulnerability scanning with automation tools for a subset of systems. Once you've fine-tuned your process, scale it across the entire organization.

- **Automate where possible, but keep human oversight**: Automation is powerful, but it's important to maintain human oversight to ensure that critical vulnerabilities are handled correctly and that no issues are overlooked.

- **Regularly update tools and processes**: Vulnerability scanning tools and automation frameworks should be regularly updated to incorporate the latest vulnerabilities, features, and best practices.

- **Monitor and measure effectiveness**: Continuously monitor the effectiveness of your integrated security workflows. Measure metrics such as time to remediation, the number of critical vulnerabilities identified and resolved, and overall security posture improvements.

- **Integrate with incident response**: Use vulnerability scanning results to enhance your incident response efforts. If a breach is detected, use the scan data to identify potential entry points and vulnerabilities that may have been exploited.

Integrating vulnerability scanning into security workflows goes beyond automating scans and deploying patches. It requires a holistic approach where security teams, tools, and processes are aligned to effectively manage vulnerabilities. This integration should extend across different security functions, from incident response to compliance, ensuring that vulnerabilities are continuously identified, assessed, and remediated.

Transitioning to deep integration with vulnerability scanning involves aligning vulnerability management with broader security workflows. This requires moving beyond basic scanning to full integration with other security tools and processes.

Deep integration with incident response

One of the most critical aspects of integrating vulnerability scanning is its alignment with the incident response process. By incorporating vulnerability data into incident response workflows, security teams can respond more effectively to security events.

Integrating automated patch management directly with incident response enables security teams to respond faster and more cohesively when threats are identified. This integration allows for immediate remediation actions, such as automated patch deployment, to follow an incident detection event, reducing the time systems remain vulnerable. By synchronizing patch management with incident response, organizations can ensure that vulnerabilities are promptly addressed in real time, strengthening the organization's overall security posture and reducing the risk of re-exploitation.

Deep integration between automated patch management and incident response workflows ensures a more cohesive and rapid response to security threats. By linking patching actions directly with incident detection and response, security teams can automatically apply patches in response to specific vulnerabilities discovered during an incident, minimizing the window for exploitation. This integration enables seamless coordination across tools and processes, enhancing the overall resilience of the system by addressing threats proactively and reducing manual handoffs between detection, response, and remediation steps. Vulnerability scanning can be used in the following ways:

- **Proactive threat hunting**: Use vulnerability scan data to proactively hunt for potential threats in your environment. For example, if a particular vulnerability is actively being exploited in the wild, scanning your systems for that vulnerability can help you identify and patch it before an attacker does.

- **Correlation with security events**: Correlate vulnerability data with security incidents detected by your SIEM system. For instance, if an **intrusion detection system** (**IDS**) flags suspicious activity on a particular server, vulnerability scan results can help identify whether that server has any unpatched vulnerabilities that might have been exploited.

- **Post-incident analysis**: After a security breach, use vulnerability scan data to understand how the attacker gained access. This information is crucial for post-incident analysis and can guide remediation efforts to prevent future attacks.

Integration with DevSecOps and CI/CD pipelines

As more organizations adopt DevSecOps practices, integrating vulnerability scanning into **continuous integration/continuous deployment** (**CI/CD**) pipelines becomes increasingly important. By embedding security scans into the development process, vulnerabilities can be identified and remediated early, reducing the risk of introducing security flaws into production.

Integrating patch management and security automation with DevSecOps and CI/CD pipelines ensures that security is embedded throughout the software development lifecycle. This approach enables automated vulnerability scanning, patching, and compliance checks to occur continuously as code moves from development to production, allowing teams to catch and resolve issues earlier. By incorporating security into CI/CD processes, organizations can maintain a consistent security posture, reduce deployment delays due to last-minute fixes, and deliver secure code faster, ultimately fostering a culture where security is a seamless part of development.

Effective security practices during development leverage automation to catch vulnerabilities early and ensure robust application security. The following concepts highlight ways to embed security into development workflows:

- **Automated code scanning**: Integrate static and dynamic code analysis tools into your CI/CD pipeline. These tools can scan code for vulnerabilities every time a developer commits code or during build processes, ensuring that security issues are caught early in the development life cycle.

- **Infrastructure as code (IaC) scanning**: Use tools such as Terraform and Ansible to define your IaC and integrate vulnerability scanning into the deployment pipeline. For example, you can scan container images for vulnerabilities before deploying them to production.

- **Shift left security**: Emphasize security earlier in the development process by integrating vulnerability scanning into unit tests, code reviews, and pre-deployment checks. This approach, known as shift left security, helps identify and fix security issues before they reach production.

Integration with compliance and regulatory requirements

Many industries are subject to strict regulatory requirements, such as the GDPR, HIPAA, and PCI-DSS, which mandate regular vulnerability assessments and remediation. Integrating vulnerability scanning into your security workflows can help meet these compliance requirements by automating assessments, tracking remediation efforts, and generating reports.

Integrating automated patch management with compliance and regulatory frameworks helps organizations meet security standards consistently and efficiently. By automating patch deployment and vulnerability reporting, companies can ensure continuous compliance with industry regulations, such as the GDPR, HIPAA, or PCI-DSS, without manual tracking. This approach not only reduces the risk of non-compliance penalties but also provides real-time visibility into security postures, enabling faster audits and reporting, and helping organizations maintain a strong defense aligned with regulatory expectations.

To effectively maintain regulatory compliance, organizations must integrate automation into their security workflows. The following strategies demonstrate how automation streamlines compliance efforts and reduces manual overhead:

- **Compliance audits**: Automate the generation of compliance reports using vulnerability scanning data. Many scanners, such as Nessus and Qualys, offer pre-built templates that align with specific regulatory standards, making it easier to demonstrate compliance during audits.

- **Continuous compliance monitoring**: Ensure continuous compliance by scheduling regular scans and integrating them with compliance monitoring platforms. This allows you to identify and address compliance gaps before they become issues during an audit.

- **Risk-based approach**: Prioritize vulnerability remediation efforts based on the risk posed to compliance. For example, focus on vulnerabilities that could lead to non-compliance with regulations, such as unpatched systems that handle sensitive data.

Advanced reporting and visualization

Advanced reporting and visualization tools in automated patch management offer critical insights into an organization's security status by presenting complex data in a clear, visual format. These tools can create dashboards, charts, and summary reports that help security teams track patching progress, vulnerability trends, and compliance status in real time. With actionable insights and easy-to-interpret visuals, teams can make informed decisions quickly, prioritize patching efforts, and communicate security metrics effectively across departments, fostering a proactive approach to risk management. Here is an example of a compliance dashboard:

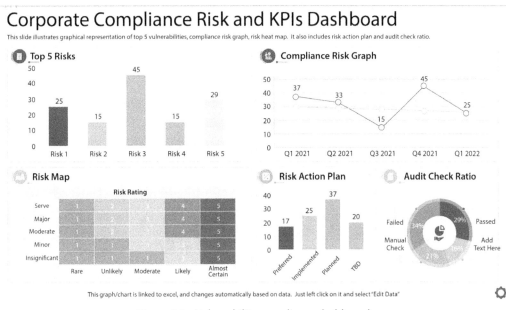

Figure 4.5 – Vulnerability compliance dashboard

Vulnerability data is only as useful as the insights you can derive from it. Advanced reporting and visualization tools can help security teams, executives, and auditors understand the current state of security and the progress made in reducing risk.

A vulnerability compliance dashboard provides a comprehensive, real-time view of an organization's compliance status by tracking vulnerabilities, patching progress, and adherence to security standards. With metrics and visual indicators, this dashboard helps security teams prioritize actions, identify areas of non-compliance, and streamline reporting for audits. By consolidating critical information into a single interface, the dashboard enhances decision-making, ensuring that security measures align with regulatory requirements and organizational risk management goals.

Effective visualization and reporting are critical for communicating vulnerability management outcomes and guiding strategic security decisions. The following approaches outline how dashboards and reports can enhance transparency and decision-making across technical and executive teams:

- **Custom dashboards**: Build custom dashboards that display key vulnerability metrics, such as the number of critical vulnerabilities, the time taken to remediate vulnerabilities, and the overall security posture. Tools such as **Tenable.io** and **Qualys** offer built-in dashboard capabilities, but you can also integrate vulnerability data into third-party visualization platforms such as Grafana and Kibana for more tailored reporting.

- **Trend analysis**: Use historical vulnerability data to identify trends in your security posture. For example, are certain systems or applications more prone to vulnerabilities? Are remediation efforts improving over time? Trend analysis can help guide future security investments and efforts.

- **Executive reporting**: Generate high-level reports for executives that summarize the overall security posture, highlighting areas of improvement and ongoing efforts to reduce risk. These reports should focus on key metrics that align with business goals, such as reducing downtime due to security incidents or meeting regulatory requirements.

Machine learning and AI-driven vulnerability management

Integrating machine learning and AI into vulnerability management is transforming the way security teams identify, prioritize, and mitigate threats, by enabling faster and more accurate detection. These technologies analyze vast amounts of data to recognize patterns and predict potential vulnerabilities, often in real time, making it possible to identify emerging threats and reduce false positives. As a result, AI-driven vulnerability management tools are becoming essential for proactive, scalable security operations that keep pace with rapidly evolving cyber threats.

The following is how machine learning and AI can be applied to enhance vulnerability management processes and address security challenges effectively:

- **Predictive risk scoring**: Use machine learning models to predict the likelihood of a vulnerability being exploited based on historical data, external threat intelligence, and environmental factors. This allows security teams to focus their efforts on the most critical issues.

- **Automated decision-making**: AI-driven tools can automate decision-making processes by recommending remediation actions based on the severity of vulnerabilities and the context of the affected systems. For example, an AI system might automatically patch a low-risk server while flagging a critical vulnerability on a high-risk server for immediate manual intervention.

- **Anomaly detection**: Machine learning models can be used to detect anomalies in vulnerability scan data, such as unusual patterns of vulnerabilities appearing in certain systems. This can help identify emerging threats or potential misconfigurations that might have been missed by traditional scanning tools.

Leveraging threat intelligence for enhanced vulnerability management

Incorporating threat intelligence into vulnerability management allows security teams to stay informed about active and emerging threats, providing context that enhances decision-making and prioritization. By integrating real-time intelligence on current exploits, attacker tactics, and threat actor profiles, organizations can focus on vulnerabilities most likely to be targeted, optimizing resource allocation and reducing risk. This proactive approach turns raw threat data into actionable insights, helping teams improve their defense strategies and stay a step ahead of potential attackers.

To effectively integrate threat intelligence into vulnerability management, consider the following best practices:

- **Real-time intelligence feeds**: Subscribe to threat intelligence feeds that provide up-to-date information on vulnerabilities being actively exploited in the wild. Integrate these feeds with your vulnerability scanning tools to automatically prioritize vulnerabilities based on real-time threat data.

- **Enriching vulnerability data**: Use threat intelligence to enrich vulnerability scan results with additional context, such as the likelihood of exploitation, the existence of known exploits, and the **tactics, techniques, and procedures** (**TTPs**) used by threat actors. This helps security teams make more informed decisions about remediation efforts.

- **Threat-informed remediation**: Prioritize remediation efforts based on the level of threat associated with specific vulnerabilities. For example, if a vulnerability has a known exploit being actively used by a threat group targeting your industry, it should be addressed immediately, even if it has a low severity score.

Integrating with multi-cloud environments

As organizations increasingly adopt multi-cloud environments, effective vulnerability management requires seamless integration across diverse cloud platforms to maintain consistent security standards. By unifying vulnerability scanning and remediation efforts across multiple clouds, security teams can address risks more efficiently, minimize configuration drift, and ensure comprehensive coverage. This approach enables greater visibility into vulnerabilities in complex cloud infrastructures, reducing the likelihood of security gaps and ensuring resilient cloud security practices across all environments.

In today's multi-cloud environments, integrating vulnerability scanning across different cloud platforms (e.g., AWS, Azure, Google Cloud) is essential. Cloud-native services and infrastructure require specialized vulnerability management strategies to ensure consistent security across all platforms:

- **Cloud-specific scanning tools**: Use cloud-specific vulnerability scanning tools, such as Amazon Inspector, Azure Security Center, or Google Cloud Security Command Center, to scan cloud-native infrastructure and services. Integrate these tools with your broader vulnerability management workflow.

- **Cross-cloud integration**: Ensure that your vulnerability scanning strategy spans across all cloud environments. Tools such as Tenable.io, Qualys, and Prisma Cloud offer cross-cloud integrations that allow you to manage vulnerabilities across multiple cloud providers from a single platform.

- **Cloud configuration auditing**: In addition to vulnerability scanning, perform regular configuration audits of your cloud environments to identify misconfigurations that could lead to security risks. Integrate these audits into your vulnerability management workflow to ensure that cloud security issues are addressed promptly.

By embedding vulnerability management into incident response, compliance, DevSecOps, and cloud security workflows, organizations can create a proactive security posture that continuously monitors and remediates vulnerabilities. Leveraging advanced technologies such as machine learning, AI, and threat intelligence can further enhance your vulnerability management efforts, ensuring that your organization stays ahead of emerging threats and reduces its overall risk.

Summary

In this chapter, we have learned how to automate vulnerability scanning using Python by leveraging libraries and tools such as Nessus and OpenVAS. We covered scripting techniques for setting up and executing scans, handling and analyzing scan results, and scheduling scans to run automatically. Additionally, we explored best practices for generating reports, setting up alerts, and ensuring scans are conducted ethically and effectively.

We covered the following in this chapter:

- **Python setup**: Successfully configuring your Python environment, ensuring the necessary libraries and tools are in place for automation.

- **Vulnerability scanning integration**: Integrating Python with popular vulnerability scanning tools and platforms, enabling the automation of scanning tasks through APIs or command-line utilities.

- **API interaction**: Gaining the ability to interact with vulnerability scanner APIs, automate scan requests, and process scan results using Python.

- **Result parsing and automation**: Automating the parsing and analysis of scan results using JSON or XML libraries, allowing faster identification of vulnerabilities.

- **Security and compliance**: Ensuring that your automated scanning processes adhere to network security policies and compliance requirements, making your scans both effective and compliant.

With these components in place, you are now well equipped to automate vulnerability scanning tasks, streamlining security operations and improving your organization's vulnerability management efforts.

In the next chapter, we'll delve into using Python to automate essential network security tasks, allowing more efficient and effective monitoring, threat detection, and response.

5

Network Security Automation with Python

In today's interconnected world, network security is a critical component of any organization's cybersecurity strategy. As networks grow in size and complexity, securing them becomes increasingly challenging. The sheer volume of devices, connections, and data traffic means that manual security management is no longer feasible. This is where automation, particularly with Python, becomes a powerful tool for network security.

Python has become the go-to language for cybersecurity professionals due to its simplicity, versatility, and extensive ecosystem of libraries tailored for security tasks. By automating network security processes, Python allows security teams to efficiently manage, monitor, and protect their networks against ever-evolving threats. Whether it's automating firewall rule updates, conducting network scans, or responding to security incidents, Python can streamline many of the time-consuming and error-prone tasks that are critical to maintaining network security. Automating network security processes not only improves efficiency but also enhances accuracy and response times. By eliminating manual tasks, security teams can focus on higher-level analysis and decision-making, leading to a more proactive and resilient network security posture.

This chapter will introduce you to the fundamentals of network security automation using Python. We'll explore how Python can be used to automate key security tasks such as network monitoring, intrusion detection, firewall management, and vulnerability scanning. You'll also learn about essential Python libraries and frameworks that are specifically designed for network security automation, such as Scapy for packet analysis, Paramiko for automating **Secure Shell** (**SSH**) tasks, and Nmap for network discovery. You'll gain hands-on experience with practical examples and scripts that demonstrate how to automate various aspects of network security using Python. Whether you're a network engineer looking to enhance your security skills or a cybersecurity professional aiming to automate your processes, this chapter will provide you with the foundational knowledge to get started with network security automation using Python.

In this chapter, we'll cover the following topics:

- Overview of common types of challenges in security automation
- Firewall management automation
- Intrusion detection and prevention automation
- Threat intelligence integration

Overview of common challenges in security automation

While network security automation offers powerful benefits, it also comes with a set of challenges that are important to acknowledge. Here's a brief overview of some common challenges in security automation:

1. **Increased complexity**: Automation can introduce complexity, especially in large-scale environments with multiple devices, policies, and processes.

   Example: Managing dependencies and ensuring scripts work harmoniously across various platforms and APIs can be challenging, requiring careful planning and testing.

2. **Risk of misconfigurations**: Automated scripts, if not thoroughly tested or properly managed, can lead to configuration errors that inadvertently open up security vulnerabilities.

   Example: An automated rule that mistakenly allows unrestricted access can expose critical systems to unauthorized users, potentially creating security gaps.

3. **Dependency on updated APIs and tools**: Automation scripts rely on APIs, libraries, or vendor tools that must remain up-to-date to function effectively.

   Example: If a vendor changes an API endpoint or deprecates a feature, it may break automation scripts and impact security operations.

4. **Alert fatigue**: Automation can increase the volume of alerts, which, without proper filtering and prioritization, may overwhelm security teams.

   Example: Automatically generated alerts for every minor anomaly can lead to desensitization, causing critical threats to be overlooked.

5. **Scalability concerns**: Scripts and tools designed for smaller networks may not scale well for larger infrastructures.

   Example: A firewall configuration script that performs well in testing may fail or slow down in production if it wasn't designed with large data volumes or high-frequency requests in mind.

6. **Skills and maintenance requirements**: Effective automation requires specialized skills, as well as ongoing maintenance to adjust for changes in network structure or compliance standards.

   Example: Organizations must invest in skilled personnel and dedicated time to maintain, update, and troubleshoot automation scripts.

I've highlighted these challenges to emphasize that while automation can greatly improve network security, it requires careful planning, skilled management, and a proactive approach to avoid potential pitfalls. Further in this chapter, we will cover how to work around these challenges and plan security automation.

Firewall management automation

Automating network security processes with Palo Alto Networks firewalls, particularly the **next-generation firewalls** (**NGFWs**) from Palo Alto Networks, can significantly streamline operations, improve response times, and ensure consistency in policy enforcement. Here's a guide to automating tasks with Palo Alto Networks, focusing on the **Pan-OS API** and **Ansible modules**, which are two commonly used automation approaches.

Automation process for Palo Alto Networks

This process can be carried out in two ways. Let's go through them.

Using the Pan-OS API

Palo Alto Networks provides a REST-based API called the PanOS API, which allows you to automate tasks such as configuration changes, policy updates, log retrieval, and system monitoring. The following are the steps to automate using the Pan-OS API:

1. **Setup and authentication**:

   A. Obtain API access credentials (API key) from the firewall.

   B. Use the firewall's management IP address to make API calls, ensuring that your environment has network access to this IP.

   C. To authenticate, send a POST request to the firewall's management interface with your admin credentials to retrieve the API key:

   ```python
   import requests

   # Replace these with actual values
   firewall_ip = "https://firewall-management-ip"
   api_username = "admin"
   api_password = "password"

   # Get the API Key
   response = requests.post(
       f"{firewall_ip}/api/?type=keygen&user={api_
   username}&password={api_password}"
   ```

```
    )
    api_key = response.json()['result']['key']
```

2. **Automating configuration changes**: Example: Automating the addition of a new security policy.

   Use the API to configure a new security rule (source IP, destination IP, application, action) by sending a POST request with the XML configuration:

   python
   ```python
   # Define the XML payload for the security rule
   security_rule = """
   <entry name="Auto-Generated Rule">
       <from><member>trust</member></from>
       <to><member>untrust</member></to>
       <source><member>10.0.0.1</member></source>
       <destination><member>192.168.1.1</member></destination>
       <service><member>application-default</member></service>
       <action>allow</action>
   </entry>
   """


   # Send the POST request to add the rule
   requests.post(
       f"{firewall_ip}/api/?type=config&action=set&xpath=/
   config/devices/entry/vsys/entry/rulebase/security/
   rules&element={security_rule}&key={api_key}"
   )
   ```

3. **Monitoring and log retrieval**:

   A. Retrieve logs or monitor events using the Pan-OS API's logging capabilities.

   B. For example, to get the latest traffic logs, use the following API endpoint with a query filter:

   python
   ```python
   log_response = requests.get(
       f"{firewall_ip}/api/?type=log&log-
   type=traffic&nlogs=10&key={api_key}"
   )
   logs = log_response.json()['result']['log']
   ```

Automating with Ansible modules for Palo Alto Networks

Palo Alto Networks offers official Ansible modules that provide an alternative for automating tasks without directly working with API calls. The following are the steps to automate with Ansible modules:

1. **Install the Ansible collection**: Use the following command to install Palo Alto's Ansible collection:

    ```bash
    ansible-galaxy collection install paloaltonetworks.panos
    ```

2. **Configure authentication**: Set up an inventory file with the firewall's IP address and login credentials, or configure them directly in your Ansible playbook.

3. **Create an Ansible playbook**: For example, add a new security rule with Ansible:

    ```yaml
    - name: Configure Palo Alto NGFW
      hosts: firewalls
      gather_facts: no
      tasks:
        - name: Add security rule
          paloaltonetworks.panos.panos_security_rule:
            provider:
              ip_address: "firewall-management-ip"
              username: "admin"
              password: "password"
            rule_name: "Auto-Generated Rule"
            source_zone: ["trust"]
            destination_zone: ["untrust"]
            source_ip: ["10.0.0.1"]
            destination_ip: ["192.168.1.1"]
            action: "allow"
    ```

4. **Automating execution**: Run this playbook to push the rule configuration to the firewall:

    ```bash
    ansible-playbook firewall-config.yaml
    ```

Key use cases

By leveraging the Pan-OS API and Ansible modules, you can automate most tasks on Palo Alto Networks firewalls, significantly improving efficiency and minimizing the potential for human error. The following use cases help track this:

*   **Automated policy updates**: Modify security rules as network changes occur, maintaining consistent access control across the organization.

- **Automated threat detection and response**: Monitor traffic for anomalies and automatically trigger responses, such as blocking suspicious IPs.
- **Logging and alerting**: Use Python scripts to automate log retrieval and feed it into **security information and event management (SIEM)** systems for real-time monitoring.

Firewalls are a critical component of network security, acting as the first line of defense by controlling inbound and outbound traffic based on security rules. As networks grow more complex and threats evolve, managing firewall rules and configurations manually can become overwhelming and error-prone. Automation of firewall management helps ensure that policies are consistently enforced, reduces the risk of misconfigurations, and frees up time for security teams to focus on more strategic tasks.

Python, with its rich ecosystem of libraries and modules, is an excellent tool for automating firewall management. Whether you're working with traditional firewalls, cloud-based firewalls, or NGFWs, Python scripts can be used to automate rule creation, modification, monitoring, and reporting.

Key tasks in firewall management automation

Automation in firewall management can encompass a wide range of tasks, including the following:

- **Rule creation and updates**: Automating the creation, modification, and deletion of firewall rules based on predefined policies or real-time security events.
- **Configuration management**: Automating backup, restoration, and auditing of firewall configurations to ensure compliance with security policies and regulatory standards.
- **Monitoring and alerts**: Continuously monitoring firewall logs and traffic patterns for suspicious activities, and automating alerts when anomalies are detected.
- **Change management**: Automating the documentation and approval of firewall changes to ensure accountability and traceability.
- **Compliance checks**: Automating regular compliance checks to ensure that firewall rules align with organizational policies and industry regulations.

By automating these tasks, organizations can reduce the chances of human error, ensure timely updates to firewall rules, and maintain a strong security posture.

Python libraries for firewall automation

Several Python libraries and modules are available to help with firewall automation. Depending on your firewall vendor and the type of firewall in use, different tools can be employed. The following are some common libraries:

- **Paramiko**: This is a Python library for SSH connections, commonly used to automate interactions with firewalls that have **command-line interfaces (CLIs)** over SSH.

- **Netmiko**: This is a multi-vendor library built on top of `Paramiko`, designed specifically for network automation, including firewall management for devices such as Cisco ASA, Palo Alto, and Juniper firewalls.

- **pyFG**: This is a Python module for managing Fortinet FortiGate firewalls via its API.

- **Palo Alto Networks API**: Many NGFWs, such as Palo Alto Networks firewalls, provide RESTful APIs that can be used with Python's requests library for automation tasks.

- **Cloud SDKs**: For cloud-based firewalls (e.g., AWS Security Groups, Azure Network Security Groups), Python SDKs provided by the cloud providers (e.g., boto3 for AWS, azure-sdk-for-python for Azure) can be used to automate firewall management.

Example use cases for firewall automation

In this section, we will learn how automating firewall management can improve security and efficiency. Let's go through how some key use cases include automating firewall rule creation and updates based on changing network conditions, integrating automated vulnerability scans to adjust firewall settings in real time, and automating responses to detected threats by blocking malicious traffic. Firewall automation helps in managing large-scale environments, reducing human error, and ensuring compliance with security policies through consistent rule enforcement.

Including examples for libraries such as `pyFG` can definitely make the content more accessible! Here's a quick example to illustrate how `pyFG` can be used in network security automation.

Using pyFG for generating network graphs

pyFG (**Python Flow Graph**) is a library that helps us visualize network flow by creating directed graphs. This can be useful in network security for mapping out connections, identifying potential attack paths, and showing communication patterns.

Let's look at an example scenario where we are trying to visualize communication paths in a network. Suppose you want to visualize communication flows between devices in your network. `pyFG` allows you to create a graph to represent these connections:

```python
from pyfg import Graph

# Create a new graph object
network_graph = Graph()

# Adding nodes (devices) to the graph
network_graph.add_node("Router")
network_graph.add_node("Web Server")
network_graph.add_node("Database Server")
```

```
# Adding directed edges (flows) between nodes
network_graph.add_edge("Router", "Web Server")
network_graph.add_edge("Web Server", "Database Server")

# Generate and display the graph (this will vary based on how you
render it)
network_graph.display()
```

This example shows the `Router` connecting to the `Web Server`, which in turn connects to the `Database Server`. Using pyFG in this way helps us visualize network relationships, making it easier to identify unapproved paths or risky connections.

Adding more of these practical examples can help you better understand the purpose and functionality of lesser-known libraries such as pyFG.

Automating firewall rule deployment with Ansible

A common scenario involves automating the deployment of new firewall rules. For example, imagine a situation where a new web server is deployed, and you need to allow traffic on ports 80 and 443 through the firewall. With Python, you can write a script that automates the creation of these rules:

```python
import paramiko

def create_firewall_rule(host, username, password, rule_command):
    ssh = paramiko.SSHClient()
    ssh.set_missing_host_key_policy(paramiko.AutoAddPolicy())
    ssh.connect(host, username=username, password=password)

    stdin, stdout, stderr = ssh.exec_command(rule_command)
    print(stdout.read().decode())
    ssh.close()

# Example rule command for Cisco ASA firewall
rule_command = "access-list outside_in extended permit tcp any host
192.168.1.100 eq 80"
create_firewall_rule("firewall_ip_address", "admin", "password", rule_
command)
```

This simple script uses `Paramiko` to connect to a Cisco ASA firewall and executes a command to allow HTTP traffic to a specific server. The same approach can be extended to other firewall vendors by modifying `rule_command`.

Automating firewall rule deployment offers significant efficiency, but it's essential to handle these processes securely and avoid some common pitfalls. Here are a few key considerations:

1. **Default or weak passwords**: Relying on default credentials or weak passwords when authenticating to the firewall.

   Solution: Always use strong, unique passwords for API authentication. Ideally, store sensitive credentials in a secure vault (e.g., HashiCorp Vault or AWS Secrets Manager) and access them programmatically.

   • **API key security**: Storing the API key or credentials directly in scripts, especially if these scripts are shared or committed to version control.

   Solution: Use environment variables or secure storage solutions for API keys. Avoid hardcoding sensitive data in scripts.

2. **Proper rule management**: Automating rule deployment without a systematic review process, which can lead to excessive, outdated, or conflicting rules, weakening firewall security.

   Solution: Implement a rule life cycle process that regularly audits, updates, and removes unused or redundant rules. Automate rule expiry by setting review periods on each rule.

3. **Testing in a staging environment**: Deploying automation directly in production without testing.

   Solution: Always test automation scripts in a staging environment first. This approach allows you to validate rule behavior and detect issues before they impact production.

4. **Logging and alerting on automation changes**: Not monitoring changes made by automation scripts, which could result in undetected misconfigurations.

   Solution: Enable logging for all automated rule changes and set up alerts for any configuration changes. This ensures visibility into rule deployments and can help in troubleshooting issues quickly.

5. **Error handling and rollbacks**: Preventing incomplete configurations or security gaps during partial rule deployments.

   Solution: Add error handling in scripts and, where possible, implement rollback mechanisms to revert to the previous configuration if a failure occurs.

6. **Rate limiting for API requests**: Making too many API requests in a short period could trigger rate limits, resulting in delays or unprocessed requests.

   Solution: Introduce delay intervals or batching in scripts to prevent excessive API requests, especially if deploying a large number of rules.

7. **Restrict API access**: Granting broad permissions to API keys used for automation.

   Solution: Restrict API access to the minimum necessary permissions. For instance, only allow rule-related actions rather than full administrative access. This minimizes the damage if the API credentials are compromised.

By following these practices, users can help ensure that their automation processes enhance security rather than inadvertently weaken it.

Firewall configuration backup automation with Ansible

Regular backups of firewall configurations are essential for disaster recovery and ensuring that changes can be tracked and rolled back if necessary. With Python, you can automate the backup process:

```python
import netmiko

def backup_firewall_config(host, username, password, device_type):
    connection = netmiko.ConnectHandler(ip=host, username=username,
password=password, device_type=device_type)
    config = connection.send_command("show running-config")

    with open(f"{host}_backup.txt", "w") as file:
        file.write(config)

    connection.disconnect()
    print(f"Backup of {host} completed.")

# Example usage
backup_firewall_config("firewall_ip_address", "admin", "password",
"cisco_asa")
```

In this script, Netmiko is used to connect to a Cisco ASA firewall, retrieve the running configuration, and save it to a file. You can schedule this script to run regularly to ensure that your firewall configurations are always backed up.

Automating compliance checks

Firewall rules need to comply with internal security policies and external regulations (e.g., PCI-DSS, HIPAA). Python can be used to automate regular checks to ensure that firewall rules are compliant:

```python
import re

def check_compliance(firewall_config, compliance_rules):
    non_compliant_rules = []

    for rule in firewall_config:
        if not any(re.search(compliance_rule, rule) for compliance_
rule in compliance_rules):
            non_compliant_rules.append(rule)
```

```
      return non_compliant_rules

# Example compliance rules: No "any" in source or destination, no
insecure ports (e.g., Telnet, FTP)
compliance_rules = [r"permit tcp \S+ eq 21", r"permit tcp \S+ eq 23",
r"permit ip any any"]

# Sample firewall configuration
firewall_config = [
    "permit ip any any",
    "permit tcp host 192.168.1.50 host 192.168.1.100 eq 22"
]

non_compliant = check_compliance(firewall_config, compliance_rules)
print("Non-compliant rules:", non_compliant)
```

This script checks a sample firewall configuration against a set of compliance rules. Non-compliant rules are flagged, allowing security teams to take corrective actions.

Automating compliance checks involves using scripts or tools to automatically assess whether a system, network, or organization meets certain security standards and regulatory requirements. Instead of manually verifying each policy, automation enables continuous monitoring and ensures that security controls are consistently enforced.

Best practices for firewall management automation

Here are some best practices for firewall management automation:

- **Test scripts in a staging environment**: Always test automation scripts in a non-production environment to avoid unintentional disruptions to the network.

- **Use version control**: Store your automation scripts in a version control system (e.g., Git) to keep track of changes and roll back if necessary.

- **Implement error handling**: Ensure that your scripts have robust error handling to prevent incomplete changes or disruptions in case of failures.

- **Schedule regular audits**: Automate regular audits of firewall configurations to ensure that they remain aligned with security policies and compliance requirements.

- **Integrate with CI/CD pipelines**: For DevSecOps practices, integrate firewall rule updates and checks into your CI/CD pipelines to ensure security controls are enforced during the deployment of new applications.

Case study – security automation in a large financial enterprise

A major financial services company, SecureBank, operates across multiple regions, managing extensive customer data and handling thousands of daily transactions. To maintain regulatory compliance and ensure robust security, SecureBank's **security operations center** (**SOC**) has automated several key security processes using Python and various automation tools.

For a comprehensive vulnerability scanning and remediation case study, here's an in-depth expansion looking at the challenges SecureBank dealt with, the best practices that followed, and what came out of it.

Challenges and initial conditions

The organization initially faced several issues—namely, fragmented scanning across different teams, inconsistencies in scan frequency, and a lack of centralized oversight. These gaps led to missed vulnerabilities and prolonged exposure to risks, affecting compliance with industry standards.

Catalysts for change

Key events that drove the shift to best practices included the following:

- **Regulatory pressure**: A recent audit revealed compliance gaps, particularly in the timeliness of patching critical vulnerabilities.
- **Incident response and lessons learned**: A previous security incident underscored the need for rapid detection and response, showing that existing processes couldn't keep up with new threats.
- **Leadership and strategy shift**: Executive leadership prioritized security as part of a broader digital transformation, emphasizing visibility and accountability in vulnerability management.

Best practices implemented

The following are some of the best practices implemented in the application of security automation:

- **Automated, continuous scanning**: The organization adopted a robust vulnerability scanning solution that enabled continuous, automated scans across endpoints, networks, and cloud environments. This allowed for real-time identification of vulnerabilities rather than waiting for scheduled scans.
- **Risk-based vulnerability prioritization**: To address overwhelming scan results, it introduced a risk-based approach to prioritize vulnerabilities by severity and exploitability. Critical vulnerabilities received immediate attention, while lower-risk items were scheduled for routine updates.
- **Remediation playbooks**: For consistent response, it developed playbooks detailing standard operating procedures for remediation, from triaging critical issues to coordinating patching activities across teams.

- **Integration with patch management systems**: The vulnerability scanner was integrated with a patch management system, automating remediation for common vulnerabilities and expediting the patch deployment process.

- **Regular security audits and reporting**: A structured audit schedule was established, verifying that remediation actions were effective and comprehensive. It also implemented detailed reporting for stakeholders, ensuring transparency.

Outcomes and benefits

The following was observed after measures were taken to tackle the initial challenges:

- **Reduced exposure time**: The organization significantly shortened the time between vulnerability discovery and remediation, minimizing the window for potential exploitation.

- **Improved compliance and risk management**: By adopting these best practices, it met compliance standards and reduced risk, with fewer findings during audits.

- **Cross-functional collaboration**: Security teams collaborated more efficiently with IT and DevOps, facilitating smoother implementations and sharing accountability for security outcomes.

This approach resulted in a proactive security stance, allowing the organization to stay ahead of vulnerabilities rather than reactively responding after incidents, creating a secure, resilient environment.

Incorporating specific tools into best practices

The tools that can be used to incorporate are as follows:

1. **Comprehensive vulnerability scanning and remediation**: SecureBank uses a combination of **Nessus** and **OpenVAS** scanners, automated through Python scripts, to perform regular vulnerability assessments across servers and workstations.

   Best practice: Scanning automation is configured to run during off-peak hours to minimize network impact, and results are piped into a central SIEM system (e.g., Splunk) for continuous monitoring.

   Example: A Python script checks daily scans, flags high-priority vulnerabilities, and creates tickets in the remediation system for IT teams to address within defined SLAs.

2. **Automated firewall and IDS updates**: SecureBank has standardized policies for firewall and IDS rule updates. It uses Ansible to push policy changes to various network devices, reducing manual errors.

   Best practice: Each policy change is first tested in a staging environment, and only reviewed rules are deployed to production, preventing configuration errors that could disrupt services.

   Example: An Ansible playbook applies a rule update across firewalls within an hour of policy approval, reducing the time for vulnerabilities to be exposed.

3. **Multi-stage alert management and incident response**: With thousands of security alerts generated daily, SecureBank employs **security orchestration, automation, and response (SOAR)** platforms such as **Splunk Phantom** to manage alert volumes.

   Best practice: Alerts are triaged into categories, with predefined playbooks handling low-risk events automatically (e.g., blocking IPs, isolating endpoints).

   Example: When an intrusion detection alert is triggered by abnormal traffic from a foreign IP, the SOAR platform automatically executes a Python script that blocks the IP in the firewall and notifies the SOC team, reducing response time to minutes.

4. **Continuous compliance audits and reporting**: Financial regulations require SecureBank to demonstrate compliance with standards such as PCI DSS. Automation scripts gather audit data and generate compliance reports.

   Best practice: Scripts automatically extract necessary logs and configurations to produce audit reports, ensuring they are both accurate and timely.

   Example: A scheduled Python job retrieves firewall configurations and network logs weekly, formatting the data into a compliance report ready for internal review or external audit.

5. **Data masking and encryption in DevOps pipelines**: SecureBank's DevOps teams ensure that sensitive data used in development or testing is masked or encrypted, preventing exposure.

   Best practice: Data masking automation applies transformations to customer data before it enters the test environment, reducing the risk of data leakage.

   Example: Python scripts apply reversible transformations to production data, allowing developers to test with realistic datasets without risking actual customer information.

By implementing these best practices, SecureBank was able to reduce its vulnerability exposure, respond to incidents more quickly, and remain compliant with industry regulations. This approach ensures that SecureBank's security automation framework is both resilient and scalable, critical for managing complex and ever-growing security demands in a large enterprise environment.

Next, let's look at some real-world considerations.

Real-world considerations

In real-world firewall automation, several key considerations must be addressed to ensure security, performance, and compliance:

- **Security and access control**: Firewalls must follow the principle of least privilege, with proper approval workflows to avoid overly permissive rules.

- **Performance impact**: Automation should optimize rules to prevent performance degradation, and balance logging needs with system resources.

- **Scalability and network complexity**: Automation must handle large, hybrid, and cloud-based environments, ensuring consistent rule application across all segments.

- **Compliance and auditing**: Firewall automation should align with regulatory requirements and maintain detailed logs for audit purposes.

- **Change management**: Automated updates must be thoroughly tested and include rollback options to mitigate the risks of misconfigurations.

These considerations help ensure firewall automation is secure, efficient, and compliant:

- **APIs versus CLI automation**: Whenever possible, prefer using APIs provided by firewall vendors for automation, as they are more stable and easier to work with than CLI automation. APIs often provide better feedback and error handling, making automation scripts more reliable.

- **Role-based access control (RBAC)**: Ensure that automation scripts run with the least privilege required. Use accounts with limited access to prevent security risks in case the automation system is compromised.

- **Logging and auditing**: Ensure that all automation actions are logged and auditable. This will help track changes made by automation scripts and comply with security best practices and regulations.

Firewall management automation with Python can drastically improve the efficiency and accuracy of managing firewall rules and configurations. By automating tasks such as rule creation, configuration backups, compliance checks, and monitoring, security teams can reduce the burden of manual management and ensure consistent enforcement of security policies. With Python's extensive library support and flexibility, you can build automation solutions tailored to your specific firewall infrastructure, enabling a more secure and resilient network environment.

For a smooth transition to automated firewall management, best practices include starting with clear policies, implementing changes gradually, incorporating approval workflows, thoroughly testing in controlled environments, and enabling continuous monitoring and logging to ensure security and compliance.

Intrusion detection and prevention automation

Intrusion detection and prevention systems (IDPSs) are essential components of modern cybersecurity strategies. These systems monitor network traffic and system activity for signs of malicious behavior and unauthorized access. **Intrusion detection systems (IDSs)** alert security teams when suspicious activities are detected, while **intrusion prevention systems (IPSs)** take immediate action to block or mitigate threats. Given the vast amount of data that flows through networks, automating the management, analysis, and response of IDPS is critical to maintaining an efficient and effective security posture.

Python, with its flexibility and extensive library ecosystem, is an excellent choice for automating various aspects of IDPS operations. From automating alert triage to creating custom detection signatures and orchestrating incident responses, Python can streamline many of the processes involved in intrusion detection and prevention.

In this section, we will cover intrusion detection and prevention automation enhancement in network security by automating the detection of and responses to potential threats in real time. This involves using tools such as IDPSs to monitor network traffic for malicious activity and immediately take actions such as blocking suspicious traffic and adjusting firewall rules. Automation improves threat detection accuracy and response times and reduces human error by integrating with security tools such as SIEM systems and leveraging **machine learning** (**ML**) for adaptive threat detection. This approach helps ensure continuous protection against evolving cyber threats with minimal manual intervention.

Key areas of automation in IDPS

Automation in IDPS can be applied to several key areas, including the following:

- **Alert triage and response**: Automating the analysis and prioritization of IDS alerts, and initiating response actions (e.g., blocking IP addresses, isolating infected hosts) based on predefined criteria.

- **Custom signature creation**: Automating the generation and deployment of custom detection signatures based on threat intelligence or specific use cases.

- **Data collection and correlation**: Automating the collection of log data from various sources, correlating it to detect complex attack patterns, and feeding it into the IDS for enhanced detection capabilities.

- **Reporting and visualization**: Automating the generation of reports and dashboards to provide visibility into detected threats and the effectiveness of prevention measures.

- **Integration with other security tools**: Automating the interaction between the IDS/IPS and other security tools (e.g., SIEMs, firewalls, endpoint detection and response tools) for coordinated threat detection and response.

By automating these processes, security teams can respond to threats more quickly and efficiently, reducing the time it takes to detect and mitigate security incidents.

Highlighting the limitations of IDPS automation offers a balanced perspective. Here are some key challenges commonly encountered:

- **High rates of false positives**: Automated IDPS systems often generate excessive alerts, many of which are false positives. This "alert fatigue" can overwhelm security teams, causing real threats to be missed or ignored.

    Example: Automated rules may flag benign network activity as suspicious, triggering unnecessary alerts. For instance, frequent file transfers between servers could be mistaken for data exfiltration.

Solution: To reduce false positives, organizations should implement more granular alert rules and use ML to distinguish typical from atypical behaviors.

- **Challenges in tuning and customization**: Properly tuning IDPS systems to the unique environment is essential but complex. Overly strict settings can result in excessive false positives, while too lenient configurations risk missing threats.

    Example: Generic rules may fail to account for normal activity in a specific network environment, such as high internal traffic, leading to unnecessary alerts.

    Solution: Regularly review and adjust detection thresholds and signature updates to match the network's activity patterns and known baselines.

- **Difficulty detecting sophisticated threats**: Traditional IDPS systems may struggle with advanced, low-profile attacks that do not trigger typical signatures.

    Example: Attackers using techniques such as encryption, tunneling, or multi-stage infiltration can bypass signature-based detection systems.

    Solution: Combine an IDPS with behavioral analytics or anomaly detection that identifies deviations in network behavior, which can highlight unknown threats.

- **Resource and performance constraints**: Continuous monitoring and high data throughput can strain network resources and affect IDPS performance, especially in high-traffic environments.

    Example: Network latency and dropped packets can occur if IDPS devices are overwhelmed by the volume of real-time traffic.

    Solution: Scale the infrastructure by distributing the IDPS across network segments and using load-balancing techniques to manage traffic volumes effectively.

- **Integration and compatibility issues**: Integrating IDPS systems with other security tools can be complex and may require custom development, particularly in heterogeneous network environments.

    Example: Legacy systems or custom-built solutions may lack native integration, requiring additional scripting or middleware.

    Solution: Use flexible APIs or middleware for seamless integration and automation, and consider IDPS systems that support standardized protocols such as REST or syslog for smoother interaction with other tools.

- **Privacy and legal concerns**: Automated IDPSs may unintentionally capture sensitive data, leading to potential privacy or legal concerns.

    Example: Logging all traffic, including sensitive communications, could raise privacy compliance issues.

    Solution: Limit data capture to necessary metadata where possible, and establish data handling policies to comply with regulatory requirements.

By acknowledging these limitations, security teams can approach IDPS automation with a realistic understanding, making it easier to optimize and maintain detection systems that align with their specific needs and network environments.

Python libraries for IDPS automation

Python offers a range of libraries and modules that are useful for automating tasks related to intrusion detection and prevention:

- **Scapy**: A powerful packet manipulation tool that can be used to create custom network traffic for testing IDS/IPS systems, as well as for automating packet analysis and detection.

- **PyShark**: A wrapper for the Wireshark packet capture tool that allows for the automation of packet analysis.

- **Elasticsearch-Py**: A Python client for Elasticsearch, often used to automate the querying and analysis of IDS logs stored in Elasticsearch indices (commonly used with tools such as the Elastic Stack).

- **Requests**: A widely used library for making HTTP requests, useful for interacting with APIs provided by IDS/IPS systems to automate tasks such as rule management and incident response.

- **SNORTPy**: A Python wrapper for managing and automating tasks with Snort, a popular open source IDS.

Use cases for IDPS automation

Use cases for IDPS automation showcase its role in enhancing network security through various automated processes:

- **Proactive threat detection**: An automated IDPS continuously monitors network traffic and system activities to identify potential threats or anomalies early on.

  Use case: Detecting unusual login attempts from foreign IP addresses and flagging them as suspicious, helping prevent unauthorized access.

- **Automated incident response**: When a threat is detected, the system can autonomously respond with corrective actions, such as blocking malicious traffic or isolating compromised systems.

  Use case: If a malware infection is detected on a device, the IDPS can automatically isolate the device from the network to prevent further spread.

- **Integration with security ecosystems**: An automated IDPS can connect with other security tools, such as SIEM systems, providing a unified view of security events for comprehensive threat management.

  Use case: Integrating with an SIEM system to correlate data across multiple sources, such as logs from firewalls and endpoints, creating a holistic view of an active threat.

- **Adaptive security measures**: Using ML, an automated IDPS adapts to new threats by recognizing and learning patterns over time, enhancing its detection capabilities.

  Use case: Identifying a previously unknown phishing attempt based on new patterns learned from recent similar incidents, reducing the chance of a successful attack.

These use cases illustrate how automation in IDPS not only improves the efficiency and effectiveness of threat detection and response but also helps maintain a robust security posture with minimal manual intervention. Let's look into them in detail.

Automating alert triage and response

One of the most valuable automation use cases in IDPS is automating the triage and response to alerts. For example, a Python script could analyze incoming alerts from an IDS and automatically determine the appropriate response, such as blocking an IP address or sending a notification to the security team:

```python
import requests

# Example: Automate response based on Snort alert data
def process_alert(alert):
    if "malicious_ip" in alert:
        # Example action: Block IP address on firewall
        block_ip(alert["malicious_ip"])

        # Notify security team
        send_notification(f"Blocked malicious IP: {alert['malicious_
ip']}")

def block_ip(ip_address):
    firewall_api_url = "https://firewall.example.com/api/block_ip"
    response = requests.post(firewall_api_url, json={"ip": ip_
address})
    return response.status_code

def send_notification(message):
    # Integrate with Slack or email notification system
    print(f"Notification sent: {message}")

# Example alert data from Snort
alert_data = {"malicious_ip": "192.168.1.100", "alert": "Detected
exploit attempt"}
process_alert(alert_data)
```

This simple example shows how Python can automate alert triage and response by processing alert data from an IDS (such as Snort) and taking appropriate action (e.g., blocking a malicious IP address via a firewall API).

Automating alert triage and response involves using scripts, tools, and workflows to handle security alerts efficiently, minimizing manual intervention and improving response times. Here's a general explanation of how this process works, including an example of what such a code might look like.

Integrating ML and AI into the IDPS triage process can significantly enhance accuracy and reduce alert fatigue. Here's how these technologies add value:

- **Reducing false positives**: ML models can analyze historical alert data to identify patterns in legitimate network behavior, helping the system recognize and ignore common benign activities that would otherwise trigger false positives.

  Example: An ML model might learn that frequent database queries are part of normal business operations, preventing these from setting off alerts unnecessarily.

  Benefit: Fewer false positives mean security teams can focus on real threats, streamlining the triage process.

- **Anomaly detection**: AI and ML algorithms can baseline normal network behavior and detect deviations, even when they don't match known signatures. This is particularly valuable for identifying unknown or advanced threats that don't trigger traditional signatures.

  Example: If an internal server suddenly starts communicating with an unknown external IP address or sends data outside typical hours, ML-based anomaly detection could flag this as potentially suspicious.

  Benefit: Anomaly detection allows for more flexible, adaptive threat detection and provides visibility into stealthy attacks.

- **Automated alert prioritization**: By analyzing context, such as device criticality, previous alert resolution, and recent network activity, AI can assign a risk score to each alert. This prioritization helps teams respond first to the most critical threats.

  Example: Alerts involving core servers with sensitive data might be automatically ranked as a higher priority compared to alerts from less critical endpoints.

  Benefit: Prioritizing alerts improves response time for significant threats, which is crucial in reducing the potential impact of an incident.

- **Context-aware correlation**: ML can analyze patterns across multiple alerts, correlating related events to highlight broader security incidents. This capability reduces noise by consolidating alerts into cohesive incidents.

  Example: If an attacker is probing several network devices, ML algorithms can link these individual alerts, identifying the activity as a coordinated reconnaissance effort.

Benefit: Correlating alerts allows analysts to respond to incidents more holistically, improving both detection accuracy and efficiency.

- **Self-learning threat intelligence**: AI-enhanced IDPS systems can continuously update their threat models based on evolving attack patterns, improving the detection of zero-day exploits and new attack methods.

  Example: After observing multiple instances of a new phishing attack, the system could automatically update detection rules to catch similar future attempts.

  Benefit: Self-learning capabilities ensure that the IDPS remains effective against new, unseen threats without requiring constant manual updates.

- **Automated response recommendations**: AI can provide response suggestions based on previous actions taken by the team for similar alerts. This functionality speeds up response time and ensures consistency in incident handling.

  Example: If a high-risk alert occurs that matches past incidents, the AI might recommend blocking an IP address, isolating a device, or increasing monitoring as the next steps.

  Benefit: Recommendations simplify decision-making for analysts, especially valuable in high-volume or high-stress situations.

By leveraging AI and ML, organizations can significantly enhance their IDPS's ability to accurately identify, prioritize, and respond to security threats, ultimately improving their security posture and reducing the burden on SOC teams.

Overview of cyber threat intelligence

The **cyber threat intelligence** (**CTI**) process is a structured approach for gathering, analyzing, and utilizing information about potential cyber threats to improve an organization's security posture. It involves several key steps:

1. **Alert generation**: Security tools (e.g., SIEMs, IDS/IPS, endpoint protection) generate alerts based on detected anomalies, threats, or breaches.

2. **Alert collection**: Alerts are collected and ingested into a central system or dashboard for processing.

3. **Alert triage**: The system classifies and prioritizes alerts based on predefined criteria such as severity, type, and potential impact.

4. **Automated response**: Based on the alert's classification, the system triggers automated responses such as blocking IP addresses, isolating affected systems, and initiating predefined workflows.

5. **Notification**: Notifications or tickets are created for human analysts if needed, and additional actions are taken based on the severity of the alert.

Custom signature generation and deployment

Automating the creation and deployment of custom IDS signatures allows security teams to rapidly adapt to emerging threats. Python can be used to generate signatures based on threat intelligence feeds or patterns identified in network traffic and automatically deploy them to the IDS:

```python
def create_snort_signature(signature_id, src_ip, dest_ip, payload):
    signature = f"alert tcp {src_ip} any -> {dest_ip} any
(msg:\"Custom Signature {signature_id}\"; content:\"{payload}\";
sid:{signature_id};)"
    return signature


def deploy_signature_to_snort(signature):
    with open("/etc/snort/rules/custom.rules", "a") as rule_file:
        rule_file.write(signature + "\n")
    # Restart Snort to apply the new rule
    os.system("sudo systemctl restart snort")


# Example usage
new_signature = create_snort_signature(100001, "192.168.1.50",
"192.168.1.100", "malicious_payload")
deploy_signature_to_snort(new_signature)
```

This script generates a custom Snort signature based on a specific IP and payload, then appends it to Snort's rules file and restarts the service to apply the changes.

Custom signature generation involves creating unique patterns to detect specific threats by analyzing malware or attack behaviors. These signatures are defined based on known indicators and are coded into a format that security tools can recognize. Once created, the signatures are deployed to security systems (e.g., antivirus systems, IDS/IPS) via updates or configuration changes. Continuous monitoring and updates ensure the signatures effectively detect evolving threats.

Automating incident response workflows

Python can also be used to automate incident response workflows, integrating with various security tools and orchestrating responses based on IDS alerts. For example, a script could automatically isolate an infected host by updating firewall rules or triggering a response in an endpoint protection system:

```python
import subprocess


def isolate_infected_host(ip_address):
    # Block all traffic to and from the infected host
```

```
    subprocess.run(["sudo", "iptables", "-A", "INPUT", "-s", ip_
address, "-j", "DROP"])
    subprocess.run(["sudo", "iptables", "-A", "OUTPUT", "-d", ip_
address, "-j", "DROP"])

    # Notify security team
    send_notification(f"Infected host {ip_address} isolated.")

def send_notification(message):
    print(f"Notification sent: {message}")

# Example usage
isolate_infected_host("192.168.1.50")
```

In this example, Python is used to interact with the host's firewall (via `iptables`) to isolate an infected system by blocking all inbound and outbound traffic.

Automating incident response workflows involves using tools to detect, analyze, and respond to security incidents with minimal human intervention. Alerts trigger predefined actions such as isolating systems or blocking threats, and automated systems log details and notify relevant personnel. This speeds up response times, reduces manual effort, and enhances overall security efficiency. Continuous updates ensure that the automation adapts to evolving threats.

Best practices for IDPS automation

Best practices for IDPS automation include defining clear security policies and response protocols to guide automated actions. Regularly update detection signatures to address new threats and minimize false positives. Continuously monitor and fine-tune the automation to ensure optimal performance and accuracy. Integrate the IDPS with other security tools for a cohesive and effective threat management strategy.

- **Thoroughly test automation scripts**: Ensure that all automation scripts are thoroughly tested in a controlled environment before deploying them to production. This will help prevent unintended disruptions or security issues.

- **Use version control**: Store all automation scripts in a version control system to track changes, collaborate with team members, and roll back if necessary.

- **Implement robust error handling**: Ensure that your scripts handle errors gracefully and log any failures or issues encountered during execution.

- **Monitor and log automated actions**: Keep detailed logs of all actions taken by automation scripts for audit and troubleshooting purposes.

- **Maintain up-to-date threat intelligence**: Continuously update your custom detection signatures and response actions based on the latest threat intelligence and emerging attack vectors.

- **RBAC**: Use the principle of least privilege to ensure that automation scripts only have access to the resources necessary for their function, minimizing potential security risks.

Real-world considerations of IDPS systems

In the real world, IDPS systems must handle high volumes of data and potential false positives, requiring careful tuning to avoid unnecessary disruptions. They need to be integrated with other security tools and workflows to provide a comprehensive defense strategy. Regular updates and maintenance are crucial to keep up with evolving threats and vulnerabilities. Additionally, ensuring that the system scales effectively with growing network environments is essential for maintaining robust security. The following factors help optimize the system's functionality while aligning with organizational security needs:

- **Scalability**: As your network grows, ensure that your automation scripts can scale to handle the increased volume of alerts, traffic, and systems.

- **Integration with other security tools**: Consider how your automation scripts can integrate with other components of your security stack, such as SIEM systems, endpoint protection platforms, and cloud security tools.

- **Compliance**: Ensure that automation processes align with regulatory and industry compliance requirements, especially in sectors where security operations are subject to audits and legal standards.

Intrusion detection and prevention automation with Python can drastically improve the efficiency of detecting and responding to threats within your network. By automating tasks such as alert triage, signature creation, and incident response, security teams can reduce the time it takes to mitigate attacks and maintain a stronger security posture. With the right tools, libraries, and practices, Python automation can become an integral part of a proactive and resilient cybersecurity strategy.

Given the critical role of IDPSs in detecting and mitigating threats, integrating threat intelligence enhances its effectiveness by providing contextual information on emerging threats and attack patterns. This transition enables a more proactive and informed approach to security, allowing IDPS systems to adapt more swiftly to evolving threats and improving overall defense mechanisms. By incorporating threat intelligence, organizations can better anticipate, identify, and respond to sophisticated attacks, ensuring a more robust and adaptive security posture.

Threat intelligence integration

Threat intelligence integration is a critical aspect of modern cybersecurity. It involves the collection, analysis, and application of threat data to enhance an organization's ability to detect, respond to, and prevent cyberattacks. By integrating threat intelligence into your security systems, you can gain real-time insights into emerging threats, understand the **tactics, techniques, and procedures** (TTPs) used by adversaries, and improve your overall defense strategy. Python, with its versatility and robust libraries, is an excellent tool for automating the integration of threat intelligence into various security processes.

Integrating threat intelligence with an IDPS enhances threat detection by providing contextual insights into emerging threats and attack patterns. This integration allows for more precise identification of suspicious activities and reduces false positives by correlating data with known threat indicators. It enables a proactive defense strategy, helping organizations anticipate and address potential attacks before they escalate. Overall, threat intelligence integration strengthens the effectiveness and adaptability of security measures.

What is threat intelligence?

Threat intelligence refers to the collection of data about potential or active threats against an organization. This data includes information about threat actors, their motives, attack vectors, and the vulnerabilities they exploit.There are certain things to consider when integrating systems with threat intelligence, shown below:

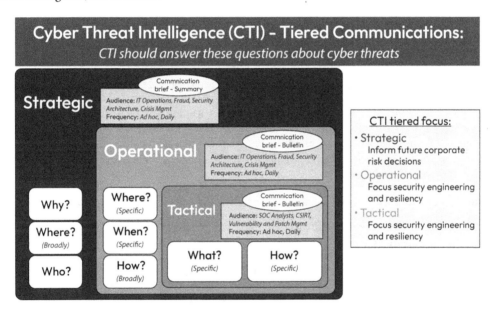

Figure 5.1 – Threat intelligence integration

Threat intelligence can be categorized into different types:

- **Strategic threat intelligence**: High-level information focused on broad trends and geopolitical threats.

- **Tactical threat intelligence**: Information on the TTPs used by threat actors.

- **Operational threat intelligence**: Data on specific incidents or attacks, often gathered in real time.

- **Technical threat intelligence**: Low-level data such as IP addresses, domains, malware hashes, and other **indicators of compromise (IOCs)**.

The goal of threat intelligence integration is to ensure that this information is continuously fed into security systems, enabling proactive defense measures and real-time threat detection.

Key areas for threat intelligence integration

Integration of threat intelligence can be applied across various security functions, including the following:

- **Automated threat detection**: Enhancing detection systems (e.g., IDS/IPS, SIEM) by continuously updating them with the latest threat indicators (IP addresses, domains, file hashes, etc.).

- **Incident response**: Enriching security alerts and incidents with context from threat intelligence feeds to improve analysis and response efforts.

- **Vulnerability management**: Prioritizing vulnerabilities based on real-world threat data, allowing security teams to focus on those most likely to be exploited.

- **Threat hunting**: Using threat intelligence to guide proactive searches for signs of compromise within an organization's environment.

Python libraries and tools for threat intelligence integration

Python offers a variety of libraries and tools that can assist with threat intelligence integration:

- **OpenCTI (Open Cyber Threat Intelligence)**: This is an open source threat intelligence platform that integrates with various threat intelligence sources and provides APIs for automation.

- **ThreatConnect SDK**: This is a Python SDK for interacting with the ThreatConnect threat intelligence platform, enabling automated retrieval and use of threat data.

- **STIX/TAXII**: The **Structured Threat Information eXpression** (STIX) and **Trusted Automated eXchange of Indicator Information** (TAXII) standards are widely used for threat intelligence sharing. Libraries such as `stix2` and `cabby` allow Python to work with STIX data and TAXII servers.

- **Maltego**: This is a tool for visualizing relationships in threat data, with Python-based automation possible via scripting.

- **Requests**: This is a versatile HTTP library for interacting with RESTful APIs of threat intelligence platforms and feeds.

- **YARA-Python**: YARA rules are used to identify and classify malware based on patterns. Python can automate the creation, management, and execution of YARA rules to detect malicious activity.

Use cases for threat intelligence automation

Threat intelligence automation can be used to streamline the detection of known threats by automatically correlating indicators with network activity and alerting security teams. It enables real-time updates and integration with security tools, enhancing response speed and accuracy. Automation can also enrich incident data with contextual information, improving analysis and decision-making. Additionally, it helps in identifying and mitigating emerging threats by continuously monitoring and adapting to new threat intelligence feeds.

The following are some of the potential sources of threat intelligence:

- Open source threat intelligence feeds include the following:

  - **AlienVault Open Threat Exchange (OTX)**: This is a widely used community-driven platform where security professionals share threat data, including IOCs such as malicious IPs, domains, and files.

  - **VirusTotal**: This provides a wealth of threat data by analyzing files and URLs submitted by users. Although primarily known for malware scanning, it also offers API access to integrate data directly.

  - **Abuse.ch**: This hosts multiple threat intelligence feeds, focusing on malware, botnets, and ransomware, particularly useful for tracking and blocking harmful domains and IPs.

  - **CIRCL Passive DNS (passive DNS replication)**: This collects passive DNS data to identify malicious domain activity, helping identify potential **command-and-control (C2)** infrastructure used by attackers.

- Government and industry sources include the following:

  - **MITRE ATT&CK**: This is a knowledge base of attacker TTPs that helps organizations understand how adversaries operate and improve detection capabilities.

  - **Automated Indicator Sharing (AIS)** from the **U.S. Department of Homeland Security (DHS)**: This allows the exchange of cyber threat indicators between public and private sectors to facilitate early warnings of potential threats.

  - **Financial Services Information Sharing and Analysis Center (FS-ISAC)**: This provides threat intelligence specifically for the financial industry, which is highly valuable for companies in this sector.

- Commercial threat intelligence providers include the following:

  - **Recorded Future, CrowdStrike, FireEye, and ThreatConnect**: These providers offer in-depth, curated threat intelligence tailored to various industries. They often provide both tactical and strategic insights, including automated threat feed integrations.

- **Splunk Threat Intelligence Management**: For users with SIEM solutions such as Splunk, many vendors offer integration with threat intelligence feeds, allowing threat data to be incorporated directly into alerting workflows.

- Community-based intelligence sources include the following:

  - **Information Sharing and Analysis Centers (ISACs)**: Sector-specific centers such as the Health-ISAC and Energy-ISAC focus on providing actionable intelligence for their respective industries, based on the unique threats they face.

  - **Reddit and GitHub security communities**: While informal, security communities often share valuable insights on newly discovered vulnerabilities and attack methods, allowing users to stay up-to-date with the latest threats.

- Internal threat intelligence includes the following:

  - **Internal logs and incident data**: Past incidents, logs, and vulnerability assessments within an organization provide highly relevant threat intelligence that can guide defense priorities and tailor threat detection.

  - **Employee reporting and phishing data**: User-reported phishing attempts and other suspicious activities often reveal targeted threat tactics specific to an organization, helping it identify trends and recurring adversaries.

By integrating these sources into security automation workflows, organizations can create a richer threat intelligence base, strengthening both proactive defense measures and rapid incident response capabilities.

Automating threat feed integration

Automating the retrieval and integration of threat intelligence feeds into security systems can greatly enhance detection capabilities. For example, Python can be used to fetch the latest IOCs from public or private threat intelligence feeds and automatically update your SIEM or firewall rules:

```python
import requests

def fetch_iocs_from_feed(feed_url):
    response = requests.get(feed_url)
    if response.status_code == 200:
        return response.json()  # Assuming the feed returns JSON
    else:
        return []

def update_firewall_rules(iocs):
    for ioc in iocs:
        if "ip_address" in ioc:
            # Example command to block IP on firewall (pseudo-code)
```

```
        block_ip_on_firewall(ioc["ip_address"])

# Example usage
ioc_feed_url = "https://example.com/threat_feed"
iocs = fetch_iocs_from_feed(ioc_feed_url)
update_firewall_rules(iocs)
```

In this example, the script retrieves IOCs from a threat intelligence feed and uses them to update firewall rules. This can be extended to integrate with any other security tool (e.g., IDS, SIEM).

Automating threat feed integration involves automatically ingesting and correlating threat intelligence from various sources into security systems. This process ensures that threat data is consistently updated and applied in real time to enhance detection and response capabilities. By integrating threat feeds seamlessly, organizations can reduce manual effort and improve the accuracy of threat identification. Automated updates and enrichment of threat data help maintain an effective and adaptive security posture.

Enriching security alerts with threat intelligence

When an alert is generated in your security systems, integrating threat intelligence can provide valuable context that helps in making informed decisions. For instance, Python can automate the enrichment of alerts by querying threat intelligence platforms to determine whether an IP address, domain, or file hash has been associated with known malicious activity:

```
import requests

def enrich_alert_with_threat_intel(ip_address):
    threat_intel_api_url = f"https://threatintel.example.com/api/ip/
{ip_address}"
    response = requests.get(threat_intel_api_url)
    if response.status_code == 200:
        return response.json()  # Return the threat intelligence data
    else:
        return None

# Example alert data
alert = {"ip_address": "192.168.1.100"}
threat_intel_data = enrich_alert_with_threat_intel(alert["ip_
address"])

if threat_intel_data:
    print(f"Enriched alert with threat intelligence: {threat_intel_
data}")
else:
    print("No threat intelligence data found for this IP address.")
```

This script takes an IP address from a security alert and queries a threat intelligence platform to retrieve information about it, enriching the alert with additional context.

Enriching security alerts with threat intelligence involves adding contextual information about threats, such as attack vectors, IOCs, and threat actors. This enhancement helps prioritize alerts based on their relevance and potential impact, enabling more informed and efficient responses. By providing additional context, enriched alerts improve decision-making and reduce the time required to address and mitigate security incidents.

Automating vulnerability prioritization

Threat intelligence can be used to prioritize vulnerabilities based on real-world exploitability. Python can automate this process by fetching **Common Vulnerabilities and Exposures (CVE)** data from a threat intelligence platform and prioritizing vulnerabilities that are actively being exploited in the wild:

```python
import requests

def fetch_vulnerability_data(cve_id):
    threat_intel_api_url = f"https://threatintel.example.com/api/cve/{cve_id}"
    response = requests.get(threat_intel_api_url)
    if response.status_code == 200:
        return response.json()  # Return the CVE threat data
    else:
        return None

def prioritize_vulnerabilities(vulnerabilities):
    prioritized_list = []
    for vuln in vulnerabilities:
        threat_data = fetch_vulnerability_data(vuln["cve_id"])
        if threat_data and threat_data["exploited_in_the_wild"]:
            prioritized_list.append(vuln)
    return prioritized_list

# Example usage
vulnerabilities = [{"cve_id": "CVE-2023-1234"}, {"cve_id": "CVE-2023-5678"}]
high_priority_vulns = prioritize_vulnerabilities(vulnerabilities)
print("High priority vulnerabilities:", high_priority_vulns)
```

In this example, the script fetches CVE data and checks whether the vulnerability is actively being exploited. If so, it's added to the high-priority list for remediation.

This code example effectively prioritizes vulnerabilities by checking whether they are actively being exploited, which is a crucial indicator of risk.

Code explanation

Here's a breakdown of the prioritization logic and how it can be adapted to meet different environments or business-critical needs.

- **Fetch vulnerability data** (`fetch_vulnerability_data` **function**):

  - This function pulls data from a threat intelligence API using the CVE ID. If the API returns a successful response (status code `200`), it retrieves the CVE data as JSON.

  - The returned threat data includes whether the vulnerability is currently being exploited in the wild (`exploited_in_the_wild`), which helps prioritize vulnerabilities that pose an immediate risk.

- **Prioritizing vulnerabilities** (`prioritize_vulnerabilities` **function**):

  - This function iterates through a list of vulnerabilities, fetches threat data for each, and checks whether each vulnerability is currently being exploited.

  - Vulnerabilities with active exploitation are appended to a `prioritized_list`, which is returned as high-priority vulnerabilities.

Adapting prioritization for different environments

Depending on the environment, several factors could influence the prioritization logic, particularly business criticality, asset sensitivity, and compliance requirements. Here's how to adapt the code:

- **Based on business criticality**:

  - Prioritize vulnerabilities on systems crucial to business operations, such as customer-facing applications or systems with sensitive data.

  - Example adjustment: Add a check to prioritize vulnerabilities based on criticality levels of affected assets, such as `"criticality": "high"`:

```python
def prioritize_vulnerabilities(vulnerabilities):
    prioritized_list = []
    for vuln in vulnerabilities:
        threat_data = fetch_vulnerability_data(vuln["cve_id"])
        if (threat_data and threat_data["exploited_in_the_
wild"]
            and vuln.get("criticality") == "high"):  # Add
criticality filter
            prioritized_list.append(vuln)
    return prioritized_list
```

- **Incorporating CVSS score or severity**:

  - Use the **Common Vulnerability Scoring System (CVSS)** score from the threat data to focus on vulnerabilities with a high impact.

  - Example adjustment: Filter vulnerabilities with a CVSS score above a threshold (e.g., cvss_score >= 7.0):

    ```python
    Copy code
    def prioritize_vulnerabilities(vulnerabilities):
        prioritized_list = []
        for vuln in vulnerabilities:
            threat_data = fetch_vulnerability_data(vuln["cve_id"])
            if (threat_data and threat_data["exploited_in_the_
    wild"]
                and threat_data.get("cvss_score", 0) >= 7.0):  #
    CVSS score filter
                prioritized_list.append(vuln)
        return prioritized_list
    ```

- **Adjusting for compliance requirements**:

  - In industries with specific compliance needs (e.g., healthcare or finance), regulatory compliance mandates could further shape priority. For example, prioritize vulnerabilities related to PCI DSS or HIPAA compliance requirements.

  - Example adjustment: Add a check to prioritize vulnerabilities associated with compliance-related systems or categories.

- **Adding risk levels for automation**:

  - To refine automation, assign a risk level to each vulnerability (e.g., "high," "medium," or "low") based on criteria such as exploitation status, CVSS score, and criticality.

  - Example adjustment: Append a risk_level attribute for further categorization or downstream processing.

In summary, this prioritization approach can be easily customized by modifying criteria such as criticality, CVSS score, and compliance requirements. Such adjustments make the code highly adaptable to various organizational needs and ensure vulnerabilities are remediated based on risk and importance to the business.

Automating vulnerability prioritization involves using algorithms and threat intelligence to assess and rank vulnerabilities based on their severity, exploitability, and impact on the organization. This automation streamlines the process by focusing remediation efforts on the most critical vulnerabilities first, improving overall risk management. By prioritizing vulnerabilities effectively, organizations can allocate resources more efficiently and reduce their exposure to potential threats.

Best practices for threat intelligence integration

When it comes to threat intelligence integration, best practices for a threat intelligence lead include ensuring seamless integration of threat feeds with existing security systems for real-time data enrichment and response. Regularly update and validate threat intelligence sources to maintain accuracy and relevance. Implement robust processes for correlating and analyzing threat data to provide actionable insights and enhance overall security posture. The following points outline key best practices to optimize threat intelligence integration and enhance security operations:

- **Select reliable sources**: Ensure that your threat intelligence feeds and platforms are reputable and provide accurate, up-to-date information. Integrating poor-quality threat intelligence can lead to false positives and wasted resources.

- **Automate updates**: Threat intelligence is dynamic, so it's crucial to automate the process of fetching and integrating new data regularly to ensure that your security systems are using the most current information.

- **Correlate with internal data**: Combine external threat intelligence with internal data (e.g., logs, events) to provide a more comprehensive view of threats and improve detection accuracy.

- **Implement RBAC**: Ensure that only authorized systems and personnel have access to threat intelligence data, particularly if sensitive information is involved.

- **Monitor and adjust**: Continuously monitor the effectiveness of your threat intelligence integration and make adjustments as necessary. This includes tuning automation scripts, updating data sources, and refining workflows based on feedback.

Real-world considerations of threat intelligence

In the real world, a threat intelligence lead must manage the integration of diverse threat data sources while ensuring the relevance and accuracy of the information. You must also address the challenge of keeping threat intelligence up-to-date and aligned with evolving attack techniques. Additionally, balancing the volume of data with actionable insights is crucial to avoid information overload and ensure effective decision-making.

- **Scalability**: As the volume of threat data increases, ensure that your automation scripts and systems can scale accordingly. This may involve optimizing data processing pipelines or distributing workloads across multiple systems.

- **APIs and rate limits**: Many threat intelligence platforms provide APIs for integration, but these APIs often come with rate limits. Be mindful of these limits and implement retry logic in your automation scripts to handle cases where the API is temporarily unavailable.

- **Threat intelligence sharing**: Consider participating in threat intelligence sharing communities or initiatives (e.g., ISACs, CERTs) to contribute to and benefit from collective knowledge about emerging threats.

- **Compliance**: Ensure that your use of threat intelligence complies with legal and regulatory requirements, particularly when dealing with sensitive information or data shared by external parties.

Integrating threat intelligence into your security operations with Python can significantly enhance your organization's ability to detect, analyze, and respond to emerging threats. By automating the retrieval, analysis, and application of threat intelligence data, you can ensure that your security systems stay up-to-date with the latest threat trends, vulnerabilities, and attack vectors. This not only improves the effectiveness of your defenses but also enables faster, more informed decision-making during incidents. With the right tools, libraries, and practices, Python can be a powerful enabler of threat intelligence integration in your security workflows.

Summary

In this chapter, we learned how to utilize Python scripts to automate tasks such as monitoring network traffic, managing firewall rules, and performing vulnerability assessments. We explored the use of Python libraries and tools to interact with network devices and security platforms, enhancing the efficiency and accuracy of security operations. The chapter emphasized the importance of automating repetitive tasks to improve response times and reduce human error. Additionally, we covered best practices for writing scalable and maintainable Python code to support robust network security solutions.

In the next chapter on *Web Application Security Automation Using Python*, we will learn how to automate the detection and testing of web application vulnerabilities using Python scripts. The chapter will cover techniques for interacting with web applications, such as automating scans for common vulnerabilities and performing security assessments. We will also explore how to integrate Python with tools and libraries to streamline security testing and reporting processes.

When diving into the next chapter, you will learn about techniques that will help you automate web application security using Python.

6

Web Application Security Automation Using Python

In today's digital world, web applications are integral to businesses and personal use, making them prime targets for cyberattacks. Ensuring the security of these applications is paramount, yet manually identifying and fixing vulnerabilities can be both time-consuming and prone to error. This is where automation steps in. In this chapter, we'll explore how Python, a versatile and powerful programming language, can be used to automate various aspects of web application security. From scanning for vulnerabilities to detecting common attack vectors such as SQL injection and **cross-site scripting** (**XSS**), Python-based tools and scripts offer efficiency and scalability in securing web applications. Whether you're a security professional or a developer, this chapter will guide you through practical techniques to enhance the security of web applications using Python.

In this chapter, we'll cover the following topics:

- Automating input validation
- Enhancing session management with web application security
- Automating session management
- Automating secure coding practices

Technical requirements

Here are the technical requirements for this chapter:

- **Python environment**: Ensure Python (version 3.x) is installed on your system. Python's versatility and extensive library support make it ideal for security automation.
- **Libraries and modules**: Install key Python libraries and modules such as the following:
  - **Requests**: For making HTTP requests to interact with web applications
  - **BeautifulSoup**: For web scraping and parsing HTML data

- **Selenium**: For automating web browsers and testing web applications

- **SQLMap**: For detecting SQL injection vulnerabilities

- **PyYAML** or **JSON**: For handling configuration files or API data formats

- **Security tool integration**: Integrate Python scripts with existing web application security tools such as the following:

  - **OWASP Zed Attack Proxy (OWASP ZAP)**: Python bindings to automate vulnerability scanning

  - **Burp Suite API**: For automating web application testing

- **Web application testing environment**: Set up a testing environment using local or cloud-based web servers, preferably with vulnerable web applications such as **Damn Vulnerable Web App (DVWA)** or OWASP Juice Shop, to practice and validate automation scripts.

- **Version control (Git)**: Use Git for managing code, version control, and collaboration on automation scripts.

- **Basic networking knowledge**: A solid understanding of HTTP protocols, headers, request methods, and status codes, which are key to automating web security processes.

These tools and resources will help streamline the automation of security tasks and enable effective web application vulnerability testing using Python.

Integrating security tools in an automated IDPS using Python

Python can be a powerful bridge for integrating various security tools in an **intrusion detection and prevention system (IDPS)** environment, enabling them to work together seamlessly. Here's an example demonstrating how Python can combine IDPS, **security information and event management (SIEM)**, and **incident response (IR)** systems for a more unified security approach.

Example – Integrating an automated IDPS with an SIEM for centralized monitoring and response

Let's consider a scenario where an organization uses the following:

- Snort (an open source IDPS) for intrusion detection

- Splunk as the SIEM for centralized log and event management

- IBM Resilient for IR automation

Here's how Python can tie these tools together:

- **Setting up Snort alerts to trigger events in Splunk**: Using Python, we can create a script that monitors Snort alert logs and sends new events directly to Splunk for centralized tracking:

```python
import requests
import json

# Function to send Snort alert to Splunk
def send_to_splunk(event):
    splunk_endpoint = "https://splunk-instance.com:8088/
services/collector/event"
    headers = {"Authorization": "Splunk <YOUR_SPLUNK_TOKEN>"}
    data = {
        "event": event,
        "sourcetype": "_json",
        "index": "main"
    }
    response = requests.post(splunk_endpoint, headers=headers,
json=data)
    return response.status_code

# Example usage
new_alert = {
    "alert_type": "Intrusion Detected",
    "source_ip": "192.168.1.100",
    "destination_ip": "192.168.1.105",
    "severity": "high"
}
send_to_splunk(new_alert)
```

- **Triggering IR actions via IBM Resilient**: Once Splunk receives an event from Snort, it can be configured to trigger automated workflows. A Python script can then initiate an IR in IBM Resilient based on specific conditions, such as high-severity alerts:

```python
def create_resilient_incident(alert):
    resilient_endpoint = "https://resilient-instance.com/rest/
orgs/201/incidents"
    headers = {"Authorization": "Bearer <YOUR_RESILIENT_API_
KEY>", "Content-Type": "application/json"}
    incident_data = {
        "name": "IDPS Alert: High-Severity Intrusion",
```

```
              "description": f"Incident detected from {alert['source_
ip']} targeting {alert['destination_ip']}.",
            "severity_code": 4  # Code 4 for high severity
        }
    response = requests.post(resilient_endpoint,
headers=headers, json=incident_data)
    return response.status_code

# Usage example
if new_alert["severity"] == "high":
    create_resilient_incident(new_alert)
```

- **Coordinating responses across systems**: Python can coordinate these responses by implementing conditions, setting alert thresholds, and ensuring each tool's actions align with the others. This streamlines processes, enabling faster containment and response.

Key benefits of Python integration in IDPS

Some of the key benefits of python integration in IDPS are as follows:

- **Real-time communication**: Python enables real-time data flow between the IDPS, SIEM, and IR systems.

- **Automated workflows**: By automating responses, Python reduces response times and ensures security events are acted upon immediately.

- **Adaptability**: Python's extensive library support means it can connect to various tools, adapting easily as the security ecosystem evolves.

This integration enhances the organization's ability to detect, analyze, and respond to threats efficiently, demonstrating Python's versatility in strengthening cybersecurity posture.

Automating input validation

Input validation is one of the most critical security practices in web application development. Poorly validated inputs can open the door to serious vulnerabilities, such as SQL injection, XSS, and **remote code execution** (RCE). Automating input validation allows security teams and developers to quickly and effectively ensure that inputs conform to expected formats, reducing the likelihood of exploitation. In this section, we will explore how Python can be used to automate the process of input validation for web applications.

Understanding input validation

Input validation ensures that any data inputted by users is checked for type, format, length, and structure before it is processed by the application. Validating inputs properly helps mitigate various attacks that stem from improper handling of data, such as the following:

- **SQL injection**: When unvalidated input is inserted directly into a SQL query, attackers can manipulate the query to steal or modify data.

- **XSS**: Malicious scripts can be injected into web applications through input fields if HTML or JavaScript is not properly sanitized.

- **Command injection**: If user input is not validated, an attacker could inject operating system commands into an application that interacts with the OS.

By implementing automated input validation, we can ensure that all inputs are screened to meet specific security standards, reducing the risk of these vulnerabilities being exploited.

Python libraries for input validation

Python offers several libraries that can help automate input validation in web applications. Here are a few key libraries commonly used in Python-based web frameworks:

- **Cerberus**: A lightweight and extensible data validation library for Python. It can be used to define validation schemas for input fields.

    The following is an example of using Cerberus for input validation:

    ```python
    from cerberus import Validator

    schema = {
        'name': {'type': 'string', 'minlength': 1, 'maxlength': 50},
        'age': {'type': 'integer', 'min': 18, 'max': 99},
        'email': {'type': 'string', 'regex': r'^\S+@\S+\.\S+$'}
    }

    v = Validator(schema)

    document = {'name': 'John Doe', 'age': 25, 'email': 'johndoe@
    example.com'}

    if v.validate(document):
        print("Input is valid")
    else:
        print(f"Input validation failed: {v.errors}")
    ```

- **Marshmallow**: A library used to convert complex data types, such as objects, into native Python data types while also performing input validation.

  Here's an example of using Marshmallow for validation:

```
from marshmallow import Schema, fields, validate

class UserSchema(Schema):
    name = fields.Str(required=True, validate=validate.
Length(min=1, max=50))
    age = fields.Int(required=True, validate=validate.
Range(min=18, max=99))
    email = fields.Email(required=True)

schema = UserSchema()

result = schema.load({'name': 'Jane Doe', 'age': 30, 'email':
'jane@example.com'})

if result.errors:
    print(f"Validation failed: {result.errors}")
else:
    print("Input is valid")
```

Automating input validation in web forms

To automate input validation in web forms, we can leverage Python frameworks such as Flask or Django, combined with validation libraries such as Cerberus or Marshmallow. This ensures that user inputs in forms are automatically validated before processing.

Here's an example of automated input validation using Flask and Cerberus in a web form:

```
from flask import Flask, request, jsonify
from cerberus import Validator

app = Flask(__name__)

schema = {
    'username': {'type': 'string', 'minlength': 3, 'maxlength': 20},
    'password': {'type': 'string', 'minlength': 8},
    'email': {'type': 'string', 'regex': r'^\S+@\S+\.\S+$'}
}
```

```
v = Validator(schema)

@app.route('/submit', methods=['POST'])
def submit_form():
    data = request.json
    if v.validate(data):
        return jsonify({"message": "Input is valid"})
    else:
        return jsonify({"errors": v.errors}), 400

if __name__ == '__main__':
    app.run(debug=True)
```

In this example, when a user submits data to the /submit route, it is automatically validated against the schema defined with Cerberus. If the validation fails, an error message is returned.

Input sanitization

In addition to validating input, it's also important to sanitize it by removing or encoding potentially harmful data. Python's built-in html.escape() function can be used to sanitize HTML input by escaping special characters:

```
import html

unsafe_input = "<script>alert('XSS')</script>"
safe_input = html.escape(unsafe_input)

print(safe_input)  # Output: &lt;script&gt;alert(&#x27;XSS&#x27;)&lt;/
script&gt;
```

Automating input sanitization ensures that potentially harmful inputs are neutralized before they can be processed by the application, protecting against attacks such as XSS.

Automated testing of input validation

Automated testing of input validation is crucial for ensuring that validation rules are correctly implemented. Python's unittest framework can be used to write test cases that check if input validation is working as expected.

Here's an example of a simple test case for input validation:

```python
import unittest
from cerberus import Validator

class TestInputValidation(unittest.TestCase):

    def setUp(self):
        self.schema = {
                'username': {'type': 'string', 'minlength': 3,
'maxlength': 20},
                'email': {'type': 'string', 'regex': r'^\S+@\S+\.\S+$'}
        }
        self.validator = Validator(self.schema)

    def test_valid_input(self):
        document = {'username': 'testuser', 'email': 'test@example.
com'}
        self.assertTrue(self.validator.validate(document))

    def test_invalid_username(self):
        document = {'username': 'x', 'email': 'test@example.com'}
        self.assertFalse(self.validator.validate(document))
        self.assertIn('minlength', self.validator.errors['username'])

    def test_invalid_email(self):
        document = {'username': 'testuser', 'email': 'invalid-email'}
        self.assertFalse(self.validator.validate(document))
        self.assertIn('regex', self.validator.errors['email'])

if __name__ == '__main__':
    unittest.main()
```

In this test case, we check if valid input passes the validation process and if invalid input triggers appropriate validation errors.

Best practices for input validation automation

Input validation is a critical security measure that ensures data entering an application is safe and trustworthy. Automating input validation processes helps prevent vulnerabilities such as SQL injection and XSS, ensuring consistent protection across all systems. Let's look at some best practices for implementing automated input validation to enhance security and reduce manual errors:

1. **Use whitelisting**: Whenever possible, validate inputs by defining a strict set of allowed values (whitelisting) rather than blocking certain inputs (blacklisting).

2. **Enforce length and format limits**: Always limit the length and format of inputs to ensure they don't exceed expected parameters and to protect against buffer overflows.

3. **Consistent validation across layers**: Ensure input validation occurs consistently across both the client side (in the web browser) and the server side (in the backend) to provide a layered defense.

4. **Automate regular testing**: Use automated testing frameworks such as unit tests to ensure that input validation rules are tested regularly, especially when the code base is updated.

5. **Log validation failures**: Implement logging for input validation failures to help identify malicious activity patterns and potential security threats.

Automating input validation with Python not only improves the security of web applications but also ensures a more efficient development workflow. By using Python libraries and frameworks, you can define strict validation rules, sanitize user inputs, and automate the process of securing web applications from common vulnerabilities. Regularly testing and refining these validation mechanisms through automation helps create a robust defense against input-based attacks, protecting your applications and data from harm.

In the next section, we will explore **automated web application vulnerability scanning**, where we will focus on detecting security flaws and integrating security scanning tools into your Python scripts.

Enhancing session management with web application security

Session management is a crucial aspect of web application security. Sessions allow web applications to maintain a state between different HTTP requests, providing continuity in a user's experience. However, if sessions are not managed securely, they can become vulnerable to attacks such as session hijacking, fixation, or replay attacks. Automating session management ensures that sessions are handled efficiently and securely, protecting users and their data. In this section, we will explore how Python can be used to automate and secure session management for web applications.

Understanding session management

Before we get into how to enhance session management, let's try and understand what it entails first. Sessions in web applications are typically managed using session IDs, which are unique identifiers assigned to users when they log in or start a session. These session IDs are often stored in cookies or as part of the URL. Secure session management involves the proper handling of these IDs to prevent unauthorized access.

Session management is crucial for maintaining the security of web applications and protecting user data. By securely handling session IDs, enforcing timeouts, and implementing proper token management, you can prevent common attacks such as session hijacking and fixation. This section will cover best practices for ensuring that session management is robust, reliable, and resistant to potential threats.

Effective session management is critical for safeguarding web applications and protecting user data. Poor session management can expose systems to vulnerabilities such as session hijacking, fixation, or unauthorized access. For example, insecure handling of session IDs or weak token management may allow attackers to intercept or reuse session credentials. Sessions that aren't properly timed out can remain open indefinitely, increasing the risk of exploitation.

By enforcing timeouts, securely handling session tokens, and ensuring that sessions are properly validated and invalidated, you can significantly reduce these risks. This section will delve into best practices for robust session management, ensuring secure user experiences and minimizing the attack surface for potential threats.

The key concepts in session management include the following:

- **Session IDs**: Unique identifiers that track user sessions
- **Session cookies**: Small pieces of data stored in the user's browser to maintain session information
- **Session timeout**: The expiration of a session after a specified period of inactivity
- **Secure Flags**: Flags such as `Secure` and `HttpOnly` that prevent session IDs from being stolen

Common session management vulnerabilities

Poor session management can lead to the following vulnerabilities:

- **Session hijacking**: When an attacker gains access to a user's session ID, allowing them to impersonate the user.
- **Session fixation**: When an attacker tricks a user into using a known session ID, enabling the attacker to take over the session.
- **Session replay attacks**: When an attacker reuses a valid session ID to gain unauthorized access.

Automating session management ensures that these vulnerabilities are mitigated through secure practices such as regenerating session IDs, setting secure flags, and implementing session timeouts.

Python libraries for session management automation

Python offers several libraries and frameworks that support secure session management. Here are a few key libraries:

- **Flask**: A lightweight web framework that has built-in session management features.
- **Django**: A high-level web framework that automatically handles session management and includes various security features for session handling.
- **Requests-Session**: Part of the Requests library, it automates the handling of session cookies and headers.

Example of automating session management using Flask

Flask allows you to automate secure session handling by utilizing its built-in session management features. Here's an example of creating and managing user sessions securely in Flask:

```python
from flask import Flask, session, redirect, url_for, request

app = Flask(__name__)
app.secret_key = 'supersecretkey'

@app.route('/')
def index():
    if 'username' in session:
        return f'Logged in as {session["username"]}'
    return 'You are not logged in.'

@app.route('/login', methods=['POST', 'GET'])
def login():
    if request.method == 'POST':
        session['username'] = request.form['username']
        return redirect(url_for('index'))
    return '''
        <form method="post">
            Username: <input type="text" name="username">
            <input type="submit" value="Login">
        </form>
    '''

@app.route('/logout')
def logout():
```

```
    session.pop('username', None)
    return redirect(url_for('index'))

if __name__ == '__main__':
    app.run(debug=True)
```

This example demonstrates a simple login/logout system that uses sessions to track whether a user is logged in. The session is created with a unique identifier (`secret_key`) to secure the session data.

Example of automating session handling with Python's Requests library

Automating session handling with Python's Requests library typically involves using Python's `requests` library to manage and maintain sessions when interacting with web applications. The main goal of this code is to do the following:

- **Establish and maintain a session**: Instead of creating a new connection each time an HTTP request is made, the code keeps the session open, which allows the reuse of session-specific data such as cookies, authentication, and tokens.

- **Handle authentication**: Sessions allow automating login processes, enabling Python scripts to authenticate once and persistently manage further requests as an authenticated user.

- **Preserve cookies and headers**: The session automatically handles cookies (such as session IDs), passing them along with subsequent requests without needing manual management.

- **Maintain state**: A session allows for the management of state across requests, such as keeping users logged in or retaining form data.

When automating interactions with web applications, the `requests` library allows you to handle session cookies automatically:

```
import requests

# Create a session object
session = requests.Session()

# Log in to the application
login_payload = {'username': 'user', 'password': 'pass'}
login_url = 'https://example.com/login'
response = session.post(login_url, data=login_payload)

# Access a protected page using the session
protected_url = 'https://example.com/dashboard'
```

```
response = session.get(protected_url)

print(response.text)  # Output the content of the page
```

In this script, the session object handles cookies and maintains the session between requests, which is particularly useful for automating interactions with multiple pages in a web application.

Automating secure session practices

To automate secure session management, you can implement several practices in your Python web applications:

- **Session ID regeneration**: Regenerate the session ID upon user login or privilege escalation to prevent session fixation attacks:

```
from flask import session
session.permanent = True  # Make session permanent
```

This ensures that the session remains secure and the session ID is not reused across multiple sessions.

- **Set Secure and HttpOnly flags**: For cookies that store session IDs, setting the Secure and HttpOnly flags ensures that the cookie is only transmitted over HTTPS and is not accessible via JavaScript (mitigating XSS attacks):

```
@app.after_request
def set_secure_cookie(response):
    response.set_cookie('session', secure=True, httponly=True)
    return response
```

- **Session timeout**: Automatically expire sessions after a certain period of inactivity to reduce the risk of session hijacking:

```
from flask import session
from datetime import timedelta

app.config['PERMANENT_SESSION_LIFETIME'] = timedelta(minutes=30)
session.permanent = True
```

This automatically expires the session after 30 minutes of inactivity.

Automated testing of session management

Automating session management also requires testing to ensure that your implementation works correctly and securely. You can write automated test cases using Python's `unittest` framework to test session functionality.

Here's an example test case for validating session management in Flask:

```python
import unittest
from app import app

class TestSessionManagement(unittest.TestCase):

    def setUp(self):
        app.config['TESTING'] = True
        self.client = app.test_client()

    def test_login_logout(self):
        # Test user login
        response = self.client.post('/login', data={'username':
'testuser'})
        self.assertEqual(response.status_code, 302)  # Redirect after
login
        self.assertIn(b'Logged in as testuser', self.client.get('/').
data)

        # Test user logout
        response = self.client.get('/logout')
        self.assertEqual(response.status_code, 302)  # Redirect after
logout
        self.assertNotIn(b'Logged in as testuser', self.client.
get('/').data)

if __name__ == '__main__':
    unittest.main()
```

This test case checks that logging in and logging out of the session work as expected. It ensures that the session is correctly maintained and cleared when the user logs out.

Best practices for secure session management

Automating session management does not mean neglecting secure practices. Here are some best practices to ensure that automated session handling is secure:

1. **Use strong session IDs**: Ensure session IDs are randomly generated and are of sufficient length to prevent brute-force attacks.

2. **Implement HTTPS**: Always transmit session cookies over HTTPS by setting the `Secure` flag on cookies.

3. **Limit session lifetime**: Use session timeouts to limit the duration of a session and prevent long-lived sessions from being hijacked.

4. **Regenerate session IDs**: Regenerate the session ID after every significant user action, such as logging in or escalating privileges.

5. **Inactivity timeout**: Expire sessions after a period of inactivity to minimize the window of opportunity for session hijacking.

6. **Monitor session activity**: Regularly monitor session activity for any unusual behavior, such as multiple logins from different locations or rapid session ID changes.

Session management is a critical component of web application security, and automating it can help ensure that your application consistently adheres to security best practices. By using Python libraries such as Flask and Requests, along with secure practices such as session ID regeneration, cookie security flags, and session timeouts, you can greatly reduce the risk of session-related attacks.

Automating the testing and management of sessions also helps identify potential vulnerabilities early in the development process, keeping user sessions secure and preventing unauthorized access. In the next section, we will explore **automating secure authentication** to further enhance user security in web applications.

Automating session management

Sessions provide the means to track user states such as login, preferences, and permissions. Automating session management can both efficiency and enhanced security by reducing vulnerabilities such as session hijacking, fixation, and replay attacks. In this section, we will discuss how Python can be used to automate session management, focusing on best practices, tools, and common vulnerabilities.

The importance of session management

Session management allows web applications to remember users between HTTP requests, which are otherwise stateless. It tracks and maintains user activity, including authentication states, shopping carts, and personalized settings. Poor session management can result in significant security breaches.

Some key concepts of session management include the following:

- **Session IDs**: Unique identifiers assigned to each user session
- **Session cookies**: Temporary storage mechanisms in users' browsers that maintain session states
- **Session timeouts**: Mechanisms that automatically expire sessions after a period of inactivity to prevent unauthorized access
- **Secure flags**: Cookie attributes such as `HttpOnly` and `Secure` that protect session cookies from exposure

Understanding session management vulnerabilities

Understanding session management vulnerabilities means recognizing potential threats that can arise if session handling is not secure. Poorly managed sessions open the door to various types of attacks, such as the following:

- **Session hijacking**: Occurs when attackers steal session IDs to impersonate users
- **Session fixation**: Involves forcing users to use known or attacker-controlled session IDs, which allows attackers to hijack their sessions
- **Session replay**: When attackers reuse valid session IDs to gain unauthorized access

Automating secure session management practices helps mitigate these vulnerabilities by enforcing strict security rules on session handling.

Python tools for automating session management

Python offers several frameworks and libraries that provide built-in support for session management. Next are some popular tools that facilitate session management automation:

- **Flask**: A lightweight web framework that has built-in session handling features, making it easy to manage sessions with minimal setup.
- **Django**: A high-level Python web framework that manages sessions automatically and provides extensive security features for session handling.
- **Requests library**: Allows for session automation in web interactions by managing cookies and maintaining sessions across requests.

Automating session management with Flask

Flask makes session management simple and secure by default, storing session data on the server side and associating it with a unique session ID. Here's how you can automate session management using Flask:

```python
from flask import Flask, session, redirect, url_for, request

app = Flask(__name__)
app.secret_key = 'supersecretkey'

@app.route('/')
def index():
    if 'username' in session:
        return f'Logged in as {session["username"]}'
    return 'You are not logged in.'

@app.route('/login', methods=['POST', 'GET'])
def login():
    if request.method == 'POST':
        session['username'] = request.form['username']
        return redirect(url_for('index'))
    return '''
        <form method="post">
            Username: <input type="text" name="username">
            <input type="submit" value="Login">
        </form>
    '''

@app.route('/logout')
def logout():
    session.pop('username', None)
    return redirect(url_for('index'))

if __name__ == '__main__':
    app.run(debug=Truc)
```

In this example, Flask automates session creation when a user logs in, storing the session information server-side. It also provides simple mechanisms to clear the session upon logout.

Automating sessions with Python's requests library

When automating interactions with web applications, the `requests` library provides easy management of session cookies, allowing the script to maintain session states across multiple requests:

```python
import requests

session = requests.Session()

# Login to the application
login_payload = {'username': 'user', 'password': 'pass'}
login_url = 'https://example.com/login'
response = session.post(login_url, data=login_payload)

# Access a protected page using the session
protected_url = 'https://example.com/dashboard'
response = session.get(protected_url)

print(response.text)  # Output the page content
```

The `session` object maintains cookies and session IDs between requests, allowing you to automate workflows that require multiple authenticated interactions with the web application.

Best practices for secure session management automation

Some of the best practices to secure session management automation are as follows:

1. **Session ID regeneration**: Regenerate session IDs upon user login and privilege escalation to prevent session fixation attacks. For example, you can regenerate a session in Flask like this:

   ```python
   session.permanent = True  # Session persists
   ```

   Regenerating session IDs ensures that session fixation attacks are avoided, as the session ID will change once the user logs in.

2. **Set Secure and HttpOnly flags**: Ensure that session cookies are protected by enabling `Secure` and `HttpOnly` flags, which prevent access to session cookies through JavaScript and ensure that cookies are only sent over HTTPS:

   ```python
   @app.after_request
   def set_secure_cookie(response):
       response.set_cookie('session', secure=True, httponly=True)
       return response
   ```

3. **Limit session lifespan**: Implement session timeouts to automatically expire sessions after a period of inactivity, limiting potential damage from a compromised session:

```python
Copy code
from flask import session
from datetime import timedelta

app.config['PERMANENT_SESSION_LIFETIME'] = timedelta(minutes=30)
session.permanent = True
```

By setting session expiration, you reduce the risk of an attacker using a stolen session ID over an extended period.

4. **Log session activity**: Log critical session events such as login, logout, and session expiration to monitor user activity and detect anomalies.

5. **Implement inactivity timeout**: An inactivity timeout will expire the session if the user has not interacted with the application for a specified period, preventing long-lived sessions from being abused.

Automated testing for session management

To ensure that session management is working securely, you can write automated test cases using Python's `unittest` framework to test login, logout, session creation, and expiration functionality.

Here is a basic example of automated testing for session management in a Flask application:

```python
import unittest
from app import app

class TestSessionManagement(unittest.TestCase):

    def setUp(self):
        app.config['TESTING'] = True
        self.client = app.test_client()

    def test_login(self):
        # Test the login process
        response = self.client.post('/login', data={'username':
'testuser'})
        self.assertEqual(response.status_code, 302)  # Should redirect
after login
        self.assertIn(b'Logged in as testuser', self.client.get('/').
data)
```

```
    def test_logout(self):
        # Test the logout process
        response = self.client.get('/logout')
        self.assertEqual(response.status_code, 302)  # Should redirect
after logout
        self.assertNotIn(b'Logged in as testuser', self.client.
get('/').data)

if __name__ == '__main__':
    unittest.main()
```

This test script checks that the session is created when logging in and destroyed when logging out, ensuring that session management processes work as expected.

Implementing multi-factor authentication in sessions

Automating session management can be further enhanced by integrating **multi-factor authentication** (**MFA**) for added security. MFA ensures that, in addition to knowing a password, a user must also verify their identity using a second factor (for example, **one-time passcode** (**OTP**) or mobile device).

Flask offers various plugins and extensions to integrate MFA into session management, ensuring that sessions remain secure even if an attacker gains access to the user's password.

These frameworks (Flask and Django) along with libraries such as Requests, provide robust tools for automating session handling. By incorporating practices such as session ID regeneration, session timeout enforcement, and secure cookie flags, you can greatly reduce the risk of session hijacking and related vulnerabilities.

Automating secure coding practices

Secure coding is essential for building robust and safe software that resists attacks and avoids vulnerabilities. While secure coding is often viewed as a manual task, automating certain practices can enhance the overall security of your software, streamline development, and ensure adherence to security guidelines across a project. In this section, we will explore how Python can help automate secure coding practices, focusing on code reviews, static analysis, and enforcing security guidelines.

Why secure coding matters

In today's digital landscape, software vulnerabilities can lead to catastrophic data breaches, financial losses, and reputation damage. Common vulnerabilities such as SQL injection, XSS, and buffer overflows are often the result of insecure coding practices. Writing secure code means proactively identifying and addressing potential security issues during the development process, preventing security flaws before they become exploitable.

Automating secure coding practices allows developers to integrate security into their workflow without excessive overhead, ensuring consistent adherence to best practices throughout the **software development life cycle (SDLC)**.

Key secure coding practices

Some fundamental secure coding practices that should be applied during development include the following:

- **Input validation**: Ensuring that all inputs are properly validated and sanitized to avoid injection attacks (for example, SQL injection, command injection).

- **Output encoding**: Encoding output to prevent attacks such as XSS.

- **Error handling**: Properly handling exceptions and errors to avoid leaking sensitive information.

- **Authentication and authorization**: Securing access to resources by enforcing proper authentication and authorization mechanisms.

- **Data encryption**: Encrypting sensitive data at rest and in transit to protect it from unauthorized access.

- **Session management**: Ensuring secure handling of user sessions, including secure session IDs and timeouts.

Automating code reviews

Code reviews are a fundamental part of secure coding practices. However, manual code reviews can be time-consuming and may miss critical issues. Automating certain parts of the review process ensures that common security flaws are identified early in the development cycle.

Python offers tools such as **pylint**, **flake8**, and **bandit** for automated code analysis, which can be integrated into **continuous integration (CI)** pipelines to enforce secure coding practices.

Example – Using Bandit for security code review

Bandit is a Python tool that automatically detects security vulnerabilities in Python code. It scans the code base for potential issues such as unsafe input handling, weak cryptography, and insecure configurations.

To automate security checks with Bandit, you can install it via `pip`:

```bash
pip install bandit
```

Then, run Bandit on your Python project to scan for security issues:

```bash
bandit -r your_project_directory/
```

Bandit will output a report highlighting security issues found in your code, such as weak cryptographic algorithms, unsanitized inputs, or the use of insecure functions.

Take a look at the following example output:

```less
[bandit]   Issue: [B301:blacklist] pickle.load found, possible security
issue.
    Severity: High    Confidence: High
    File: /path/to/your/code.py    Line: 42
```

This automated scan identifies potential vulnerabilities and provides recommendations to fix them, streamlining the secure coding review process.

Static code analysis for security

Static analysis tools analyze code without executing it, identifying potential security vulnerabilities, code quality issues, and adherence to secure coding guidelines. Automating static code analysis ensures that every piece of code is checked for security risks before it is merged into production.

Popular static analysis tools for Python include the following:

- **SonarQube**: Provides in-depth code analysis, identifying security hotspots, bugs, and code smells. It supports Python and integrates easily into CI/CD pipelines (where **CD** refers to either **continuous deployment** or **continuous delivery**).

- **Pylint**: Analyzes code for style errors, programming errors, and logical issues, ensuring code adheres to security guidelines.

SonarQube is a tool that can be configured to scan Python code for security vulnerabilities and quality issues as part of an automated build process. Here's how you can set up SonarQube for automated static analysis:

1. Install and configure SonarQube in your environment.

2. Add the following `sonar-project.properties` file to your project root:

```bash
sonar.projectKey=my_python_project
sonar.sources=.
sonar.language=py
sonar.python.version=3.x
```

3. Run the analysis using the SonarQube scanner:

    bash
    ```
    sonar-scanner
    ```

    This command will scan your Python project, analyzing it for code quality, security issues, and adherence to secure coding standards. The results will be uploaded to the SonarQube dashboard, where you can review security issues and take corrective action.

Enforcing secure coding standards with linters

Linters such as `flake8` and `pylint` can enforce coding standards, helping developers write more secure, clean, and consistent code. You can configure these linters to check for security-specific issues, such as the use of deprecated or unsafe functions.

Here's an example of how to set up `flake8` to enforce secure coding practices:

1. Install `flake8`:

    ```
    pip install flake8
    ```

2. Create a configuration file (`.flake8`) in your project directory to enforce security guidelines:

    ```
    [flake8]
    max-line-length = 100
    ignore = E203, E266, E501, W503
    exclude = .git,__pycache__,docs/conf.py,old,build,dist
    ```

3. Run `flake8` on your project directory to automate security checks:

    ```
    flake8 your_project_directory/
    ```

Linters catch issues such as the use of hardcoded credentials, unsanitized inputs, and potential security vulnerabilities related to coding patterns.

CI for secure coding

Automating secure coding practices through CI ensures that security checks are run automatically on every commit. This approach integrates secure coding practices into the regular development workflow, preventing security vulnerabilities from being introduced into production code.

Here's an example of a CI pipeline configuration that includes automated secure coding checks:

1. **Static code analysis**: Use SonarQube or Bandit to scan the code for security vulnerabilities.

2. **Automated unit tests**: Include unit tests that validate the secure handling of input/output and other security-critical functions.

3. **Automated linting**: Run `flake8` or `pylint` to enforce secure coding practices.

Here's an example Jenkinsfile that automates these steps:

```groovy
pipeline {
    agent any
    stages {
        stage('Linting') {
            steps {
                sh 'flake8 your_project_directory/'
            }
        }
        stage('Static Analysis') {
            steps {
                sh 'bandit -r your_project_directory/'
            }
        }
        stage('SonarQube Scan') {
            steps {
                sh 'sonar-scanner'
            }
        }
        stage('Unit Tests') {
            steps {
                sh 'pytest'
            }
        }
    }
}
```

This pipeline automatically runs linting, security scans, and unit tests, ensuring that code is reviewed for security issues on every build.

Best practices for automating secure coding

Automating secure coding practices requires adhering to best practices that ensure code is continuously checked for vulnerabilities without sacrificing performance or development speed. Here are some best practices to follow:

- **Shift left in security**: Integrate security checks early in the development process. Automate security checks as part of your CI pipeline to catch vulnerabilities before they reach production.

- **Use pre-commit hooks:** Set up pre-commit hooks with tools such as `pre-commit` to automatically run security checks before code is committed.

- **Monitor for security updates**: Continuously monitor libraries and dependencies for security vulnerabilities using tools such as `safety` or `pyup`.

- **Enforce coding standards**: Use tools such as `pylint` and `flake8` to enforce secure coding standards and ensure code is consistently reviewed for security issues.

Secure coding practices are vital for building resilient software that can withstand attacks. Automating secure coding processes with tools such as Bandit, SonarQube, and linting tools allows developers to focus on writing functional code while ensuring that security issues are caught early. By integrating these tools into CI pipelines, developers can ensure that security is a continuous part of the development life cycle.

Summary

In this chapter, we explored how Python can be used to automate key aspects of web application security testing and management. Automating tasks such as input validation, session management, and secure coding practices helps streamline security processes, detect vulnerabilities early, and ensure continuous protection against attacks. By integrating automated tools such as Selenium, OWASP ZAP, and static analysis libraries into a CI/CD pipeline, developers can enforce security standards across the development life cycle. Automation not only enhances the efficiency of security testing but also ensures that security is embedded into web application development from the start.

The next chapter will explore how SecureBank, a financial institution, leveraged Python to enhance its security operations. Through case studies, we will examine how Python automation was applied to areas such as fraud detection, threat monitoring, and IR, helping SecureBank strengthen its overall security posture.

Part 3:
Case Study and Trends in Security Automation Using Python

As organizations increasingly adopt automation to enhance their security practices, Python has emerged as a leading language for developing efficient security solutions. In this section, we will explore real-world case studies showcasing the successful implementation of Python in automating various security tasks, from threat detection to incident response. Additionally, we will examine the latest trends in security automation, highlighting how Python is driving innovation and addressing evolving cybersecurity challenges. This part provides a practical understanding of how Python can empower security teams to stay ahead of threats in an automated environment.

This part has the following chapters:

- *Chapter 7, Case Studies - Real-World Applications of Python Security Automation*
- *Chapter 8, Future Trends - Machine Learning and AI in Security Automation with Python*
- *Chapter 9, Empowering Security Teams Through Python Automation*

7

Case Studies – Real-World Applications of Python Security Automation

In this chapter, we'll take a look into real-world case studies that showcase how Python has been used effectively to automate security processes across various industries. By examining practical implementations, we'll highlight how organizations have leveraged Python's flexibility and powerful libraries to streamline vulnerability management, **incident response** (**IR**), and threat detection. These case studies will demonstrate the tangible benefits of security automation, including enhanced efficiency, improved accuracy, and a stronger overall security posture. Through these examples, we'll explore the versatility of Python in tackling complex security challenges.

We'll cover the following in this chapter:

- IR automation – case studies
- Vulnerability management automation – Real-world examples
- Threat hunting automation – practical implementations

Technical requirements

To follow the case studies and implement Python-based security automation in real-world scenarios, the following technical requirements are necessary.

Python libraries and tools for security automation

You'll require the following:

- **Python 3.x:**

  - **Purpose**: The latest version of Python provides enhanced libraries, support for concurrent programming, and improved security features that are critical for automation tasks

  - **Relevance**: It's essential for leveraging modern libraries and features, enabling efficient and secure code development

- **Requests:**

  - **Purpose**: A library for automating HTTP requests, making it easier to interact with REST APIs

  - **Relevance**: It's used to communicate with various security tools, threat intelligence platforms, and data feeds to automate tasks such as data retrieval, vulnerability assessments, and threat analysis

- **Paramiko**:

  - **Purpose**: It supports the SSH protocol for remote command execution and secure file transfers

  - **Relevance**: It's ideal for automating security tasks on remote servers, such as deploying updates, monitoring files, and executing scripts for compliance checks

- **Scapy**:

  - **Purpose**: A powerful library for packet manipulation and network traffic analysis

  - **Relevance**: It's used for tasks such as crafting packets, monitoring network traffic, detecting suspicious activity, and testing network defenses

- **PyYAML**:

  - **Purpose**: It parses and generates YAML files, so it's commonly used for configuration management

  - **Relevance**: It's essential for reading and modifying configurations in security tools and managing structured data, such as rulesets or access controls, in an easily readable format

- **pandas and NumPy**:

  - **Purpose**: These libraries are used for data processing (pandas) and numerical computation (NumPy)

  - **Relevance**: They're useful in analyzing large security datasets, such as logs, vulnerability reports, and threat feeds, allowing for trends and insights to be garnered that inform defensive strategies

Security tools integration

You'll require the following:

- **OWASP ZAP or the Burp Suite API**:

  - **Purpose**: APIs for automating web application security testing

  - **Relevance**: They enable security teams to conduct regular scans on applications, detect vulnerabilities (for example, SQL injection and XSS), and incorporate findings into automated reporting or remediation workflows

- **Nmap**:

  - **Purpose**: A network scanning tool that identifies open ports, services, and potential vulnerabilities

  - **Relevance**: It can be automated to monitor network security postures, detect unauthorized devices or services, and assess exposure to vulnerabilities regularly

- **Metasploit API**:

  - **Purpose**: Provides a framework for penetration testing

  - **Relevance**: Automates testing workflows, from vulnerability exploitation to post-exploitation analysis, allowing teams to continuously assess the effectiveness of security defenses

Development and deployment essentials

You'll require the following:

- **Version control (Git)**:

  - **Purpose**: Manages code versions, enabling collaboration and tracking changes

  - **Relevance**: It keeps the security automation code base organized, secure, and versioned, helping teams work together efficiently while maintaining a log of updates and changes

- **Cloud/server access**:

  - **Purpose**: Provides infrastructure for running automated scripts on cloud or on-premises systems

  - **Relevance**: This is necessary for deploying, testing, and executing security automation tasks across diverse environments, including AWS, Azure, or local networks

IR automation – case studies

Incident Response (IR) is a cornerstone of cybersecurity that's essential for quickly identifying, managing, and mitigating security incidents to protect organizational assets. In practice, automation has transformed IR, making it possible to react to threats in real time, close potential attack windows faster, and reduce human error during critical moments. Automation in IR not only enhances speed but also introduces consistency and scalability – qualities that manual processes can't match under high-volume or high-stress situations.

For example, automated workflows can trigger predefined actions, such as isolating compromised systems or notifying response teams within seconds of an alert, drastically minimizing damage and exposure. This agility is especially valuable in complex environments such as financial services, where even minor delays can lead to significant financial and reputational losses.

Unlike other forms of automation (such as vulnerability scanning or compliance reporting), which emphasize thoroughness and breadth, IR automation focuses on immediacy and precision. These systems are designed to work under strict time constraints, often using Python scripts to parse logs, filter noise, and isolate high-priority threats, allowing teams to maintain robust defenses even as incident volume rises. The case studies in this section illustrate how organizations across various industries have leveraged Python-driven IR automation to handle specific threats with efficiency, helping them stay resilient against evolving attack landscapes.

Each case study aims to showcase specific goals that highlight the benefits of automation in different aspects of IR:

- **Time savings**: Demonstrating how Python-based automation reduces response times by quickly identifying and isolating compromised assets.

- **Accuracy**: Showing how automation minimizes human error in incident analysis and response actions.

- **Scalability**: Exploring automated IR workflows that handle high volumes of alerts, which is useful for large-scale operations or enterprises.

- **Consistency**: Illustrating how automation ensures that IR processes are followed consistently, improving adherence to security policies and standards.

Through these case studies, you'll gain a practical understanding of how Python can enhance IR processes, enabling faster, more accurate, and scalable responses to security threats.

Case study 1 – automating phishing IR for a financial institution

Background: A major financial institution was frequently targeted by phishing attacks directed at its employees and clients. The manual processes that were used for identifying, analyzing, and responding to these incidents were time-consuming, often resulting in delays in threat mitigation.

Solution: The organization implemented a Python-based automation solution to streamline its phishing IR. Here are the key components of the solution:

- **Email parsing and analysis**: Python scripts leveraged the `email` library to parse incoming emails, extracting URLs and attachments for automated analysis.

- **Threat intelligence integration**: Using Python's `requests` library, the system connected to threat intelligence feeds to verify the legitimacy of URLs and attachments.

- **Automated alerts**: Python's `smtplib` was used to send automated alerts, notifying security teams and affected users of potential phishing threats in real time.

- **Incident tracking**: A Python-based dashboard provided a centralized view to track and manage phishing incidents via real-time updates and reporting capabilities.

Outcome: Automation reduced the average response time to phishing incidents by 60%, enhanced the accuracy of threat detection, and allowed the security team to focus on complex, high-priority security tasks.

Case study 2 – automated malware analysis and response for a healthcare provider

Background: A healthcare provider experienced a ransomware attack that encrypted critical patient data. The manual analysis and response to malware infections were slow, risking significant operational disruptions.

Solution: To automate malware analysis and response, the organization implemented a Python-based system with the following components:

- **Malware sandbox**: They developed a sandbox environment using Python scripts to automatically execute and analyze suspicious files.

- **Behavioral analysis**: Python scripts monitored filesystem changes, network activity, and process behavior to identify malicious activities.

- **Automated response**: They integrated with an endpoint protection platform to automatically quarantine infected systems and initiate remediation processes.

- **Reporting and documentation**: They automated the process of documenting malware incidents and responses using Python libraries so that they could generate reports and logs.

Outcome: The automation solution reduced the time to detect and respond to ransomware attacks by 75%, significantly minimizing operational impact and enhancing incident handling efficiency. Additionally, automation helped alleviate stress levels among the IR team by reducing their manual workload, enabling them to shift focus toward proactive threat hunting and strategic planning. As a result, the team's workflow became more streamlined, and they experienced greater job satisfaction and reduced burnout.

This approach highlights both the measurable improvements and the positive changes in the team's work environment, providing a well-rounded view of the automation solution's value.

Case study 3 – network intrusion detection and response automation for an e-commerce platform

Background: An e-commerce platform experienced multiple network intrusions and DDoS attacks, overwhelming its manual IR team. The complexity of the attacks made it challenging to respond quickly and effectively.

Solution: The e-commerce platform employed a Python-based automation solution for network intrusion detection and response:

- **Intrusion detection system (IDS) integration**: They automated the process of collecting data from IDS logs using Python's pandas library to analyze network traffic patterns.
- **Automated alerts and actions**: They implemented scripts to automatically trigger alerts and response actions, such as blocking IP addresses and isolating affected systems.
- **Anomaly detection**: They used Python libraries such as `scikit-learn` to build machine learning models for detecting anomalous network behavior and potential intrusions.
- **Incident tracking and reporting**: They developed a Python-based dashboard to track ongoing incidents, visualize attack patterns, and generate detailed reports.

Outcome: This automation improved the detection of network intrusions, reduced the time to respond to attacks by 50%, and enhanced the overall security posture of the e-commerce platform.

Case study 4 – automated log analysis and IR for a telecommunications company

Background: A telecommunications company struggled with analyzing and responding to large volumes of log data generated by its infrastructure. Manual log analysis was inefficient and prone to missed critical alerts.

Solution: The company implemented a Python-based automation framework for log analysis and IR:

- **Log aggregation and parsing**: They automated the process of collecting and parsing logs from various sources using Python's `loguru` and `pyyaml` libraries.
- **Pattern detection**: They developed Python scripts to detect predefined patterns and anomalies in log data, indicating potential security incidents.
- **Automated incident generation**: They created scripts to generate and prioritize incident tickets based on log analysis results and their severity.

- **Integration with ticketing systems**: They integrated with existing ticketing systems to automate the process of creating and assigning incident tickets for faster resolution.

Outcome: The automation framework improved the efficiency of log analysis, reduced false positives, and expedited IR, leading to more effective handling of security incidents.

Best practices for IR automation

Based on these case studies, several best practices for implementing effective IR automation can be identified:

- **Integrate with existing tools**: Ensure that automation solutions are compatible with existing security tools and systems to streamline integration and maximize effectiveness.

- **Customize for specific needs**: Tailor automation scripts and processes to address the unique security requirements and threat landscape of the organization.

- **Continuous monitoring and improvement**: Regularly monitor the performance of automation solutions and make adjustments as needed to address evolving threats and vulnerabilities.

- **Ensure human oversight**: While automation enhances efficiency, maintain human oversight to handle complex incidents and validate automated responses.

- **Maintain documentation and training**: Document automated processes and provide training to security teams to ensure they understand and can manage automated IR systems effectively.

The case studies presented in this section demonstrate the significant benefits of automating IR using Python. By leveraging automation, organizations can enhance their ability to detect, respond to, and mitigate security incidents effectively. Python's versatility and extensive library support make it an ideal choice for developing customized automation solutions that address specific security challenges. As cyber threats continue to evolve, integrating automation into IR strategies will remain crucial for maintaining robust and resilient security postures.

Vulnerability management automation – real-world examples

Vulnerability management is an aspect of cybersecurity that involves identifying, assessing, and mitigating vulnerabilities within an organization's systems. In vulnerability management, automation enhances efficiency, accuracy, and speed, allowing organizations to address potential security threats proactively. This section explores real-world examples of how automation has been applied in vulnerability management, illustrating the practical benefits and outcomes of integrating automated solutions.

While automation significantly enhances the efficiency and effectiveness of vulnerability management, it also introduces several risks and challenges that organizations must navigate. Here are some of them:

- **False positives**: Automated vulnerability scanning tools may generate false positives, identifying issues that don't pose actual threats. For instance, a security team might receive alerts about outdated software that has already been patched, leading to wasted resources on unnecessary investigations. This can divert attention from genuine vulnerabilities that require urgent remediation.

- **Over-reliance on automation**: Organizations may become overly reliant on automated tools, leading to complacency in manual review processes. For example, a company that automates its vulnerability assessments may neglect the importance of regular manual penetration testing, which can uncover complex security issues that automated scans might miss. This reliance could create gaps in the overall security posture since human insight is essential for understanding the context of identified vulnerabilities.

- **Integration challenges**: Integrating automated vulnerability management solutions with existing security infrastructures can be complex. For instance, a business deploying a new vulnerability management tool may encounter compatibility issues with its existing **Security Information and Event Management** (**SIEM**) system, leading to fragmented data and an incomplete picture of its security landscape.

- **Skill gaps**: While automation reduces the need for manual tasks, it may also create skill gaps within the security team. A lack of expertise in understanding the output of automated tools can hinder effective vulnerability remediation. For example, if a team isn't trained to interpret the findings of an advanced scanning tool, they may miss critical vulnerabilities or misprioritize them.

Incorporating awareness of these challenges into a vulnerability management strategy can help organizations leverage the benefits of automation while mitigating its risks.

Case study 1 – automated vulnerability scanning for a financial institution

Background: A leading financial institution faced challenges in keeping up with frequent vulnerability scans due to the large scale of its IT infrastructure. Manual scanning and patching processes were labor-intensive and prone to delays, increasing the risk of exposure to vulnerabilities.

Solution: The institution implemented an automated vulnerability management system with the following components:

- **Scheduled scans**: They automated the process of scheduling vulnerability scans using tools such as **Qualys** and **Nessus**, running scans regularly to identify new vulnerabilities.

- **Integration with ticketing systems**: They integrated vulnerability management with the IT ticketing system to automatically create and assign tickets for identified vulnerabilities, streamlining the remediation process.

- **Automated reporting**: They developed Python scripts to generate and distribute vulnerability reports, providing insights and tracking progress on remediation efforts.

Outcome: Automation reduced the time required for vulnerability scans by 70%, improved the accuracy of vulnerability detection, and accelerated the remediation process, leading to a more secure and resilient IT environment.

Case study 2 – real-time vulnerability assessment for a healthcare provider

Background: A healthcare provider managed sensitive patient data and required real-time vulnerability assessments to comply with regulatory requirements and protect against data breaches. The manual assessment process was slow and didn't provide timely insights into emerging threats.

Solution: The healthcare provider adopted a real-time vulnerability management system with the following features:

- **Continuous scanning**: They implemented continuous vulnerability scanning using **Rapid7 InsightVM** to identify vulnerabilities as they emerged.

- **Automated risk assessment**: They utilized automated risk scoring algorithms to prioritize vulnerabilities based on their potential impact and exploitability.

- **Integration with a SIEM system**: They integrated with SIEM systems to correlate vulnerability data with real-time threat intelligence, providing a comprehensive view of security posture.

Outcome: Automation provided real-time insights into vulnerabilities, enabling quicker responses to emerging threats. The provider achieved compliance with regulatory requirements and enhanced protection for patient data.

Case study 3 – patch management automation for a global e-commerce company

Background: A global e-commerce company faced challenges with managing and applying patches across a diverse and extensive IT infrastructure. Manual patch management was inefficient and often resulted in delayed patch deployment.

Solution: The company implemented an automated patch management solution with the following components:

- **Patch deployment automation**: They automated the process of deploying patches using tools such as `WSUS` and `BigFix`, scheduling patch installations during off-peak hours to minimize disruption.

- **Automated testing**: They developed a Python-based testing framework to automatically test patches in a staging environment before deployment, ensuring compatibility and stability.

- **Compliance monitoring**: They integrated with compliance monitoring tools to track patch status and generate reports on patch deployment progress.

Outcome: Automation significantly reduced the time required for patch deployment, improved patch testing accuracy, and ensured timely application of security updates, reducing the risk of vulnerabilities being exploited.

Case study 4 – vulnerability prioritization for a technology firm

Background: A technology firm faced difficulties in prioritizing vulnerabilities due to the sheer volume of issues that were identified during scans. Manual prioritization was time-consuming and often resulted in suboptimal allocation of resources.

Solution: The firm implemented an automated vulnerability prioritization system with the following features:

- **Risk-based prioritization**: They used automated tools to assess the risk associated with each vulnerability based on factors such as exploitability, impact, and asset criticality.

- **Integration with threat intelligence**: They integrated vulnerability prioritization with threat intelligence feeds to incorporate current threat data into the prioritization process, focusing on vulnerabilities actively being exploited.

- **Automated remediation workflow**: They developed Python scripts to automate the creation of remediation tasks based on prioritized vulnerabilities, ensuring timely resolution.

Outcome: Automation improved the accuracy and efficiency of vulnerability prioritization, allowing the firm to address high-risk vulnerabilities first and optimize resource allocation.

Best practices for vulnerability management automation

From these case studies, several best practices for implementing effective vulnerability management automation can be identified:

- **Integrate with existing tools**: Ensure that automation solutions are compatible with existing vulnerability management tools and systems to enhance efficiency and effectiveness.

- **Customize automation workflows**: Tailor automation workflows so that they meet the specific needs of the organization while considering factors such as infrastructure size, regulatory requirements, and threat landscape.

- **Continuous monitoring and improvement**: Regularly review and update automation processes to address evolving vulnerabilities and improve detection and remediation capabilities.

- **Ensure proper configuration and testing**: Thoroughly test automation scripts and configurations to avoid false positives and ensure accurate vulnerability detection and reporting.

- **Maintain human oversight**: While automation enhances efficiency, maintain human oversight to handle complex issues and validate automated actions.

The real-world examples presented in this section highlight the significant benefits of automating vulnerability management processes. By leveraging Python and other automation tools, organizations can improve the efficiency, accuracy, and speed of vulnerability detection, assessment, and remediation. Automation not only streamlines the vulnerability management process but also enhances overall security posture, allowing organizations to stay ahead of potential threats and reduce their risk exposure. As cyber threats continue to evolve, integrating automation into vulnerability management strategies will be crucial for maintaining robust and resilient security defenses.

Threat hunting automation – practical implementations

Threat hunting involves proactively searching for signs of malicious activity and vulnerabilities within an organization's IT environment. In threat hunting, automation enhances the efficiency, scope, and accuracy of identifying potential threats, enabling faster responses and improved security posture. This section explores practical implementations of threat-hunting automation through real-world examples and outlines how organizations can leverage automated solutions to bolster their threat detection and response capabilities.

Case study 1 – automated threat detection in a financial services firm

Background: A financial services firm faced significant challenges in detecting sophisticated threats amid a high volume of security data. Manual threat-hunting efforts were insufficient for identifying **advanced persistent threats** (APTs) and other stealthy attacks, which necessitated a more robust approach to threat detection.

Solution: The firm implemented an automated threat-hunting solution with the following components:

- **Behavioral analytics**: The integration of automated behavioral analytics tools allowed anomalies in user and network activity to be identified. Tools such as Elastic Stack and Splunk were employed to set up automated alerts for unusual behavior patterns. This shift from manual monitoring to automated analytics enabled the security team to detect deviations from normal behavior more rapidly and accurately. For instance, while manual efforts might miss subtle changes in user behavior due to fatigue or oversight, automated tools continuously analyze vast amounts of data, ensuring a higher detection rate for potential threats.

- **Machine learning models**: By developing machine learning models to analyze historical data, the firm could identify potential threats based on deviations from established norms. Utilizing Python libraries such as scikit-learn and TensorFlow for model training and deployment allowed the team to harness advanced algorithms that can learn from historical attack patterns and adapt to new threats. This capability significantly increases detection rates compared to traditional methods, where patterns must be predefined and can't adapt to new attack vectors easily.

- **Automated investigation**: The implementation of automated scripts to gather contextual information and correlate alerts from multiple sources drastically reduced manual investigation time. In traditional setups, analysts might spend hours manually sifting through logs and data to establish connections between seemingly unrelated alerts. In contrast, automation can quickly compile and analyze relevant information, allowing analysts to focus on high-priority incidents rather than getting bogged down in data collection. This efficiency not only speeds up response times but also minimizes the likelihood of human error in the investigative process.

Outcome: Automation improved the detection of advanced threats and reduced the time required for investigations, enhancing overall threat visibility. By enabling quicker responses to potential security incidents, the firm was able to mitigate risks more effectively. The ability to automate repetitive tasks allowed the security team to engage in more strategic activities, such as developing proactive security measures and refining response protocols, ultimately fortifying the organization's cybersecurity posture.

Case study 2 – automated threat intelligence integration for a healthcare provider

Background: A healthcare provider needs to integrate threat intelligence feeds into their threat-hunting process to stay ahead of emerging threats. Manual integration was time-consuming and often delayed the incorporation of new threat data.

Solution: The provider adopted an automated threat intelligence integration system with the following features:

- **Threat feed aggregation**: They automated the process of aggregating threat intelligence feeds using Python scripts and APIs from providers such as **ThreatConnect** and **Recorded Future**.

- **Automated correlation**: They developed automated correlation engines to match threat intelligence data with internal security logs and alerts, identifying potential threats in real time.

- **Alert management**: They used automated alert management systems to prioritize and route threat intelligence alerts to appropriate teams for further investigation.

Outcome: Automation streamlined the integration of threat intelligence, providing timely insights into emerging threats and enhancing the provider's ability to detect and respond to potential security issues.

Case study 3 – network traffic analysis and anomaly detection for an e-commerce platform

Background: An e-commerce platform faced difficulties in analyzing large volumes of network traffic to identify potential threats. Manual analysis was inefficient and often missed subtle indicators of malicious activity.

Solution: The platform implemented an automated network traffic analysis solution with the following components:

- **Traffic monitoring**: They deployed automated network monitoring tools to capture and analyze network traffic in real time. Tools such as **Zeek** (formerly Bro) and **Suricata** were utilized for this purpose.

- **Anomaly detection**: They implemented machine learning algorithms to detect anomalies in network traffic patterns, using libraries such as **scikit-learn** and **Keras** for model development.

- **Automated response**: They integrated with **security orchestration, automation, and response (SOAR)** platforms to automatically trigger responses such as blocking suspicious IP addresses or isolating affected systems.

Outcome: Automation improved the platform's ability to detect and respond to anomalies in network traffic, reduced the time required for threat detection, and enhanced the overall security of the e-commerce platform.

Case study 4 – automated endpoint threat detection and response for a technology firm

Background: A technology firm requires a robust solution for detecting and responding to threats on endpoints, including laptops and servers. The manual approach to endpoint security was slow and lacked comprehensive coverage.

Solution: The firm implemented an automated endpoint threat detection and response system with the following features:

- **Endpoint monitoring**: They deployed automated endpoint monitoring tools to collect and analyze data from endpoints. Tools such as **CrowdStrike Falcon** and **Carbon Black** were used for this purpose.

- **Threat detection**: They integrated automated threat detection algorithms to identify malicious activity based on behavioral analysis and known threat signatures.

- **Automated response**: They developed automated response workflows to quarantine infected endpoints, deploy patches, and remediate detected threats.

Outcome: Automation enhanced the firm's ability to detect and respond to endpoint threats in real time, improved overall endpoint security, and reduced the manual effort required for incident handling.

Best practices for threat hunting automation

From these case studies, several best practices for implementing effective threat-hunting automation can be identified:

- **Integrate with existing security tools**: Ensure that automation solutions are compatible with existing security tools and platforms to maximize effectiveness and efficiency.

- **Leverage machine learning and AI**: Utilize machine learning and AI to enhance threat detection capabilities, providing more accurate and timely insights into potential threats.

- **Automate routine tasks**: Automate routine and repetitive tasks such as data collection, log analysis, and alert generation to free up resources for more complex threat-hunting activities.

- **Continuously update and improve**: Regularly update automation scripts and models to adapt to evolving threats and improve detection accuracy.

- **Maintain human oversight**: While automation enhances efficiency, maintain human oversight to validate automated findings and handle complex investigations.

The practical implementations presented in this chapter highlight the significant benefits of automating threat-hunting processes. By leveraging automation, organizations can enhance their ability to detect and respond to threats more efficiently and accurately. Python's versatility, combined with advanced tools and machine learning algorithms, provides a powerful foundation for developing effective threat-hunting automation solutions. As cyber threats continue to evolve, integrating automation into threat-hunting strategies will be crucial for maintaining a proactive and resilient security posture.

Summary

This chapter explored several real-world case studies demonstrating the practical applications of Python in security automation. Through diverse examples, we illustrated how Python's flexibility and powerful libraries have been leveraged to enhance security processes across various domains. The case studies highlighted the successful implementation of automated solutions for tasks such as vulnerability management, IR, threat hunting, and more. By showcasing tangible benefits such as improved efficiency, accuracy, and responsiveness, this chapter emphasized Python's role in advancing security automation and reinforcing organizational defenses against evolving cyber threats.

The next chapter will explore how advanced technologies such as machine learning and AI are transforming cybersecurity by automating threat detection, response, and prevention. It will also delve into the process of integrating Python to develop AI-driven security solutions, enabling more efficient and scalable defenses against evolving cyber threats.

8

Future Trends – Machine Learning and AI in Security Automation with Python

In the modern cybersecurity landscape, the complexity and volume of threats necessitate advanced, intelligent solutions to stay ahead of potential breaches. **Artificial intelligence (AI)** has emerged as a transformative force in security, enabling more sophisticated threat detection, analysis, and response mechanisms. Python, with its rich ecosystem of AI libraries and frameworks, is well suited to develop and implement these cutting-edge security solutions.

This chapter introduces the fundamentals of leveraging AI for security applications using Python. We will explore how AI-driven approaches can enhance various aspects of cybersecurity, including threat detection, anomaly detection, predictive analysis, and automated response. Through practical examples and case studies, we will demonstrate how Python's robust libraries and tools can be utilized to build intelligent security systems that adapt and evolve with emerging threats. By the end of this chapter, you will have a solid understanding of how to integrate AI into your security strategy using Python, equipping you with the skills to enhance your organization's defenses.

We will cover the following topics:

- Introducing **machine learning (ML)** and AI in security automation
- Applications of ML in cybersecurity
- Implementing AI-driven security solutions with Python

Technical requirements

To successfully implement AI-driven security solutions with Python, several technical components and tools are necessary:

- **Python environment**:

  - **Python version**: Python 3.6 or higher to ensure compatibility with modern AI libraries.

  - **Virtual environment**: Set up a virtual environment using `venv` or `virtualenv` to manage dependencies.

- **AI libraries and frameworks**:

  - **TensorFlow** or **PyTorch**: For building and training ML and **deep learning** (**DL**) models.

  - **scikit-learn**: For implementing traditional ML algorithms and model evaluation.

  - **Keras**: A high-level **neural network** (**NN**) API running on top of TensorFlow for easier model building.

  - **pandas** and **NumPy**: For data manipulation and numerical operations.

- **Data sources**:

  - **Security data**: Access to relevant security data such as logs, alerts, and network traffic. This can include data from **security information and event management** (**SIEM**) systems, **intrusion detection systems** (**IDSs**), or **threat intelligence** (**TI**) feeds.

- **Data preprocessing tools**:

  - **Data cleaning**: Tools for cleaning and preprocessing data to ensure it is in a suitable format for AI models (for example, removing noise and handling missing values).

  - **Feature engineering**: Techniques and tools for transforming raw data into meaningful features that can be used for model training.

- **Model training and evaluation**:

  - **Training infrastructure**: Access to computational resources, such as GPUs or TPUs, for training complex models efficiently.

  - **Evaluation metrics**: Techniques for evaluating model performance, such as accuracy, precision, recall, and F1 score.

- **Integration and deployment**:

  - **API development**: Tools and frameworks for developing APIs to integrate AI models with existing security systems (for example, Flask, FastAPI).

- **Automation tools**: Platforms for automating the deployment and updating of AI models, such as Docker for containerization and **continuous integration/continuous deployment (CI/CD)** pipelines.

- **Security and compliance**:

  - **Access control**: Implement proper access controls to protect AI models and sensitive data used for training.

  - **Compliance**: Ensure AI solutions comply with relevant regulations and standards, such as the **General Data Protection Regulation (GDPR)** or the **Health Insurance Portability and Accountability Act (HIPAA)**, depending on your industry.

- **Monitoring and maintenance**:

  - **Monitoring tools**: Set up tools to monitor the performance and accuracy of AI models in production.

  - **Regular updates**: Implement processes for updating models and retraining them with new data to adapt to evolving threats.

By meeting these technical requirements, you will be well equipped to develop and deploy AI-driven security solutions using Python, enhancing your ability to detect and respond to cybersecurity threats effectively.

Introducing ML and AI in security automation

In modern cybersecurity, ML and AI are revolutionizing the ability to detect and respond to threats with unprecedented speed and precision. One of the most impactful uses of these technologies is automated threat detection. By analyzing historical threat data, ML algorithms can identify patterns in network traffic that may signal a potential attack. For example, a **supervised learning (SL)** algorithm can be trained on labeled data containing both benign and malicious network behaviors. Once trained, this model can automatically flag suspicious activities, such as unexpected data exfiltration, without human intervention.

Additionally, AI-based anomaly detection systems can be deployed to monitor user behavior, detecting deviations from normal patterns that might indicate a compromised account or insider threat. These systems use **unsupervised learning (UL)** to build baselines of normal behavior, dynamically adjusting to each user or endpoint in the network. When a significant deviation occurs—such as access to sensitive data outside normal business hours—the system can trigger alerts, launch automated investigations, or even execute predefined remediation actions such as quarantining an endpoint or revoking access.

By integrating ML and AI into security automation workflows, organizations can not only detect threats earlier but also automate responses, reducing manual intervention and allowing security teams to focus on more strategic tasks. This section will dive into key techniques, algorithms, and tools used to automate security processes with the power of ML and AI.

ML and AI have revolutionized various industries by enabling systems to learn from data and make intelligent decisions without explicit programming. In cybersecurity, these technologies are increasingly being used to enhance security automation, providing advanced methods for detecting, analyzing, and responding to threats.

AI refers to the broader concept of creating machines that can perform tasks that typically require human intelligence. AI encompasses a range of techniques, including ML, **natural language processing (NLP)**, and **computer vision (CV)**.

ML, a subset of AI, focuses on algorithms that enable systems to learn from and make predictions based on data. ML models are trained using historical data to identify patterns and make informed decisions. Key types of ML include the following:

- **SL**: The model is trained on labeled data, where the correct output is known. It learns to map inputs to outputs based on this data, making it suitable for classification and regression tasks.

- **UL**: The model works with unlabeled data to find hidden patterns or groupings. It is used for clustering and anomaly detection, where the goal is to identify unusual patterns or group similar data points.

- **Reinforcement learning (RL)**: The model learns by interacting with an environment and receiving feedback in the form of rewards or penalties. It is used for decision-making tasks where the model learns to optimize actions to achieve a goal.

Applications of ML and AI in security automation

Let's explore how ML and AI are reshaping cybersecurity, providing tools that enhance the speed and accuracy of threat detection, response, and prevention. By automating repetitive security tasks and evolving with new data, these technologies enable security teams to focus on complex challenges, reducing response times and improving overall security posture. This section will explore specific use cases and techniques in AI/ML-driven security automation, focusing on areas such as malware detection, phishing analysis, and anomaly-based intrusion detection.

Malware detection with ML

ML-driven malware detection replaces traditional signature-based methods with advanced algorithms capable of identifying zero-day threats. Techniques such as decision trees, **support vector machines (SVMs)**, and NNs classify files by analyzing their behavior, metadata, and network activity. For instance, an NN trained on behavior-based features can spot sophisticated malware variants before they're widely recognized. By continuously learning from new data, these models enhance detection accuracy and reduce dependency on signature updates.

Phishing detection with NLP

AI-powered phishing detection applies NLP to analyze email content, structure, and metadata. By examining factors such as sender authenticity, URL patterns, and textual clues, NLP models can accurately identify phishing attempts. For example, an NLP-based classifier trained on common phishing markers can parse subtle indicators in real time, such as domain mismatches or irregular language. This real-time analysis significantly reduces the chances of phishing links reaching end users.

Anomaly-based intrusion detection

UL algorithms enable ML-driven IDSs to establish baselines of normal network behavior. When unusual activity deviates from these baselines—such as high data transfers or unfamiliar IP access—the system generates alerts and can take automated action, such as blocking traffic or isolating compromised endpoints. This approach enables adaptive security that evolves with changing network conditions, enhancing response readiness against novel threats.

Threat detection and classification

AI and ML can analyze vast amounts of data to detect and classify potential threats. By training models on historical attack data, these technologies can identify patterns indicative of malicious activity. Here are some examples of this:

- **Malware detection**: ML algorithms can analyze files and behavior to classify them as benign or malicious. Techniques such as static analysis and dynamic analysis are used to examine code and runtime behavior.

- **IDSs**: AI-powered IDSs can monitor network traffic and detect anomalous patterns that may indicate an intrusion. ML models can adapt to new attack vectors by learning from evolving data.

Anomaly detection

Anomaly detection involves identifying deviations from normal behavior that may signify potential threats. AI and ML excel in this area in the following ways:

- **Behavioral analysis**: ML models can learn normal user and system behaviors, flagging deviations that may suggest insider threats or compromised accounts.

- **Network anomalies**: AI can detect unusual patterns in network traffic, such as unexpected data flows or unauthorized access attempts, which could indicate a network breach.

Predictive analysis

Predictive analysis uses historical data to forecast future threats. AI and ML can provide the following:

- **Risk scoring**: AI models can evaluate the likelihood of future attacks based on past incidents and current TI, helping prioritize security measures.

- **Threat forecasting**: ML algorithms can analyze trends and emerging threats to predict potential attack vectors and advise on proactive defenses.

Automated response

AI can automate responses to detected threats, reducing the time between detection and mitigation. This includes the following:

- **Incident response (IR) automation**: AI-driven systems can automatically execute predefined responses to certain threats, such as isolating affected systems or blocking malicious traffic.

- **Adaptive security measures**: AI can adjust security policies and configurations based on real-time threat data, ensuring that defenses are always up to date.

Key techniques and tools

Let's have an in-depth look at foundational methods and essential technologies that drive security automation using AI and ML. This section highlights critical algorithms, frameworks, and platforms that enable the seamless integration of automation into cybersecurity workflows. By understanding these techniques and tools, security professionals can effectively leverage AI to streamline threat detection, analysis, and response.

SL algorithms

SL algorithms, alongside other ML and AI techniques, are transforming cybersecurity by automating threat detection, response, and prevention processes. These technologies enable security teams to tackle increasingly complex cyber threats while reducing response times and improving accuracy. This section delves into specific use cases and advanced methodologies—such as malware detection, phishing analysis, and anomaly-based intrusion detection—showcasing how AI and ML are enhancing security automation across industries:

- **Decision trees**: Used for classification tasks, decision trees create a model that predicts the value of a target variable based on input features.

- **SVMs**: Effective for classification tasks, SVMs find the optimal hyperplane that separates different classes in the data.

- **NNs**: These algorithms are inspired by the human brain and are used for complex tasks such as image and speech recognition. They are the foundation of many advanced AI applications.

UL algorithms

UL algorithms play a crucial role in security automation by identifying hidden patterns and anomalies in data without the need for labeled training sets. Here are some examples of their use:

- **K-means clustering**: A popular method for grouping data into clusters based on similarity. It is used for discovering hidden patterns in data.

- **Principal component analysis (PCA)**: A dimensionality reduction technique that transforms data into a set of orthogonal components, making it easier to visualize and analyze.

RL algorithms

RL algorithms offer a powerful approach to security automation by enabling systems to learn optimal responses through trial and error, continuously improving their decision-making in dynamic and evolving threat environments. Here are some examples:

- **Q-learning**: An algorithm used to find the best actions to take in a given state to maximize rewards. It is often used in decision-making scenarios.

- **Deep Q-Network (DQN)**: An extension of Q-learning that uses NNs to approximate the Q-values, enabling it to handle more complex environments.

Tools and frameworks

To effectively implement security automation with AI and ML, a variety of tools and frameworks are available, each designed to streamline development, deployment, and integration into existing security workflows:

- **TensorFlow**: An open source framework for building and training ML models, developed by Google.

- **PyTorch**: An open source ML library that provides tools for DL and is favored for its flexibility and ease of use.

- **scikit-learn**: A library for ML in Python that provides simple and efficient tools for data analysis and modeling.

Challenges and considerations

Data plays a critical role in the success of AI and ML models in security automation. This section addresses common issues of poor data quality, insufficient data, and potential biases that can arise, which may compromise the accuracy and effectiveness of automated security solutions. Let's explore strategies for ensuring high-quality data collection and handling to maximize the potential of AI-driven cybersecurity systems:

- **Data quality and quantity**: AI and ML models require high-quality, relevant data to function effectively. Inaccurate or insufficient data can lead to poor model performance and unreliable results.

- **Model bias and fairness**: AI models can inadvertently incorporate biases present in the training data, leading to unfair or discriminatory outcomes. It is essential to address and mitigate biases to ensure equitable and accurate results.

- **Explainability and transparency**: AI models, especially DL models, can be complex and opaque. Ensuring that models are interpretable and their decisions are understandable is crucial for gaining trust and facilitating effective decision-making.

- **Security and privacy**: Implementing AI in security automation must be done with careful consideration of data privacy and security. Protecting sensitive information and ensuring compliance with regulations is paramount.

ML and AI are powerful tools that can significantly enhance security automation by providing advanced threat detection, predictive analysis, and automated responses. By understanding the fundamentals of these technologies and their applications, you can harness their capabilities to improve your organization's security posture and stay ahead of emerging threats. This section has laid the groundwork for integrating AI and ML into your security strategy, setting the stage for a deeper exploration of practical implementations in the following sections.

Applications of ML in cybersecurity

As cybersecurity threats become increasingly sophisticated, traditional methods of defense are often inadequate. ML offers a powerful approach to enhancing security measures by enabling systems to learn from data and make informed decisions. This section explores various applications of ML in cybersecurity, highlighting how these techniques can be employed to detect, analyze, and respond to cyber threats more effectively.

Introducing ML in cybersecurity

ML, a subset of AI, involves training algorithms to recognize patterns and make decisions based on data. In cybersecurity, ML can be used to automate and improve various security tasks, such as threat detection, anomaly detection, and IR. By leveraging large volumes of data and advanced algorithms, ML can identify potential threats and vulnerabilities more accurately and quickly than traditional methods.

Threat detection

Threat detection focuses on the application of AI and ML in identifying and responding to potential security threats. This section explores how advanced algorithms can analyze vast amounts of data in real time to detect anomalies, malicious activities, and emerging threats more effectively than traditional methods. It also highlights the advantages of automated threat detection in reducing response times and enhancing overall cybersecurity resilience.

Malware detection

Malware detection is one of the most common applications of ML in cybersecurity. Traditional signature-based detection methods are limited to known threats and often fail to detect new or modified malware variants. ML-based approaches address these limitations in the following ways:

- **Behavioral analysis**: ML models analyze the behavior of files and processes to identify malicious activities. Techniques such as feature extraction and behavioral profiling help in detecting anomalies that may indicate malware.

- **Static and dynamic analysis**: ML algorithms can process both static attributes (for example, file metadata) and dynamic behavior (for example, execution patterns) to classify files as benign or malicious. This approach helps in identifying previously unknown threats.

Phishing detection

Phishing attacks exploit social engineering to trick users into revealing sensitive information. ML enhances phishing detection in the following ways:

- **Content analysis**: ML models analyze email content, URLs, and attachments to identify phishing attempts. NLP techniques help in understanding the context and detecting deceptive language.

- **URL classification**: ML algorithms can classify URLs based on their features, such as domain names and URL structures, to identify suspicious links and prevent users from accessing malicious sites.

Anomaly detection

We'll now delve into the use of ML techniques to identify unusual patterns or behaviors that may indicate security threats or system vulnerabilities. This section explores how AI models are trained to distinguish between normal and suspicious activities, enabling proactive detection of potential breaches or attacks. By automating anomaly detection, organizations can improve threat visibility and reduce the risk of undetected intrusions.

Network anomaly detection

Anomaly detection involves identifying deviations from normal network behavior, which may indicate a potential security breach. ML techniques for network anomaly detection include the following:

- **Statistical methods**: ML algorithms use statistical models to establish baseline network behavior and detect deviations. Techniques such as clustering and time-series analysis help identify unusual patterns in network traffic.

- **DL**: Advanced ML models, such as **autoencoders (AEs)** and **recurrent neural networks (RNNs)**, can analyze complex network traffic patterns and identify anomalies with high accuracy.

User behavior analytics

User behavior analytics (**UBA**) focuses on detecting deviations in user behavior that may indicate compromised accounts or insider threats. ML-based UBA involves the following:

- **Behavioral profiling**: ML models create profiles of normal user behavior based on historical data. Anomalies in user activities, such as unusual login times or access to sensitive data, are flagged for further investigation.

- **Anomaly scoring**: ML algorithms assign scores to user activities based on their deviation from established norms. High-scoring anomalies are prioritized for investigation, enabling timely responses to potential threats.

TI and prediction

This section explores how AI and ML are transforming the way organizations gather, analyze, and utilize TI to predict potential security incidents. It highlights how predictive models can identify emerging threats by analyzing patterns in historical data, enabling proactive measures to mitigate risks before they materialize. By leveraging AI-driven TI, organizations can stay ahead of evolving cyber threats and enhance their overall security posture.

Threat forecasting

Predictive analytics uses historical threat data to forecast future threats and vulnerabilities. ML techniques for threat forecasting include the following:

- **Trend analysis**: ML models analyze historical attack data and identify trends and patterns that may indicate emerging threats. This information helps organizations prepare for future attacks.

- **Risk scoring**: ML algorithms assess the risk level of potential threats based on historical data and current TI. Risk scores guide security teams in prioritizing mitigation efforts.

Attack simulation

ML can simulate potential attack scenarios to evaluate the effectiveness of existing security measures. Techniques include the following:

- **Adversarial ML**: ML models simulate attack strategies and test defenses against these simulated attacks. This approach helps identify weaknesses and improve security posture.

- **Red team exercises**: ML-based red teaming involves using automated tools to mimic real-world attack techniques, providing insights into vulnerabilities and potential improvements.

Automated IR

This section examines how AI and ML streamline and accelerate the process of responding to security incidents and explores how automation tools can identify, prioritize, and remediate threats in real time, reducing manual intervention and minimizing response times. By leveraging automated IR, organizations can mitigate the impact of cyberattacks more efficiently and ensure a more resilient security infrastructure.

Automated threat mitigation

AI and ML can automate responses to detected threats, reducing the time between detection and remediation. Key approaches include the following:

- **Automated containment**: ML models can trigger automated actions to isolate affected systems or block malicious network traffic, minimizing the impact of an attack.
- **Response orchestration**: ML-driven systems integrate with security infrastructure to automate IR workflows, such as updating firewall rules or deploying patches.

Incident analysis

ML can assist in analyzing and understanding incidents in the following ways:

- **Root cause analysis (RCA)**: ML algorithms analyze incident data to determine the root cause of attacks and provide actionable insights for remediation.
- **Post-incident review**: ML models help in reviewing past incidents to identify patterns and improve future IR strategies.

Challenges and considerations

Some of the challenges and considerations are as follows:

- **Data quality and volume**: ML models require large volumes of high-quality data for training and accurate predictions. Ensuring data accuracy and completeness is crucial for effective ML-based security solutions.
- **Model bias and fairness**: ML models can inherit biases from training data, leading to unfair or inaccurate results. Addressing biases and ensuring fairness is essential for reliable security solutions.
- **Explainability and transparency**: AI and ML models can be complex and difficult to interpret. Ensuring that models are transparent and their decisions can be explained is important for building trust and facilitating effective decision-making.

- **Security and privacy**: Implementing ML in cybersecurity requires careful consideration of data privacy and security. Protecting sensitive data and ensuring compliance with regulations is critical.

ML offers powerful tools for enhancing cybersecurity through advanced threat detection, anomaly detection, predictive analysis, and automated response. By leveraging ML, organizations can improve their ability to identify and respond to cyber threats, ultimately strengthening their overall security posture. Understanding the applications and challenges of ML in cybersecurity equips security professionals with the knowledge needed to implement effective and intelligent security solutions.

Implementing AI-driven security solutions with Python

The application of AI in cybersecurity is revolutionizing the way organizations protect their systems, data, and users. AI, particularly when combined with Python, offers powerful tools for detecting, analyzing, and responding to cyber threats in real time. Python's vast ecosystem of libraries and its simplicity make it an ideal choice for building AI-driven security solutions. In this section, we will explore how to implement AI-based security systems using Python, from threat detection to automating IR.

Introducing AI in security

AI in cybersecurity refers to the use of intelligent systems that can autonomously learn from data, detect patterns, and make decisions to enhance the security posture of an organization. AI-driven security systems leverage ML, DL, and NLP to automate and optimize threat detection, vulnerability analysis, and response strategies.

Python plays a central role in AI and ML development due to its readability, community support, and comprehensive libraries such as TensorFlow, PyTorch, and scikit-learn. These tools enable security professionals to develop sophisticated AI models for various security applications, including malware detection, network monitoring, UBA, and more.

Setting up the Python environment for AI-driven security

Before implementing AI-driven security solutions, it's essential to set up a Python development environment with the necessary libraries and tools. The following steps guide you through the setup process:

1. **Install Python**: Ensure that Python (version 3.6 or higher) is installed on your system. Python's latest versions come with features and optimizations suitable for AI tasks.

2. **Set up a virtual environment**: Create a virtual environment to isolate your project dependencies. This helps manage different versions of libraries and ensures consistency across various projects:

   ```bash
   python3 -m venv ai_security_env
   ```

```
source ai_security_env/bin/activate  # On Windows use: ai_
security_env\Scripts\activate
```

3. **Install required libraries**: Install libraries for AI and ML development:

```
pip install numpy pandas scikit-learn tensorflow keras
matplotlib seaborn
```

The libraries installed are the following:

- **NumPy** and **pandas** for data manipulation

- **scikit-learn** for traditional ML algorithms

- **TensorFlow** and **Keras** for DL models

- **Matplotlib** and **Seaborn** for data visualization

Once your environment is set up, you're ready to begin building AI-based security solutions.

AI for threat detection

One of the most effective applications of AI in security is threat detection. AI models can analyze network traffic, user behavior, and system logs to identify abnormal patterns that may indicate a security breach. In this section, we will develop a simple anomaly detection system using ML.

Data collection and preprocessing

The first step in building a threat detection model is to collect relevant data. Security logs, network traffic data, and system events are typical sources of information. Preprocessing involves cleaning, normalizing, and structuring the data for analysis.

For this example, let's assume we have network traffic data in a CSV file. We'll load and preprocess the data using pandas:

```python
import pandas as pd

# Load network traffic data
data = pd.read_csv('network_traffic.csv')

# Normalize data (scaling features between 0 and 1)
from sklearn.preprocessing import MinMaxScaler
scaler = MinMaxScaler()
scaled_data = scaler.fit_transform(data)
```

Building an anomaly detection model

Anomaly detection can be achieved using UL techniques. One popular algorithm is the Isolation Forest algorithm, which isolates anomalies by creating partitions in the data. We can implement it using scikit-learn:

```
from sklearn.ensemble import IsolationForest

# Train the Isolation Forest model
model = IsolationForest(contamination=0.05)   # Assume 5% of the data
are anomalies
model.fit(scaled_data)

# Predict anomalies
anomalies = model.predict(scaled_data)

# Identify anomalies (-1 indicates an anomaly)
anomalous_data = data[anomalies == -1]
print(anomalous_data)
```

In this example, the model will detect anomalies in network traffic based on patterns and behavior. Once detected, these anomalies can trigger further investigation or automated response mechanisms.

AI for malware detection

Malware detection is another area where AI shines. Traditional antivirus systems rely on signature-based detection, which is ineffective against new or polymorphic malware. AI, however, can detect malware by analyzing the behavior and characteristics of files.

Feature extraction from files

To build a malware detection system, we first need to extract meaningful features from files (for example, metadata, API calls, and file size). This feature extraction process can be automated with Python.

For example, we can extract file attributes using the `pefile` library for **Portable Executable** (**PE**) files:

```bash
pip install pefile
```

```python
import pefile
```

```
# Load a PE file
pe = pefile.PE('malicious_file.exe')

# Extract relevant features (e.g., number of sections, entry point,
imports)
num_sections = len(pe.sections)
entry_point = pe.OPTIONAL_HEADER.AddressOfEntryPoint
imports = len(pe.DIRECTORY_ENTRY_IMPORT)

print(f'Number of sections: {num_sections}, Entry point: {entry_
point}, Imports: {imports}')
```

Training a malware classification model

We can use SL to train a malware classification model. Let's use a dataset of benign and malicious file features to train a decision tree classifier:

```
from sklearn.tree import DecisionTreeClassifier
from sklearn.model_selection import train_test_split

# Load feature data and labels (0 = benign, 1 = malicious)
features = pd.read_csv('file_features.csv')
labels = pd.read_csv('file_labels.csv')

# Split data into training and testing sets
X_train, X_test, y_train, y_test = train_test_split(features, labels,
test_size=0.2)

# Train a decision tree classifier
classifier = DecisionTreeClassifier()
classifier.fit(X_train, y_train)

# Evaluate the model
accuracy = classifier.score(X_test, y_test)
print(f'Model accuracy: {accuracy * 100:.2f}%')
```

By automating feature extraction and using AI-driven models, this malware detection system can quickly identify and block malicious files.

AI for automating IR

AI can also be applied to automate IR workflows. By integrating AI into SIEM systems, organizations can streamline the identification, containment, and resolution of security incidents.

Automated incident triage

AI models can classify incidents based on their severity and type. For instance, a model can analyze security logs and categorize events as low, medium, or high priority, allowing security teams to focus on the most critical issues.

Here's a basic example of classifying incidents using an SVM model:

```python
from sklearn.svm import SVC

# Load incident data
incidents = pd.read_csv('incident_data.csv')
severity = pd.read_csv('incident_severity.csv')

# Split data into training and testing sets
X_train, X_test, y_train, y_test = train_test_split(incidents,
severity, test_size=0.2)

# Train an SVM model
svm_model = SVC()
svm_model.fit(X_train, y_train)

# Predict and evaluate the model
predictions = svm_model.predict(X_test)
print(predictions)
```

Response orchestration with AI

After triaging incidents, AI systems can automate responses by integrating with existing security tools. For instance, once a high-priority incident is detected, AI can trigger automated actions such as isolating compromised systems, updating firewall rules, or notifying security teams.

Python's integration with APIs allows for seamless automation:

```python
import requests

# Example: Trigger an API call to isolate a compromised system
def isolate_system(system_id):
    response = requests.post(f'https://security-platform/api/isolate/
{system_id}')
    return response.status_code
```

```
# Isolate system with ID '12345'
status = isolate_system('12345')
if status == 200:
    print("System successfully isolated.")
```

Challenges in implementing AI-driven security solutions

While AI holds immense potential for cybersecurity, it comes with its own set of challenges:

- **Data quality**: AI models rely on high-quality data for accurate predictions. Poor or incomplete data can lead to false positives and negatives.

- **Model interpretability**: Many AI models, especially DL models, are considered "black boxes," making it difficult to explain their decisions.

- **Bias in data**: If the training data is biased, the AI model may produce biased results, potentially missing threats or overreacting to benign events.

- **Security of AI models**: AI models themselves can be vulnerable to adversarial attacks, where attackers manipulate input data to deceive the model.

Implementing AI-driven security solutions with Python opens new doors for automating threat detection, malware analysis, and IR. Python's rich ecosystem of libraries and frameworks simplifies the development of intelligent systems capable of handling complex cybersecurity tasks. While AI presents challenges in terms of data quality and interpretability, the benefits of AI in enhancing security far outweigh the difficulties.

By leveraging AI in cybersecurity, organizations can respond faster, more accurately, and more effectively to the ever-growing landscape of digital threats. The future of cybersecurity will undoubtedly see deeper integration of AI, and Python will continue to be at the forefront of this innovation.

Summary

As cybersecurity challenges evolve, ML and AI are increasingly pivotal in shaping the future of security automation. This chapter provided a comprehensive overview of how ML and AI, particularly through Python, are transforming security practices and their future potential. Let's summarize how they are doing this:

- **Advancements in threat detection**: ML and AI are enhancing threat detection capabilities by analyzing vast amounts of data to identify patterns and anomalies that signify potential threats. Future advancements will likely include more sophisticated models that can detect increasingly complex and subtle cyber threats.

- **Enhanced anomaly detection**: AI-driven systems are becoming more adept at identifying deviations from normal behavior, which helps in detecting unknown threats. As these models improve, they will offer more precise and timely alerts, reducing false positives and improving overall security efficacy.

- **Automated IR**: AI is streamlining IR by automating routine tasks and decision-making processes. This includes the automation of threat containment, mitigation, and recovery, which will enable faster and more efficient responses to security incidents.

- **Integration of AI with emerging technologies**: The integration of AI with other emerging technologies, such as the **Internet of Things** (**IoT**) and cloud computing, will drive the development of more comprehensive security solutions. This integration will enhance the ability to manage and secure complex, distributed systems.

- **Ethical and privacy considerations**: As AI technologies become more prevalent in cybersecurity, addressing ethical concerns and ensuring data privacy will be crucial. The future will see a greater focus on creating transparent, fair, and secure AI systems that protect both user data and privacy.

In summary, the integration of ML and AI into security automation with Python is set to revolutionize how organizations approach cybersecurity. With continuous advancements and a focus on addressing emerging challenges, AI will play a central role in shaping the future of security solutions. The next chapter will emphasize how Python's versatility and powerful libraries enable security teams to build and scale automation solutions for enhanced threat management. By integrating Python into security workflows, teams can improve efficiency, reduce manual tasks, and better respond to evolving cyber threats, ultimately strengthening organizational defenses.

Empowering Security Teams Through Python Automation

In today's rapidly evolving cybersecurity landscape, automation has become a key enabler for security teams to stay ahead of sophisticated threats. Python, with its versatility and rich ecosystem, has emerged as a powerful tool to drive automation across various security tasks. This chapter brings together the insights you've gained throughout this book, illustrating how Python-based automation can empower security teams to be more efficient, proactive, and responsive.

By leveraging Python, teams can streamline vulnerability management, incident response, threat detection, and more. This empowers them to focus on strategic decision-making rather than getting bogged down by manual processes. As security challenges continue to grow, automating tasks with Python will remain critical in fortifying an organization's defenses and enhancing the agility of security operations.

In this chapter, we'll cover the following topics:

- Recapitulating Python automation in security
- Leveraging Python for enhanced threat response
- Empowering security teams for future challenges

Recapitulating Python automation in security

As cybersecurity threats become more sophisticated, automation has proven to be a critical component in enhancing the efficiency and effectiveness of security operations. We've covered the following aspects of Python automation throughout this book:

- **The power of Python in security**: Python has earned its place as one of the most popular programming languages for cybersecurity due to its simplicity, flexibility, and the extensive range of libraries available. Whether it's automating network scans, analyzing logs, or integrating with security tools, Python enables security teams to tackle a wide array of tasks without being bogged down by complex code structures. Its ability to interface with popular security platforms and tools such as Nmap, Scapy, and SIEM systems further underscores its value in streamlining operations.

- **Vulnerability management automation**: Throughout this book, we explored how Python can be used to automate vulnerability management, making it easier to identify, assess, and remediate weaknesses in an organization's infrastructure. By integrating Python scripts with vulnerability scanning tools, security teams can automatically schedule scans, process results, and prioritize vulnerabilities based on risk, allowing for faster and more effective responses.

- **Incident response automation**: One of the most impactful applications of Python automation is incident response. With Python, security teams can automate repetitive tasks such as log parsing, alert triage, and executing predefined responses to common threats. Incident response workflows, such as automatically isolating a compromised system or collecting forensic data, can be triggered by Python scripts, ensuring that incidents are handled swiftly and consistently.

- **Threat intelligence integration**: Another major area where Python has shown its strength is threat intelligence. By automating the process of ingesting threat feeds and enriching security alerts, Python enables security teams to stay up to date with the latest threats without manual intervention. Python's ability to fetch data from APIs such as VirusTotal and OTX and correlate it with internal telemetry helps security teams make more informed decisions about potential threats.

- **Machine learning (ML) and artificial intelligence (AI) in security**: Looking forward, ML and AI are becoming integral parts of security automation. Python's rich ecosystem of libraries such as TensorFlow, scikit-learn, and Keras provides powerful tools for building AI-driven security solutions. From anomaly detection to predictive analytics, Python empowers security teams to create more advanced, proactive defenses that evolve alongside emerging threats.

- **Integrating Python with existing tools**: Throughout the journey, we also learned how Python seamlessly integrates with existing tools and platforms used in security operations. Whether working with SIEM systems, firewalls, or cloud environments, Python's ability to automate and orchestrate across various systems makes it indispensable for modern security teams. Additionally, by leveraging APIs, Python allows data to be exchanged between different security tools, enabling unified and automated workflows.

- **Future trends in Python security automation**: As security challenges grow in complexity, so too will the role of automation. Future trends will see Python continuing to evolve, incorporating more sophisticated AI and ML capabilities to predict and prevent threats before they materialize. Additionally, with the rise of the **Internet of Things (IoT)** and cloud services, Python will be instrumental in securing these distributed, dynamic environments.

In summary, Python has proven to be a powerful asset in security automation, enabling teams to streamline processes, enhance their security posture, and respond to threats with greater speed and precision. As new cybersecurity challenges emerge, Python will remain a vital resource in developing adaptive, scalable, and efficient defenses. In a nutshell, Python has become a go-to ally for security teams, bringing a level of efficiency and speed that wasn't possible before. By automating routine tasks and improving how we handle threats, Python allows teams to focus on the complex stuff that needs a human touch. And as the cybersecurity landscape keeps evolving, Python is set to remain an essential tool – helping us stay one step ahead of the latest challenges with adaptable, powerful defenses.

As you explore these automation techniques, think of Python as more than just code. It's an enabler that helps lighten the load, make smarter choices, and keep our systems safe.

Leveraging Python for enhanced threat response

As cyber threats grow in both volume and sophistication, timely and efficient threat response has become a cornerstone of effective cybersecurity. Security teams are often overwhelmed by the sheer number of alerts and incidents they need to process daily, making automation a critical part of enhancing their threat response capabilities. Python, with its versatility and extensive library support, has emerged as one of the most powerful tools for automating threat response tasks, enabling teams to respond more effectively and efficiently to potential security incidents.

Why automate threat response?

Manual threat response processes are not only time-consuming but also prone to errors. Security teams need to analyze logs, cross-check threat intelligence, isolate compromised systems, and remediate vulnerabilities, often under the pressure of rapidly escalating incidents. Automating these tasks with Python allows security teams to reduce response times, ensure consistency in actions taken, and free up valuable resources to focus on high-level analysis and strategy.

Python can automate the following aspects:

- **Alert triage**: Automatically assess and prioritize alerts based on severity and context.

- **Incident investigation**: Gather relevant forensic data, including system logs, network traffic, and user activity.

- **Remediation actions**: Trigger automated responses, such as blocking an IP address, isolating a compromised system, or closing vulnerable ports.

Key Python libraries for threat response

A variety of Python libraries can be used to automate different aspects of threat response. Some of the most commonly used ones are as follows:

- **Requests**: Used to interact with APIs, allowing Python to retrieve data from threat intelligence platforms, SIEMs, and other external systems.

- **Scapy**: A powerful tool for network packet analysis and manipulation that enables detailed inspection of network traffic during an incident investigation.

- **Paramiko**: Automates SSH sessions to manage remote systems. This makes it ideal for executing commands on compromised machines or collecting logs remotely.

- **Pytest and Unittest**: Testing libraries that ensure that automated responses are functional and don't introduce new risks into the environment.

- **Logging**: Python's built-in logging module helps track actions and document the entire threat response process, something that's critical for post-incident reviews and compliance.

Automating key threat response processes

Python can be leveraged to automate several key processes in threat response, making incident handling faster and more efficient:

- **Automated threat enrichment**: Once an alert is triggered, Python can automatically query threat intelligence sources to enrich the alert with context about the IP address, domain, file hash, or malicious activity. This helps security analysts make faster, more informed decisions.

- **Incident triage and prioritization**: Security teams are often flooded with alerts, many of which are false positives. Python scripts can analyze logs and alerts to determine their severity, impact, and legitimacy, helping teams prioritize critical incidents and avoid alert fatigue.

- **Dynamic containment**: One of the most time-sensitive tasks in threat response is isolating the compromised system or account to prevent further damage. Python scripts can trigger containment measures such as blocking IPs, disabling user accounts, or segmenting a network in real time.

- **Forensic data collection**: Python can gather logs, system snapshots, network traffic, and other relevant data for forensic analysis during or after an incident. This automation ensures that no crucial information is overlooked and that it's collected promptly.

Real-world use cases of Python in threat response

Python's ability to automate and streamline threat response is increasingly being utilized across industries to improve security operations. The following are some real-world use cases to consider:

- **Automated phishing response**: When a phishing attempt is detected, Python scripts can be configured to automatically analyze the suspicious email, extract malicious URLs, check them against known phishing databases, and then quarantine the message or block the URL across the network.

- **Ransomware response**: During a ransomware attack, Python can automatically detect abnormal encryption behavior, isolate the affected systems, notify security teams, and initiate a snapshot recovery process to restore systems from backups.

Phishing response

Phishing attacks remain a prevalent threat. Automating the detection and response to phishing attempts can significantly reduce response times and minimize the impact of such attacks. Here's a simple example of how to use Python to check whether an email domain is known for phishing:

```python
import requests

# Function to check if a domain is in a known phishing database
def is_phishing_domain(domain):
    url = f"https://api.phishtank.com/v2/get_phish.
php?domain={domain}"
    response = requests.get(url)
    return response.json()  # Returns True if phishing, else False

# Example usage
email_domain = "example.com"
if is_phishing_domain(email_domain):
    print(f"The domain {email_domain} is known for phishing.")
else:
    print(f"The domain {email_domain} is safe.")
```

This snippet uses a hypothetical API (PhishTank) to check whether the provided domain is associated with phishing. In a real-world application, you would replace the URL with a valid API endpoint.

Ransomware detection

Detecting ransomware can involve monitoring file changes and suspicious behaviors. Here's a basic example of using Python to monitor file modifications in a specified directory:

```python
import os
import time
# Directory to monitor
directory_to_monitor = "/path/to/directory"
file_mod_times = {}

def monitor_directory():
    while True:
        for filename in os.listdir(directory_to_monitor):
            file_path = os.path.join(directory_to_monitor, filename)
            if os.path.isfile(file_path):
                mod_time = os.path.getmtime(file_path)
                # Check if the file has been modified
                if filename in file_mod_times:
                    if mod_time != file_mod_times[filename]:
                        print(f"File modified: {filename} at {time.
ctime(mod_time)}")
                file_mod_times[filename] = mod_time
        time.sleep(5)   # Monitor every 5 seconds

# Start monitoring
monitor_directory()
```

In this example, the script monitors a specified directory for any file modifications. If a file is modified, it logs the change, which could be a sign of ransomware activity (for example, rapid file encryption). In a more advanced setup, you could integrate this with alerting systems or SIEM tools.

Looking at these practical examples, you can see how Python can be applied to real-world cybersecurity challenges such as phishing response and ransomware detection. These hands-on code snippets will enhance your ability to implement similar solutions in your environments.

Integrating Python with security platforms

Python's flexibility allows seamless integration with a variety of security platforms, enhancing automation and enabling more efficient responses. The following are some common integrations:

- **SIEM systems**: Python scripts can be used to pull data from SIEMs such as Splunk or Elasticsearch, enabling automated log data analysis and responses to be executed based on predefined rules.

- **Endpoint detection and response (EDR)**: Python can interface with EDR tools to automate tasks such as system scans, quarantining compromised endpoints, and running remote investigation scripts.

- **Threat intelligence platforms (TIPs)**: By connecting Python with TIPs such as VirusTotal or Open Threat Exchange, security teams can automatically ingest threat feeds and correlate these with internal logs, enriching alerts and enhancing real-time threat insights.

Building scalable threat response workflows

While automating individual tasks is beneficial, Python enables the development of end-to-end workflows for handling complex incidents from detection to remediation. For instance, an alert from a SIEM system can trigger a Python script that aggregates data from threat intelligence sources, analyzes network traffic, and automatically isolates affected systems. These workflows can be customized and scaled to fit an organization's unique needs and threat landscape.

Potential pitfalls in automated security workflows

However, as valuable as automation is in strengthening security, there are potential pitfalls that organizations must consider to maintain balance and prevent unintended risks:

- **False positives**:

  - **Challenge**: Automated systems can generate a high volume of false positives, overwhelming security teams and diverting attention from genuine threats.

  - **Mitigation strategies**: Regularly tuning and calibrating automated tools, incorporating contextual analysis, and establishing feedback loops with security analysts can significantly reduce noise from false positives.

- **Maintenance requirements**:

  - **Challenge**: Automation tools require consistent upkeep; outdated scripts or tools may miss new vulnerabilities or threats.

  - **Mitigation strategies**: Conduct periodic reviews, keep documentation updated, and ensure team members receive training in the latest automation techniques.

- **Security of automation tools**:

  - **Challenge**: Automation tools themselves are targets for attackers, who may attempt to gain unauthorized access to modify security processes.

  - **Mitigation strategies**: Employ strict access control, conduct regular vulnerability assessments, and maintain detailed audit logs to secure these tools.

- **Over-reliance on automation:**

  - **Challenge**: Excessive dependence on automation can foster complacency, with security teams potentially missing nuanced threats that require human judgment.

  - **Mitigation strategies**: Strike a balance by combining automation with human oversight, providing ongoing training, and conducting regular incident response drills.

In conclusion, Python enables robust, scalable automation in cybersecurity, from SIEM data handling to threat intelligence integration and comprehensive incident response workflows. However, by acknowledging and mitigating potential pitfalls, organizations can harness automation's power responsibly. This balanced approach ensures that automation serves as a vital tool for enhancing security without compromising reliability or readiness.

Empowering security teams for future challengesTop of Form

As the cybersecurity landscape continues to evolve, so too must the strategies and tools used by security teams. The sheer volume and complexity of cyber threats, coupled with the rise of advanced technologies, make it imperative for security teams to adapt and prepare for future challenges. In this section, we'll explore how modern security teams can leverage tools such as automation, AI, and continuous learning to remain agile and proactive in the face of increasingly sophisticated threats.

The evolving threat landscape

The nature of cyber threats is constantly changing. Attackers are employing increasingly complex methods, including **advanced persistent threats** (**APTs**), zero-day vulnerabilities, and social engineering attacks. Additionally, the expansion of cloud services, remote work, and IoT has created more opportunities for threat actors to exploit.

For security teams, this means that traditional, manual approaches to security are no longer sufficient. Teams must be equipped with the skills and tools necessary to predict, detect, and respond to threats in real time, often across a diverse and rapidly changing environment.

The role of automation in future security

Automation has already proven to be a game-changer in cybersecurity, and its importance will only grow as future challenges emerge. Automating repetitive tasks such as threat detection, vulnerability scanning, incident response, and log analysis allows security teams to focus on higher-level strategy and threat hunting. As cyber-attacks become more sophisticated, automation helps with the following:

- **Scaling security operations**: Security teams can handle an increasing number of alerts and incidents without being overwhelmed by manual processes.

- **Improving response times**: Automation reduces the time it takes to detect and respond to threats, which can minimize damage and prevent the spread of an attack.

- **Consistency and accuracy**: Automated workflows ensure that security policies and procedures are followed consistently, reducing the risk of human error.

Python, with its versatility and extensive library support, plays a critical role in enabling automation in security operations. By using Python scripts to automate tasks such as incident response, log parsing, or threat intelligence integration, security teams can efficiently manage a larger scope of security operations with fewer resources.

As cybersecurity challenges continue to evolve, the role of automation will expand, particularly through the integration of AI and ML. These technologies are poised to enhance the capabilities of security operations significantly. Let's look at some key trends and emerging tools that professionals should consider.

Enhanced threat detection with AI and ML

AI and ML are becoming integral to improving threat detection capabilities by analyzing vast amounts of data and identifying patterns indicative of malicious behavior:

- **Emerging tools**:

  - **Darktrace**: This AI-powered cybersecurity platform uses ML to detect and respond to cyber threats in real time. It employs an autonomous response system that mimics the human immune system, adapting to new threats dynamically.

  - **Cylance**: Using advanced ML algorithms, Cylance provides proactive threat detection and prevention, focusing on endpoint protection without relying on traditional signature-based methods.

Automated incident response

Automation in incident response is evolving with AI and ML, enabling faster and more effective handling of security incidents:

- **Emerging tools**:

  - **IBM Resilient**: This incident response platform leverages AI to provide contextual insights and automate workflows, allowing security teams to respond to incidents more efficiently. Its orchestration capabilities enable integration with various security tools for a streamlined response process.

  - **Palo Alto Networks Cortex XSOAR**: This **security orchestration, automation, and response** (**SOAR**) platform combines threat intelligence, automated playbooks, and incident management to enhance response capabilities.

Proactive threat hunting

AI and ML technologies are enabling organizations to shift from reactive to proactive threat hunting by continuously analyzing network behavior and identifying anomalies:

- **Emerging tools**:

  - **Elastic Security**: This solution uses ML to analyze data in real time, enabling security teams to detect threats early. It provides advanced analytics and customizable dashboards for effective threat hunting.

  - **Sumo Logic**: This cloud-native platform offers ML-driven insights that help security teams identify and respond to anomalies within their systems, enhancing proactive threat detection.

Behavioral analytics

Behavioral analytics powered by AI and ML allows organizations to understand user behavior and identify deviations that may indicate potential threats:

- **Emerging tools**:

  - **Exabeam**: This platform specializes in **user and entity behavior analytics** (**UEBA**), using ML to create user profiles and detect anomalies in real time, helping to identify insider threats and compromised accounts.

  - **Splunk User Behavior Analytics**: Leveraging ML, this tool enhances security monitoring by providing insights into user behavior, enabling security teams to detect unusual activities and potential threats.

Automation of compliance and risk management

As regulatory requirements grow, automation tools that integrate AI can help organizations maintain compliance and manage risk effectively:

- **Emerging tools**:

  - **Drata**: This compliance automation platform leverages AI to continuously monitor and assess an organization's security posture against compliance requirements, streamlining the audit process and reducing manual effort.

  - **RiskLens**: Focused on risk management, RiskLens uses quantitative risk analysis powered by AI to help organizations prioritize risks based on potential financial impact, facilitating more informed decision-making.

As the cybersecurity landscape continues to evolve, embracing automation, AI, and ML will be crucial for organizations aiming to stay ahead of emerging threats. By exploring and implementing these emerging tools and frameworks, security professionals can enhance their capabilities, improve incident response times, and maintain a proactive security posture. The integration of these technologies will ultimately empower organizations to navigate the complexities of modern cybersecurity challenges more effectively.

AI and ML in security

AI and ML are becoming pivotal technologies in cybersecurity, enabling more intelligent and adaptive security systems. AI can analyze vast amounts of data faster than human analysts, identifying patterns and anomalies that might indicate a threat. ML models can be trained to detect suspicious behavior, flagging potential attacks before they cause significant harm.

The following are some of the applications of AI and ML in future cybersecurity operations:

- **Anomaly detection**: ML algorithms can identify deviations from normal network traffic or user behavior, alerting security teams to potential threats that may go unnoticed using traditional rule-based detection methods.

- **Threat prediction**: By analyzing historical data, ML can predict the likelihood of certain types of attacks, enabling security teams to proactively implement defenses.

- **Behavioral analytics**: AI can analyze the behavior of users, devices, and applications to detect unusual or suspicious activity, helping to mitigate insider threats and account takeovers.

While AI and ML won't replace human security experts, they will augment their abilities, helping them to make faster and more accurate decisions when responding to threats. Python, with libraries such as TensorFlow, scikit-learn, and Keras, provides a platform for developing AI-driven security solutions that can be integrated into existing security operations.

The integration of AI and ML in cybersecurity is transforming how organizations detect, respond to, and mitigate threats. These technologies enhance traditional security measures by providing advanced analytics, predictive capabilities, and automation. Let's take a look at some key applications of AI and ML in security, along with notable tools and frameworks that professionals should explore.

Threat detection and prevention

AI and ML models analyze large volumes of data to identify patterns and anomalies indicative of potential threats, enabling proactive defense mechanisms.

- **Emerging tools**:

  - **CrowdStrike Falcon**: A cloud-native endpoint protection platform that uses AI to detect and respond to advanced threats in real time. It employs ML algorithms to identify suspicious behavior and respond to incidents automatically.

  - **Fortinet FortiAI**: This tool uses ML to enhance threat detection across networks, offering automated incident response and reducing the time required to identify and mitigate threats.

UEBA

AI-powered UEBA solutions monitor user behavior to detect anomalies that may suggest compromised accounts or insider threats:

- **Emerging tools**:

  - **Sumo Logic**: Offers real-time analytics for monitoring user behavior and identifying anomalies using ML models, helping security teams respond quickly to potential threats.

  - **Splunk UBA**: A solution that leverages ML to analyze user behavior across an organization, providing insights into potential insider threats and account takeovers.

Automated incident response

AI and ML streamline incident response processes, enabling organizations to respond to threats more quickly and efficiently.

- **Emerging tools**:

  - **IBM Security QRadar SOAR**: This platform integrates AI capabilities to automate incident response workflows, providing security teams with context-rich insights and orchestrating actions across multiple security tools.

  - **Cortex XSOAR by Palo Alto Networks**: This SOAR platform utilizes ML to enhance incident response by automating repetitive tasks, integrating threat intelligence, and orchestrating responses across the security stack.

Phishing detection

AI and ML algorithms can identify phishing attempts effectively by analyzing email content, metadata, and user behavior:

- **Emerging tools**:

  - **Avanan**: This email security solution uses AI to detect phishing emails and prevent them from reaching users' inboxes. It analyzes various factors, including sender reputation and email content, to assess threats.

  - **Proofpoint**: Employs ML to enhance email security by identifying and blocking phishing attempts, as well as analyzing user interactions to improve detection capabilities.

Risk assessment and compliance

AI and ML tools can automate risk assessments and ensure compliance with regulatory requirements by continuously monitoring and analyzing security postures:

- **Emerging tools**:

  - **Drata**: An automation platform that leverages AI to streamline compliance efforts by continuously monitoring security controls and generating real-time reports on compliance status.

  - **RiskLens**: Uses quantitative risk analysis powered by AI to assess cybersecurity risks and provide insights into the financial impact of potential threats, helping organizations prioritize risk management efforts.

As AI and ML technologies continue to evolve, their applications in cybersecurity will expand, offering security professionals powerful tools to enhance their defense mechanisms. By exploring these emerging tools and frameworks, organizations can leverage AI and ML to improve threat detection, automate incident response, and maintain compliance, ultimately strengthening their overall security posture.

Building a culture of continuous learning

In an environment where threats are constantly evolving, security teams must foster a culture of continuous learning. Cybersecurity professionals need to stay up to date with the latest tools, techniques, and best practices. This means ongoing education, certifications, and hands-on experience with new technologies.

The following are key aspects of continuous learning:

- **Collaboration**: Security teams should work closely with other departments, such as IT, development, and compliance, to share knowledge and improve the organization's overall security posture.

- **Threat intelligence sharing**: Participating in threat intelligence communities can help security teams stay informed about new threats and vulnerabilities.

- **Regular training**: Providing regular training on emerging threats and tools ensures that security teams can adapt to new challenges. This includes hands-on training with new automation and AI tools to ensure that teams are well-prepared to use them effectively.

Cross-functional collaboration for security success

As security threats impact every part of an organization, future security teams must adopt a more collaborative, cross-functional approach. Security should no longer be siloed within an isolated department but rather integrated into every aspect of the business.

Let's go through why it's important to have teamwork across various departments, including IT, development, and security, to build a robust and resilient cybersecurity strategy:

- **DevSecOps integration**: Security should be embedded into the development life cycle, with security teams collaborating with developers and operations to build secure code and infrastructure from the ground up.

- **Board-level engagement**: Security teams need to work closely with leadership to communicate the importance of cybersecurity in business strategy and risk management. By aligning security initiatives with business goals, security teams can gain the necessary support and resources to protect the organization effectively.

- **Cloud and IoT security**: As businesses increasingly adopt cloud services and IoT devices, security teams need to collaborate with cloud architects and IoT specialists to ensure that security policies are enforced across these environments.

The importance of adaptive and scalable security

As organizations grow and adopt new technologies, their security needs will evolve. Security teams must focus on creating adaptive and scalable defenses that can grow with the organization. This means leveraging cloud-based security tools, investing in automation and AI, and continually assessing and adjusting security strategies based on changing business needs and threat landscapes:

- **Scalability through automation**: Automation will allow security operations to grow alongside the organization's digital infrastructure, handling more alerts and larger datasets without requiring additional manual labor.

- **Adaptive AI systems**: AI and ML systems will evolve with the business, learning from past incidents and adjusting detection models to better identify new and emerging threats.

Looking ahead – preparing for the future of cybersecurity

The future of cybersecurity will be shaped by ongoing technological advancements, the increasing use of automation and AI, and the need for more agile and collaborative approaches. Security teams that adopt these tools and practices will be better equipped to face future challenges, ensuring the protection of their organizations against evolving threats.

Empowering security teams for the future involves more than just technical solutions – it requires building a culture of innovation, adaptability, and resilience. By focusing on continuous improvement and leveraging the full potential of automation and AI, security teams will be well-prepared to defend against the challenges of tomorrow.

As we move into an era of more complex and unpredictable cyber threats, security teams must evolve to meet these challenges head-on. By leveraging Python for automation, integrating AI and ML, fostering a culture of continuous learning, and adopting a cross-functional approach, security teams will be well-equipped to face the future of cybersecurity. The need for agile, scalable, and adaptive security strategies has never been more critical, and by embracing these practices, security teams can protect their organizations with confidence and efficiency.

Summary

This chapter highlighted how leveraging Python's simplicity and flexibility enables security professionals to automate routine tasks, enhance threat detection, and respond to incidents more efficiently. We learned about the following aspects:

- **Leveraging automation for efficiency**: Python's versatility enables security teams to automate repetitive and complex tasks, improving response times, reducing human error, and allowing teams to focus on strategic security initiatives.

- **Integrating AI and ML**: As threats become more sophisticated, AI-driven tools, powered by Python, help security teams analyze vast amounts of data, identify threats, and predict potential risks, making cybersecurity more proactive and adaptive.

- **Scalability and adaptability**: Automation ensures that security operations can scale with growing organizations, adapting to evolving threats and technological changes without requiring an overwhelming increase in manual work.

- **Continuous learning and collaboration**: Future-ready security teams prioritize ongoing education, collaboration across departments, and the integration of security into all aspects of the business, positioning themselves to tackle the next wave of cybersecurity challenges effectively.

Throughout this journey, you've learned about key concepts in security automation, including ML applications, anomaly detection, and automated incident response, while gaining hands-on experience with Python libraries and tools. By embracing these techniques, you're now better prepared to implement effective security solutions, foster collaboration within your organization, and proactively address the ever-changing landscape of cyber threats. As you move forward, remember that continuous learning and adaptation are crucial in the fight against cybercrime, and Python will be a powerful ally in your efforts to protect valuable digital assets, foster collaboration within your organization, and proactively address the ever-changing landscape of cyber threats.

Collaboration between security and other departments, such as DevOps and IT, is essential for the success of security automation initiatives. By fostering a culture of cooperation and integrating security practices into all stages of development and operations, organizations can enhance their security posture, streamline processes, and respond more effectively to threats. The examples and case studies illustrate the tangible benefits of cross-functional collaboration, providing a roadmap for organizations looking to improve their security automation efforts.

As you reflect on the insights presented in this chapter, consider how you can incorporate these automation techniques into your daily security practices. Here are some actions you can take:

- **Evaluate your current processes**: Assess your current security workflows to identify areas where automation can reduce manual effort and enhance efficiency. Look for repetitive tasks that could benefit from automation.

- **Integrate security into development**: Work closely with your DevOps teams to integrate security measures into your CI/CD pipelines. Implement automated security testing tools to identify vulnerabilities early and reduce risk.

- **Leverage collaboration**: Foster strong communication between security, IT, and development teams. Conduct joint training sessions and incident response drills to improve coordination and readiness for potential threats.

- **Adopt emerging tools**: Explore and implement emerging automation tools that align with your organization's needs. Invest in solutions that enhance threat detection, incident response, and compliance monitoring.

- **Commitment to continuous improvement**: Stay informed about the latest trends in security automation, AI, and ML. Regularly revisit your automation strategies to ensure they remain effective in addressing evolving threats.

By taking these steps, you can not only strengthen your organization's security posture but also create a more agile and resilient security framework. Embrace automation as a vital component of your security strategy and empower your team to focus on more strategic initiatives that enhance overall cybersecurity.

Index

Z

Packtpub.com

Subscribe to our online digital library for full access to over 7,000 books and videos, as well as industry leading tools to help you plan your personal development and advance your career. For more information, please visit our website.

Why subscribe?

- Spend less time learning and more time coding with practical eBooks and Videos from over 4,000 industry professionals

- Improve your learning with Skill Plans built especially for you

- Get a free eBook or video every month

- Fully searchable for easy access to vital information

- Copy and paste, print, and bookmark content

Did you know that Packt offers eBook versions of every book published, with PDF and ePub files available? You can upgrade to the eBook version at packtpub.com and as a print book customer, you are entitled to a discount on the eBook copy. Get in touch with us at customercare@packtpub.com for more details.

At www.packtpub.com, you can also read a collection of free technical articles, sign up for a range of free newsletters, and receive exclusive discounts and offers on Packt books and eBooks.

Other Books You May Enjoy

If you enjoyed this book, you may be interested in these other books by Packt:

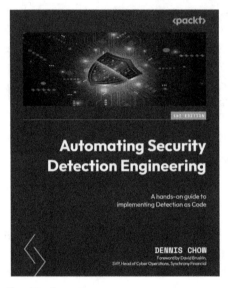

Automating Security Detection Engineering

Dennis Chow

ISBN: 978-1-83763-641-9

- Understand the architecture of Detection as Code implementations
- Develop custom test functions using Python and Terraform
- Leverage common tools like GitHub and Python 3.x to create detection-focused CI/CD pipelines
- Integrate cutting-edge technology and operational patterns to further refine program efficacy
- Apply monitoring techniques to continuously assess use case health
- Create, structure, and commit detections to a code repository

Offensive Security Using Python

Rejah Rehim, Manindar Mohan

ISBN: 978-1-83546-816-6

- Familiarize yourself with advanced Python techniques tailored to security professionals' needs
- Understand how to exploit web vulnerabilities using Python
- Enhance cloud infrastructure security by utilizing Python to fortify infrastructure as code (IaC) practices
- Build automated security pipelines using Python and third-party tools
- Develop custom security automation tools to streamline your workflow
- Implement secure coding practices with Python to boost your applications
- Discover Python-based threat detection and incident response techniques

Packt is searching for authors like you

If you're interested in becoming an author for Packt, please visit `authors.packtpub.com` and apply today. We have worked with thousands of developers and tech professionals, just like you, to help them share their insight with the global tech community. You can make a general application, apply for a specific hot topic that we are recruiting an author for, or submit your own idea.

Share your thoughts

Now you've finished *Security Automation with Python*, we'd love to hear your thoughts! Scan the QR code below to go straight to the Amazon review page for this book and share your feedback or leave a review on the site that you purchased it from.

`https://packt.link/r/1805125109`

Your review is important to us and the tech community and will help us make sure we're delivering excellent quality content.

Download a free PDF copy of this book

Thanks for purchasing this book!

Do you like to read on the go but are unable to carry your print books everywhere?

Is your eBook purchase not compatible with the device of your choice?

Don't worry, now with every Packt book you get a DRM-free PDF version of that book at no cost.

Read anywhere, any place, on any device. Search, copy, and paste code from your favorite technical books directly into your application.

The perks don't stop there, you can get exclusive access to discounts, newsletters, and great free content in your inbox daily

Follow these simple steps to get the benefits:

1. Scan the QR code or visit the link below

https://packt.link/free-ebook/978-1-80512-510-5

2. Submit your proof of purchase
3. That's it! We'll send your free PDF and other benefits to your email directly